FACES
of the
ISLANDS

When Pacific Islander and American Ways Meet

Willard C. Muller

Book Design by Kathy Campbell

Printed by Gorham Printing
Rochester, Washington

First Edition

Printed in the United States of America

ISBN 0-9637370-1-5
Library of Congress Control Number 2002102872

Produced by Lincoln Square Publishing Company
In cooperation with Binford and Mort Publishing Company, Hillsboro, Oregon

DEDICATED to the memory of Chief Petrus Mailo. He was freely and widely acknowledged by other chiefs throughout the Truk District—now Chuuk State—as first among equals. With his natural humility, high intelligence and wisdom, he showed his people by the way he lived what is important and unimportant in life: what is passing and what endures.

"This is a warm and thoughtful description of the first years of U.S. civilian administration of Truk—part of the Caroline Islands—after World War II. Rather than dwell on the clash of cultures, Muller portrays the gentle adjustment of ancient traditions to more modern ways He and other young Americans, far from home, teach and yet learn themselves, press forward new ideals, yet understand the subtleties of the old—all aimed at a better life for an island people. It is an inspiring history of nation-building"

Charles T. Cross
Ambassador of the United States of America (ret.)

"Willard Muller, first U.S. civilian District Administrator on Truk (now Chuuk) has produced, in the tradition of Arthur Grimble, an engagingly written account of his five years in Micronesia. This book will reward both the general reader and the area specialist. The author was clearly a culturally sensitive administrator who frequently traveled to even the most remote islands and villages of the District. The general reader, along with historians and other specialists, will appreciate the clarification he provides regarding many issues confronted in those early years of the Trust Territory government. They ranged from civilian-military rivalries, through political and economic development, to the importance of the cultural education provided U.S. administrators by the staff anthropologist."

William H. Alkire
Professor of Anthropology, Emeritus
University of Victoria.

"In this fascinating memoir, Will Muller, the young District Administrator, helps us see vividly the old Truk District in the middle Carolines. Along with many others, readers will meet the renowned Chief Petrus Mailo, and Tosiwo Nakayama, who was born on one of the smallest and most remote islands, yet grew up to become the first President of a new Pacific nation. It is fortunate for us all that we now have this record of the that past era, for policy decisions and challenges that were faced then are today very much a part of the scene as the Micronesian people, with American and other foreign cooperation, steer their course into the 21st century."

> Karen M. Peacock, PhD
> Pacific Curator
> University of Hawai'i Library

"Here is a graceful and warmly written account of Willard Muller's five years as District Administrator and American Consul in the middle Carolines. The author gathers you up and takes you right along with him as he and his staff work to understand, befriend and counsel the islanders in the effort to help enhance their lives. America's interests in the Pacific must continue to note the strategic importance of this entire area. Muller's work points us clearly in that direction and emphasizes our need to understand cultures other than our own."

> Robert B. McClinton
> Rear Admiral, USN (Ret.)

CONTENTS

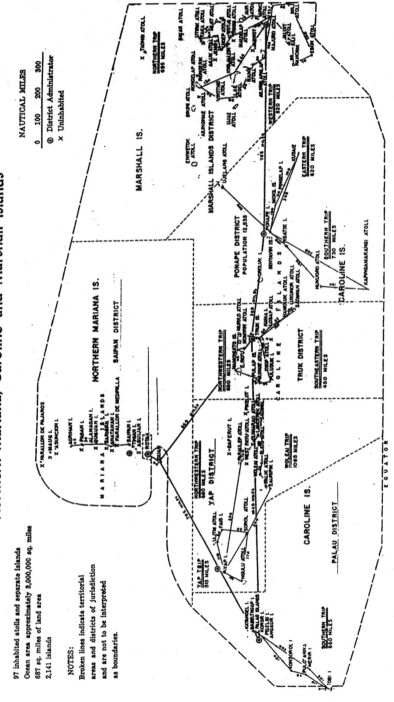

TRUST TERRITORY OF THE PACIFIC ISLANDS
Northern Mariana, Caroline and Marshall Islands

97 inhabited atolls and separate islands
Ocean area approximately 8,000,000 sq. miles
687 sq. miles of land area
2,141 islands

NOTES:

Broken lines indicate territorial areas and districts of jurisdiction and are not to be interpreted as boundaries.

NAUTICAL MILES

0 100 200 300

⊕ District Administrator
✕ Uninhabited

ACKNOWLEDGMENTS

My gratitude to those who helped me in writing this book goes to far more people than can be mentioned here. But I must express my strong gratefulness for assistance received from certain people who lived and worked in the islands, some of them no longer with us, who provided information and helped me recall vividly experiences and observations: Dr. Clark Richardson, Russell and Verna Curtis, Herb Wilson, Lou Gardella, John Smith, John and Sue Davis, Tosiwo Nakayama,—all personalities whom readers will meet in the pages which follow. I am deeply grateful to our staff anthropologist, Frank Mahony, for the education he gave to all of us Americans about the islands' culture. Many thanks to staff members of the National Oceanic and Atmospheric Administration (NOAA) in Hawaii and Seattle who provided basic information on *tsunamis*.Grateful thanks to Richard Miller and Joe McDermott in the U.S. Department of Interior's Office of Insular Affairs, and Dr. Michael Levin from the U.S. Bureau of Census, who patiently answered my questions, provided background materials and reviewed the Epilogue chapter. I am very grateful to anthropologists Tom Gladwin and John "Jack" Fischer for their help, direct and indirect, and to the Bank of Hawaii, Harvard University Press, Saturday Evening Post for permission to quote them, and to the University of Hawai'i Press—the latter for quoting Father Hezel's writings.

Special gratitude goes to Father Francis X. Hezel, S.J., who has spent nearly forty years living and working in the former Truk District and other parts of Micronesia I have quoted him extensively in the Epilogue chapter. I am indebted to Dr. Karen Peacock, Pacific Curator at the University of Hawai'i Library. She helped and encouraged me in many ways as I wrote this book. I am very grateful to others for reading parts or all of the manuscript in draft: former FSM President Tosiwo Nakayama, Dr. Harold Hanlin, Horace "Pony" Marshall, Raymond Clarke, Stuart and Jon Van Dyke, and Hollis Coe. Grateful thanks to artists Catherine Cranford for the cover painting, Alexandria Edouart and Bob Golightly for their pen and ink sketches, and to John and Jerry Behrens for their talented help on computer matters.

Finally, but first in so many ways, gratitude to my beloved wife, Carolyn, who shared many island experiences with me, encouraged me to write this book, and helped greatly with content and editing suggestions.

"In those developing countries of more than half the world, village life is an important key to the culture. When you go abroad, if you are to have a successful experience, whether you go as a tourist, represent our government, a private business, church, or other group, your chances for the best possible experience will be greatly improved if you try to understand the culture."

Want a Job in the South Sea Islands?

Twelve of us boarded the little amphibian plane. The flight to Truk Lagoon would take about four hours from Guam. This would be the final leg of my 9,000-mile flight from Washington, D. C., with a stopover in Hawaii and two-hours at Wake Island for refueling. I was beginning to feel travel-weary, and lonesome for Carolyn and our two tiny girls. But my excitement grew as I thought about my new assignment: District Administrator and American Consul for the thirty-nine populated islands in the Central Carolines, with Moen, the headquarters island, about 650 miles to the southeast.

Most of the passengers were Navy men and wives returning to their respective island groups after a week on Guam for holidays and shopping, or to conduct business at Navy offices. A few minutes later we were airborne. While a Navy man across the aisle engaged my seatmate in conversation, I sat back with my nose to the window, watching Guamanian villages drift by below. Then we came to a high cliff and were over blue water. I settled back and began to think about events of the past few weeks.

This whole turn of events had begun on a bright spring day in Washington, D.C. about a month earlier. I was having lunch with Van Dyke at one of those little outdoor restaurants. He had been my boss in Germany, and I highly respected his ability and advice. Every time I thought about an administrative job located in Washington, D. C., which I'd been offered a week before this meeting with him, I would begin to have visions of the Olympic National Park country in western Washington, where I had worked as a seasonal ranger during three college summers. Happy memories would flood back, of snow-capped peaks, alpine meadows fragrant with avalanche lillies, tall evergreen trees mirrored in blue lakes. I'd think about winding forest trails, how saddle and packhorses' hoofs sound on cedar puncheon bridges, and about the rangers and fireguards I worked with. It all made me homesick. I still had tucked in the back of my mind the thought that I'd really like a career in the National Park Service.

"If you feel that strongly," Van Dyke said, "why don't you do something about it? You say no ranger jobs are open. Think about taking some other professional level job with the Park Service or some other Interior Department agency. Then look for a chance to switch to ranger."

He told me about one of his Maxwell graduate school classmates who was now Acting Director of Planning in the Office of the Secretary, U.S. Department of the Interior. Van Dyke ended up making an appointment for me.

The Planning Director, who looked much under forty, began with small talk. I attributed his cordiality mainly to his friendship with Van Dyke and a little, perhaps, because I also was from the Maxwell Graduate School of Citizenship and Public Affairs. My Dean at Stanford had recommended it to me as one of the two best graduate schools of public administration in the country. We were only a few minutes into our meeting when Mr. Craine told me there weren't any possibilities for ranger jobs for a year or two, and he started to tell me about "...a lot of South Sea islands Interior's going to take over from the Navy..."

"Now," he concluded on that subject a few minutes later, still sounding far more cheerful than I felt, "why don't I set up an appointment for you with this fellow who's coming in from Honolulu to interview people for several management positions out there? A guy by the name of McConnell."

Three days later I returned to the Interior Department, this time to its Office of Territories. After a short wait, I was led to one of the inner offices where I met Mr. James McConnell. The receptionist had told me his official title was Deputy High Commissioner, Trust Territory of the Pacific Islands, and that he had arrived the previous afternoon from his new headquarters in Hawaii. He stood to shake hands with me and motioned me to a chair in front of his desk. He looked about fifty, stocky, fit, and dignified, with heavy gray hair and mustache. A light blue suit accentuated his deep tan. He spent the first few minutes asking about my work experience in Germany. Then he picked up my resume from the desk top, studied it briefly, laid it down and asked, "What do you know about the Trust Territory islands?"

I knew precious little. Since my meeting with Mr. Craine, I had been curious enough to take the bus down Pennsylvania Avenue to the Library of Congress and read some Congressional reports on the islands and sketchy material from an encyclopedia. Now his blue eyes leveled on me, waiting for a reply.

"I know that between the two World Wars they were assigned to Japan by the League of Nations to administer until they could be permanently returned to their rightful owners, and that they were wrested from the Japanese military in some of the bloodiest Pacific battles of WWII. At war's end they were occupied by U.S. Navy military government teams. In 1947, they became part of the U.N. Trusteeship system, with the U.S. government designated to administer them on behalf of the U.N. I understand President Truman decided they should be under civilian administration. Interior's Office of Territories was given the task to prepare those islanders for self-government or independence.

"I know that the islands, some just above the equator, are scattered across an ocean area of about 3,000,000 square miles. They range from the Western Carolines, roughly 500 miles south of the Philippines, to the Marshalls, about 2,300 miles southwest from Hawaii. Less than 100 of them are permanently occupied."

The well was about dry. Mr. McConnell continued to look at me steadily.

"I believe," I continued, struggling to remember what else I had read, "the total population is around 60,000. "The people are mainly in the Micronesian ethnic group and speak a combination of Malaysian and Polynesian. A few islands are pure Polynesian. The people live by fishing, making copra, and are subsistence farmers..."

The Deputy High Commissioner continued to look steadily at me.

"Mmm—well," he said, rumbling, "let me tell you how the Trust Territory will be administered under Interior." He described clearly, and with an economy of words, the main tasks of the new islands agency and the structure of the staff being assembled in Hawaii, its headquarters, and in each of the six island groups far out in the Pacific.

For more than an hour Mr. McConnell questioned me about my background. Having worked my way through college during the depression years, I didn't finish graduate school until I was twenty-six. I ticked off for him jobs I'd held before starting college, and summer work during college years: government postal clerk in my little Washington state home town, deckhand on a tugboat, part-time newspaper reporter, and that great Olympic National Park ranger assignment.

I told him about my brief stint with the War Food program in Washington right after finishing graduate school, then three years in the war-time Navy. That left me with only six years of postwar management experience, part of which were in Washington, tied in with the United Nations Relief and Rehabilitation program, and with the U.S. military government in Bavaria, as a civilian in the fields of food, agriculture and forestry. In 1949, the U.S. High Commission for Germany—forerunner of the American Embassy in West Germany—took over from military government, and I was transferred to it. I simply had no experience in the Pacific islands to show, except, as a junior officer on a destroyer, sailing and fighting our way through some of them.

During my growing-up years I had been fascinated by the writings about the South Seas by Robert Louis Stevenson. Several of my high school friends—sons of naval officers and enlisted men who, with their families, had been stationed at American Samoa—brought back fascinating stories about life in those islands. Following the war, I was captivated by Michener's timeless stories of the South Sea islands.

Two days after the interview, I received a call from the Office of Territories, telling me I had been accepted as Administrator of the Truk District. Would I please come in and sign the necessary papers?

Now, sitting in the little plane on the way to Truk, my palms suddenly became sweaty as there surfaced from my sub-conscious mind a question Mr. McConnell had asked me during the Washington interview. *What is there in your background that makes you believe you are qualified to administer a group of Pacific Islands?*

A cloud of self-doubt enveloped me. I was about to be propelled several hours from now into a strange new world with a very different culture, about which I'd have everything to learn. This was my first management assignment where I'd have independent duty. My immediate boss, the High Commissioner, would be back in Hawaii.

My seatmate, a gentle, soft-spoken man with silver hair, who taught vocational subjects at a Honolulu high school, was on his way to Truk for the summer under a volunteer program to teach islanders how to repair shortwave radio equipment. He turned and started asking me questions about the islands. As I responded, I felt my self-deprecation easing. A reassuring thought was forming in my mind.

In 1951 there were very few Americans anywhere, other than a small handful of Naval and other military officers in the Pacific, who had experience in island administration. Most officers still in the Navy six years after the war had opted for naval careers. The few interested in resigning to join the Trust Territory civilian program already had applied, been screened, and some were hired. I felt certain there had been no candidates for District Administrator who were expert in more than one—possibly two—of the half-dozen technical fields, and the financial and administration skills required in the islands. I was a trained, and at least somewhat experienced, manager—like an orchestra conductor. And that, I told myself, was what was needed to get doctors, nurses, engineers, surveyors, agriculturists, educators, a cultural anthropologist, craftsmen, and those with other assorted skills, to work well together and with the islanders in carrying out the Trust Territory's purposes.

Well, I'd give it my best.

"The Civilians Are Coming..."

Our little plane lost altitude. Looking downward to my right, I saw the distant outline of the entire Truk Lagoon, set almost in the center of the Truk District. Waves breaking over the great barrier reef looked snowy white against the cobalt blue sea. Scattered inside were a dozen emerald green mountainous islands and several low ones on the reef itself. On several islands I saw scattered villages. Breadfruit and palm trees added to their lush appearance. From the air it all looked great to me.

The plane touched down onto Moen Island's coral airstrip near the water's edge and gradually rolled to a stop. We were on the Navy's district headquarters island. Someone wheeled a wooden ramp alongside the plane. The flight crewman motioned for me to leave first. Stepping onto the ramp with growing excitement, I saw a lone Naval officer standing near the bottom step. Lieutenant-Commander Robert Law, the man I was to replace, greeted me. Tall, tanned, dressed in Navy khaki shorts, blouse and overseas cap, he shook hands and smiled warmly as he introduced himself. I had an immediate favorable impression of him—a body chemistry reaction strongly confirmed in the days that followed.

He led me to the front of a white quonset at the edge of the field, where a group of Americans who had come down to meet the weekly flight were waiting. He first introduced me to Captain Samuel Anderson, USN. I had learned in my Honolulu briefings that Captain Anderson was Chief Field Administrator, responsible for coordinating all Navy operations in the six districts of the Trust Territory. The captain shook hands perfunctorily, without smiling. Like Commander Law, he wore khaki shorts. The rest of his outfit included a colorful, faded aloha shirt, worn outside his shorts, and open-toed sandals. He was bareheaded and had what looked like a two-days' growth of beard.

Commander Law then led me over and introduced me to a cluster of other Naval officers, two American Jesuit priests who said they had come to meet the new District Administrator, and several civilians who had arrived ahead of me and would be members of my staff. Then he drove me in his gray military jeep about a half mile inland, climbing gradually to the Navy hotel.

He told me as we entered that he liked to be called Bob. Two of the newly recruited Interior Department civilians, Cicely "Cy" Pickerill, the lady who was to be principal of the islander boarding high school, and Charles "Reck" Reckefus, our new head of the Finance and Supply department, arrived in other jeeps. We were joined a few minutes later by Captain Anderson and several other Naval officers. They invited us newcomers over to the bar for a drink.

The captain walked up to me and, with no preliminaries, asked in the voice of a stern superior, "How are you civilians going to handle cargo? The big freighters can't come in to Baker dock. How are you going to keep the generators and reefer banks operating twenty-four hours a day? What will you do about diesel fuel supply for the base?"

Before I could say anything, he rattled off several more similar questions. From his tone, it was clear to me that he considered each of these items a major, urgent challenge to the incoming civilian staff. Furthermore, it was incomprehensible to him, his manner and inflections told me, that we new civilians, lacking knowledge and experience concerning the complexities of forward base operations and maintenance under difficult tropical conditions, could cope with them. Bob Law and his counterparts in the other districts had sizable staffs of enlisted personnel and officers, along with a few Navy civilians, and years of experience in forward base operations. The Navy had shown good foresight at war's end in arranging, in cooperation with Stanford

University, for the creation of a School of Naval Administration. Many of the Navy's future Pacific islands administrators had received training there.

When I was a junior Naval officer, I seldom saw a captain—"four-striper"—but I thought of them as standing in power and authority just a couple of notches below God. Now I found myself having to fight off a tendency to be awed. Any captain who dresses like this one does during duty hours, I thought, must have his human side.

"I don't know the answers," I told him. "But by July first I will." To myself I added, prayerfully: *I hope!*

Interior planned to assign to the Truk District about half as many Americans as the Navy had used. The captain's questions did underscore a serious problem: while eventually I'd have about thirty-five U.S. and 200 islander employees, less than half of the Americans would be at Truk in time to get briefings from their Navy counterparts and to help get ready for the turnover. Some would arrive a month or two late.

These islands had been the Navy's responsibility from the day a Marine brigadier general accepted the Japanese surrender at war's end aboard a U.S. destroyer off Truk's barrier reef. Mr. McConnell had told me in Hawaii he had the distinct impression the Navy was not happy about turning them over to Interior.

Less than thirty minutes after we arrived at the hotel, we Interior civilians found ourselves alone. Before leaving, one of the officers informed me I'd be billeted with Lieutenant Bob Beck, who would come by for me after dinner. At mealtime three civilian employees—lady school teachers at the intermediate school and the two-year high school—came into the hotel and joined us. They were among the few Navy civilians who had been hired by Interior, and would become part of my staff. We newcomers found them very cordial and helpful in answering our steady stream of questions.

"Captain Anderson has been dropping in here almost every evening," one of them told us, "and he says in an ominous voice, loud enough for everyone in the dining room to hear, 'Well, in a few weeks the civilians are coming. Then look out!'"

After dinner Lieutenant Beck, a handsome, dark-haired young bachelor and Naval Academy graduate, arrived at the hotel in a jeep to pick me up. Seeing some of the other Navy houses—white quonsets with added rooms, screened porches and window "eyebrows" and well-kept yard with colorful tropical flowers—as we drove up "Telegraph Hill," I was not prepared for my first view of Bob's place.

Standing alone in a grove of trees at the top of the hill was a slightly sagging tent with a steeple-shaped canvas roof. It was secured to a wooden platform and had weathered wooden siding about four feet high. From where the siding ended, up to the beginning of the canvas roof was screen wire. The entire inside of the tent felt damp from recent rains. I felt a flash of indignation. I didn't know why Lieutenant Beck chose to live in a place like this, but I thought it was not the place to house the man who had come to take over from the Navy administrator. It certainly wasn't my young host's fault. To hell with it! I could put up with this for two weeks. I wasn't going to let Captain Anderson or any other Navy person think my feathers were ruffled.

At bedtime, two minutes after Bob and I said good night and he turned off the light, his change in breathing told me he was already fast asleep. I lay in my bunk bed wide awake, listening to the tropical night sounds: soft, strange bird calls in the distance, and a gentle trade wind breeze rustling breadfruit and banana plant leaves. Sleep eluded me. It was, I thought, the cumulative effect of having flown through so many time zones—even since leaving Hawaii, where I'd been instructed by Mr. McConnell to stop over. That first visit to our new Honolulu headquarters had been a very busy four days: meetings with him and the High Commissioner and other key headquarters staff there at Fort Ruger, a former U.S. Army post. Mr. McConnell, coatless and wearing a short-sleeved shirt, spent most of his time with me emphasizing all the things my new staff and I would need to do in a two-week period between when I arrived at Truk and the Navy turned the islands over to us on July 1.

High Commissioner Elbert Thomas, who held a rank equivalent to ambassador, was a gentle, scholarly man from Utah. He had been a Mormon missionary in Japan, a professor of history at Brigham Young University and, for many years, a towering figure in the United States Senate. Doing most of the talking in a thirty-minute meeting, he told me our main task was to prepare the islanders for self-government.

"We must encourage them," he said, "to keep the best features of their own culture, while adopting the best of Western and other cultures..." Near the end of our meeting, he said, "Keep in mind that the islands hold an extremely important place in America's line of defense."

Cy Pickerill, Reck Reckefus, Pete Becker and I sat at breakfast with the teachers in the hotel dining room the next morning when the phone rang. It was Bob Law. "I'll be down in a few minutes and we'll take a tour of the base."

We began at the administration building. It was a large, gleaming white metal building with a pitched roof, located several hundred feet down the hill from the hotel. Designed for the tropics, it had many windows, all screened, and office partitions several feet above door height, so air could flow easily through it. Bob showed me his office, Captain Anderson's and those of their senior staff members.

He led me out the back door of the building, and we climbed several steps to a large paved square. Here seven white quonsets, all looking freshly painted, were neatly aligned on three sides. The main administration building closed the square. The quonsets housed the post office, telephone exchange, a barber shop, the Education, Finance and Supply, and the anthropologist's offices. I met for the first time Trukese office employees and several of my new American staff, who had arrived on the flight a week earlier. The Americans were being briefed by Navy counterparts.

While driving up with Bob from the airfield the previous afternoon I had studied with great interest the men, women and children walking along the road. Anxious to meet and actually talk with some Trukese, I had introduced myself to several workers at the hotel. Here in the offices, these young men and Lydia, the only Trukese lady employee I'd yet seen, looked to be in their early to mid-twenties. They were a little shorter than the Americans, their skins were light to medium brown, and they had dark eyes. Lydia, typical, I learned later, of many Trukese young women, had thick straight hair that hung nearly to her waist. Those I chatted with spoke English quite well.

When we left them, I said to Bob, "The Trukese staff I've met so far seem very likable."

"You'll like them. I'm going to miss them a lot," he said with emotion.

We returned to the front of the administration building, got into his jeep again and drove along the main road, which curved to the left past the front of the building, then straightened. A quarter-mile down that road Bob turned to the right and soon we climbed steeply another graveled road, past a dozen American houses on our right, until we reached the top of "Nob Hill," where

Captain Anderson's big home stood. I was particularly interested in it, because Mr. McConnell had suggested in Honolulu that it should become the district administrator's residence. It was constructed from several quonsets joined together, with the addition of porches, louvred windows, and "eyebrows" which jutted out at sloping angles to shade the windows. The inside walls were of bright, colorful hardwood panels which looked like cherry wood. Most of the rooms were spacious and cheerful looking.

A few hundred yards behind the house loomed a 1,200-foot ridge, covered with a rich green growth of tall grass, bushes, and a scattering of coconut palms. It extended along almost one whole side of the valley in which the Navy base headquarters was located. We walked around to the front of the house and stood for a few minutes on the lawn, which provided a sweeping view over half of the valley below and an inlet part of the lagoon to the right. I looked around with keen interest.

In Captain Anderson's yard and those of his neighbors on the hillside below us, I saw pineapple and banana plants, papaya, mango, and coconut trees, and a riot of colorful tropical flowers: frangipani, hibiscus, ginger, gardenia, poinciana, and several kinds of orchids. Bob pointed straight ahead to the south, across the valley, to the ridge beyond, with a knobby, leaning peak: Mt. Tonachau.

He identified for me, among the white quonset buildings neatly aligned in rows along the valley floor, the intermediate boarding school, base chapel, Public Works shops, and the quonsets which housed the High Court—the Trust Territory's Supreme Court. On the far side of the main road which ran through the valley were the diesel generator plant, commissary, Constabulary headquarters, and the two-year Pacific Islands Central School—only high school in the Trust Territory.

That evening Reck, Pete Becker, the deadly serious, loquacious civil engineer who would head our Public Works department, and I sat down together in a corner of the hotel lounge area. They, too, had spent most of the day with their counterparts inspecting sections of the Navy base of particular interest to them.

"I've never seen such a goddam pile of junk for rolling stock!" Pete said mournfully. "Some of those trucks and jeeps must have seen every campaign in the Pacific!"

"By the looks of the warehouses," Reck added, "we're going to be short of lots of items we ought to have right away—except paint—until we can get our own requisitions filled. They tell me it takes three months for stateside orders to arrive."

"Mr. Muller," Pete said, nodding vigorous agreement with Reck's comments, "we're in trouble!" He spent the next five minutes sketching a grim picture of the Public Works shops and the boat pool (group of small craft) situation.

"In the past week an officer and two different sailors told me the Navy's madder'n hell about Interior's coming in here," he went on. "They wanted to stay. I hear they shipped a lot o' shop hand tools back to Guam. The engine in the landing craft sounds rough and the self-propelled barge is all fouled up—won't run. We can't load copra to ships out in the harbor without 'em! I hear they offered to sell the marine railway to the local trading company!" His voice became more intense. "And I hear rumors they're even sending the 'YOGI' (big diesel fuel barge) back to Guam. Without the YOGI, we won't have a place to bulk-store for the base." He sat back glumly.

What I'd seen confirmed some of their observations. Still, I felt good about the overall picture. With the exception of the worn-out refrigeration plant and one or two of the five diesel generators, the Navy base looked in good shape to me. Most of the vehicles I'd seen looked and sounded quite good.

More important, the Navy had done a fine job during the previous six years in training Trukese workers. Among the approximately 200 islander employees were several who could stand generator plant watches and operate the dock crane. They could help considerably to repair vehicles and diesel engines, perform much of the carpentry and plumbing work and, under supervision, refuel planes. Several had some training in refrigeration and radio shack work. The Navy also had sent several carefully hand-picked young Trukese women to Guam for nurse training and a few young men to Fiji to study medicine, dentistry, and sanitation.

I pulled out my own briefing notes. "Pete, you'll be happy to learn that the Navy has several replacement trucks on order. And Commander Law says we'll get them. The marine railway wasn't sold. The fuel barge stays. How does the Public Works staff look to you?"

Pete brightened. "I saw a Trukese crane operator working on the dock this morning. He could make it stateside. The lieutenant in charge of Public Works tells me their Trukese power plant foreman's as good as some of his sailors. The boat pool's got good Trukese boat handlers. But a Navy chief told me Captain Anderson won't let the natives touch the picket boat. Only American sailors can crew it. Captain Anderson's the only one who skippers it."

I was reminded of Pete's last remark several days later, when I asked Bob Law to have someone check out Ray Hann, our new diesel mechanic and boat pool supervisor, on the picket boat. It was a beautiful forty-five foot cabin cruiser—former Navy crash boat—with a wheelhouse forward, and a cabin aft that had a little galley and folding bunks. Its brasswork shone and the hull was white and spotless.

"Damn, I'd like to," Bob said apologetically. "But Captain Anderson's the only one who handles it."

I was on Moen Island a week before I met Frank Mahony, who was to be our staff anthropologist. He had returned that morning on a freighter from Navy's final field trip to a group of outer islands. Later that day we sat down together in the temporary office Bob Law had set up for me near his, and I asked Frank many questions about the twenty-four populated islands which lay far outside the Truk Lagoon's fifteen populated islands. Some were scattered up to 160 miles to the west and northwest of Truk Lagoon. Others were about an equal distance to the south and southeast.

Frank was fairly tall, lean, with dark hair, blue eyes, and a deep tan. While he talked, his enthusiasm for his work often surfaced. He had joined Bob's staff about a year earlier as a civilian anthropologist right out of graduate school. It was his good fortune to have had his tutelage at Truk under Tom Gladwin, head of the Navy's Native Affairs department there. (We later changed it to Island Affairs.) Tom had initially come to Truk under a program called the Coordinated Investigation of Micronesian Anthropology (CIMA). It was funded by Office of Naval Research and coordinated by the Pacific Science Board—part of the National Research Council. The Micronesian islands to be studied were parceled out to universities with major departments of anthropology. Yale University was assigned Truk; Harvard got Yap, and so on.

After Tom had completed his CIMA research, he was hired by Lieutenant-

Commander Law to head up the Native Affairs office. Since Tom found himself part of the chain of command, he convinced Bob Law that he should have on his staff a cultural anthropologist who could be neutral when our government made decisions affecting the lives of islanders. Jack Fischer, also a former CIMA anthropologist at Truk, was hired, served one year on Tom's staff, then was transferred to the Ponape District, about 400 miles east of the Truk District, to be their anthropologist. Frank took his place at Truk.

He told me briefly about monthly meetings the Truk Lagoon chiefs held on Moen island. "Have you met Chief Petrus yet?" he asked. I said I had not, but my priorities list included trying to meet some island chiefs in Truk Lagoon before July 1.

"Petrus Mailo is Chief of Moen," he said. He's also Island Judge and on the Board of Truk Trading Company. It's the only wholesale trading company in the district, and the only one in the Trust Territory owned entirely by the islanders. Because of Petrus' wisdom, personality, and *itang* status, he's the most widely respected leader in all the islands. He's accepted by the other chiefs as their natural leader. His father, Mailo, was a great chief before Petrus, and trained him."

"I heard about Chief Petrus in Washington," I said. "At a Navy Department briefing. An officer who'd been on Truk said good things about him—the only chief he mentioned by name. What's *itang*?"

"Oh," he said, grinning, and his blue eyes lit up again, "that's a long story. Maybe I should explain it later when you have more time."

Several days later I saw Frank down at the dock. "I understand Chief Petrus is at his house this morning working on his boat," he said. "Can you take time to go over and meet him now?"

We walked the short distance past Truk Trading Company's "elephant" quonset warehouses, along a tree-shaded dirt road through the village and entered the chief's yard. He was out in back, near the beach, kneeling by his boat, which was propped up on one side by several sticks.

Frank greeted him in Trukese, then introduced me. The chief got to his feet. His forehead was damp with sweat. Taller than medium height, he had graying hair, a stocky, thickset body and powerful forearms. His dark eyes signaled animation. He was dressed in a faded, checkered sport shirt with the bottom hanging loose outside baggy trousers, and was barefooted. The chief

14

extended a big, strong hand and greeted me in his own language. Frank interpreted.

"He says he is honored to meet the new *kepina* (governor). He thanks you for coming to Truk to help his people."

"I'm very happy to meet you, Chief Petrus," I said. "I look forward to getting better acquainted with you and working with you and your people."

We stood for several seconds, our hands still clasped. His steady gaze seemed to look deeper than my face—to search for the essence of me, while I tried to sense the makeup—the instincts and spirit—of this big, brown, smiling man.

Frank waited for one of us to speak again, and when the chief did, the anthropologist turned to me.

"Chief Petrus thanks you for coming to help make things better in the islands. He says he tries in his small way to help the people here on Moen, but he doesn't know what to do. He says we Trukese are poor, simple people. We lack the white man's superior mentality, so we make little progress."

I couldn't help grinning. This had a familiar ring. It sounded like pure Stanley Andrews—one-time editor of the *Arkansas Democrat* and later an Assistant Secretary of Agriculture. Still later, he was sent by our government to West Germany on a key assignment for the U.S. High Commission there. He had disarmed one senior German official after another with his "I'm just a country boy" routine; then in conversations and actions which followed, his intellect, high competence and urbanity showed clearly. The chief, still smiling, looked steadily into my eyes. Frank faced me expectantly, a trace of a worried frown appearing around his eyes.

I concentrated fully, trying to phrase an appropriate response and I wanted it to be as clear and brief as an epigram. The decent interval of silence had passed. Though it was only a few seconds, it seemed like minutes.

"Chief Petrus," I said, "I have no reason to believe that we Americans are any more intelligent or wiser than you Trukekse. You and I have both met wise people who didn't spend much time in school. We both know there are many different ways to learn. I hope you Trukese leaders and your people and we Americans can work well together to help the people." Frank translated.

The chief nodded slightly. He said he and the other Trukese wanted to work in a good way with me and the other Americans. We talked a little more.

Then I turned to examine the caulking job he had nearly finished, and we talked about it. Frank told me later the chief was surprised that the new *kepina* knew anything about caulking boats.

On June 28, the Navy arranged a brief, formal turnover ceremony at the intermediate school auditorium. It was attended by teachers from the intermediate school and high school, Trukese workers, Navy people and Americans who would be on my staff. Bob Law had invited chiefs from the islands within Truk Lagoon, and most of them came.

Dressed in Navy whites, with gold stripes on shoulder boards, Bob made a speech, reviewing the Navy's years and accomplishments in the islands. He was friendly in his remarks about Interior's taking over in four days. When I was introduced, following him, I told the Trukese that while we civilians coming in to replace Navy lacked experience in the islands, we brought with us good academic backgrounds and work experience in medicine, agriculture, education, and other specialized fields of knowledge, and we were prepared to work hard and share it with them. We were here to carry on the fine start the Navy had made. We would try to help them improve their living conditions and prepare them to govern themselves. We were sure there were many things we American would learn from the Trukese.

The day we civilians had been preparing for was almost at hand. Then we would become accountable for helping the people on each of these thirty-nine populated islands to have a better quality of life. The experienced Navy people would still be around for another week—until one of their big transport planes flew down to take them to Guam. I was hoping for a smooth transition.

First Crisis

July 1—turnover day—fell on a Sunday. I was enjoying a second cup of coffee in the hotel at breakfast with several members of my new staff, when Frank walked in and hurried over to me.

"I'd like to talk with you privately—something urgent," he said in a half-whisper. I excused myself and left the table. We walked down the road toward the administration building.

"Two Trukese friends came to my quarters a few minutes ago," he said, his voice intense. "They told me all Trukese workers are going on strike tomorrow morning."

That would be the first working day under civilian administration. The base would be paralyzed.

"But—why? Why are they going to strike now?" I asked, as much puzzled as shaken. "They haven't even worked one day for us."

"They're going to ask for pay raises," Frank said.

"What about hospital workers?" That was my first sinking thought. "Will they strike, too?"

"Everyone, I was told. But I'll check again."

If every Trukese employee walked out of the hospital, that would leave

Dr. Hagentornas, acting director of the Medical department, and a young administrative assistant to take care of all bed patients and out-patients twenty-four hours a day.

Pulling out my pocket notebook, I scanned the list of American Interior civilians now at Truk. Besides the two medical people, Frank and me, there were Reck and his Supply department assistant, Pete Becker and three of his Public Works department craftsmen, one radio operator, and three teachers. Chief Warrant Officer Harry Reed was going to stay on for a year, under a special Navy-Marine Corps arrangement with Interior, to complete training the Constabulary, which had district-wide responsibilities. The middle-aged Marine officer had been very helpful and friendly to me and other civilians during the past two weeks. One thing in our favor was that all students at the intermediate school and high school—both boarding schools—were back at their home islands on summer vacation.

Until today the Navy was in charge. I had met, both on an individual basis and in small groups, with members of my staff, including several former Navy civilians recruited by the Trust Territory. Now I called a meeting with all of the American staff.

They gathered at mid-morning in my office, and I told them about the planned strike. There were a few seconds of stunned silence. Then came an outburst of responses. Mostly, they sounded surprised. They expressed feelings ranging from frustration and guarded neutrality to anger by one person that the islanders decided to strike in this manner. We agreed we had to learn whether pay was the whole issue. If not, what were we facing? Looking around the semi-circle, I listened to them and studied their expressions. Their responses in the first minutes that followed were encouraging. We began to check off tasks that had to be performed to keep the District center operating: hospital, generator plant, water supply, refrigeration plant, and radio shack. We had to refuel for the first time the weekly plane flight arriving the next day, and refuel a freighter passing through a day or two later. We had to maintain law and order.

"Since I talked with you after breakfast," Frank said, "I was told by one of the Trukese who is, I think, a strike leader, that a half-dozen key hospital workers, including the nurses, won't strike."

Several others started to speak at the same time. I nodded to Harry Reed.

"The entire Constabulary force—all thirty of 'em—will stay on duty. They won't strike," he said, with a note of pride in his voice.

We began to realize that in this little cluster of American civilians and the marine officer, and with the help of non-striking Trukese, we had the capability of carrying out bare-bones operations for weeks. Our biggest problems would be to care for the hospital patients and to operate the generator plant twenty-four hours a day. Of the Americans, only Ray Hann, our heavy equipment mechanic, knew how to keep the big diesel generators going.

Right after the meeting ended, I drove up to Bob Law's. He was in the yard, about to get into his jeep and drive to Captain Anderson's house. Bob hadn't heard about the strike. With no hesitation, he agreed to my request to use two sailors temporarily—both machinist mates—to stand power plant shifts.

The next morning after breakfast I stepped out of the hotel, looked down the hill and saw something that sent my spirits soaring. Dozens of Trukese workers in a steady stream walked past the administration building. This was great! Someone had given Frank the wrong information. Or the workers had changed their minds. What a way, I had thought on Sunday morning, to begin our first work day on Monday. I walked down to the administration building, greeting workers as I crossed the road, and entered the building. Pete Becker, our Public Works director, stood in the hallway talking with Warrant Officer Reed.

"What's going on?" I asked them.

The screen door at the entrance flew open. Frank entered and hurried toward us. His face was flushed.

"They're not coming to work," he said, sounding breathless. "They're just here to collect their pay." He turned and hurried back outside.

The workers gathered and talked in groups in the headquarters area. Frank soon returned to where we still stood in the hallway and told me their strike spokesmen just informed him they all want a meeting with the *kepina* to demand pay raises.

I agreed with their request to meet with them at the intermediate school auditorium in a half-hour. Frank said he'd go down to the school, toward which groups of workers were now beginning to move, to tell their leaders I'd meet with them. Before leaving, he turned back to me and said, "I'll see you there. I'll translate for you. I suggest you mostly listen to them, with no censure at this point..."

Becker told me he had to help Hann at the dock area, and Reed hurried over to Constabulary headquarters. I walked down the hallway and sat alone in my office during the next twenty minutes. *What the heck do I do now?* I asked myself. I had no experience in strike negotiations. Only a couple of college courses in labor relations. I knew that in the U.S. such talks often were tense, drawn out. Sometimes they stretched into months. Yes, I *would* mainly listen. I'd just have to wait until they spoke to decide what my closing message to them would be.

When it was time to go, I drove a pool jeep down the graveled road to the intermediate school and entered the auditorium. It was crowded and echoed with the din of around 130 Trukese workers, talking, calling to each other, some laughing. Many heads turn toward me as I walked up the center aisle toward the front, where Frank stood near a podium.

"Many of them understand English," Frank said. He stood beside me, ready to interpret for the rest.

Turning to face them, I saw for the first time most of the Trukese workers on my staff. I began almost subconsciously to study row after row of faces. They didn't fit my stereotype of strikers. What I saw was reassuring. These employees, most I guessed to be in their twenties and thirties, looked back at me, many of them smiling. I thought they mainly looked friendly and curious.

My antenna picked up no trace of hostility. I had begun to feel tense in the past half hour as I considered the prospect of a confrontation with a big room full of strikers—strangers to me—with their list of demands. My tension eased a little.

Now Frank turned to me with that same anxious look he'd worn when he waited for me to reply to Chief Petrus in his yard a week earlier.

I focused on several individual faces and found it easy to smile back at them.

"*Ran anim ami meinisen,*" (Greetings to all of you) I began, thereby spending a portion of the three dozen Trukese words I had learned by now.

"*Ran anim, kepina!*" they thundered back.

Following Frank's suggestion, I invited their spokesmen to talk first. This would, he said, give the workers a chance to blow off steam.

Apiner, the generator plant foreman, about forty, and one of the oldest, most senior employees, stood up. "*Kepina*, we are all," he waved a hand toward his assembled companions, "workers for you—the Americans. We thank you for coming here to listen to our poor words. First we worked for the Japanese. They did not train many of us, but make us do simple labors. Then the American Navy come to us when war ended. The Navy trained us. Today we are good workers. We worked hard for the Navy. We want to do good work for you. But it is hard for us to do good work when our hearts are heavy because we know we do not get enough *peioff* (pay) to live." Apiner spoke on for another minute, then concluded in the same level, matter-of-fact voice in which he delivered his opening words.

"We demand today for more pay for all Trukese workers. We ask you to help our need." He again swept his hand toward the assembled workers. "Thank you, *kepina*." He sat down.

The next speaker, one of the senior boat pool workers, looked deadly earnest as he faced me. He spoke in English without Frank's help. "My brother stays in our village on Uman and he does not have to buy some foods. I bring foods here from my island, but when it is finish, I must buy on Moen. I must buy work clothes. But my brother does not need to buy much clothes, because he just make *taka* (copra) and bring in *pula* (taro) and catch *ik* (fish).

"*Kepina*," he, like the first speaker, concluded in a quiet, conversational voice, "we demand more pay for the works. We cannot live without more pay. You are our father; we ask you help us."

The third spokesman stood up, smiling, and made the workers' case in the same equable tone. "Sir, we workers must leave our islands and our families for the work. We cannot go each night to our home island. There is no boat. Sometimes there is a boat, but we must pay and we have no money. So we just stay on Moen Island, and we must only go to our family when the work is finish on Friday." He concluded with a smiling demand for more pay for all workers.

Four or five others spoke briefly, saying the same things in slightly different words.

Frank asked the Trukese if any more workers wished to speak. A worker stood, spoke one brief sentence and sat down. "He says," Frank translated, "they are now ready to hear from the *kepina*."

With Frank still interpreting, I thanked them for giving me the opportunity to hear their feelings. "As you know," I said, trying to sound as agreeable and relaxed as they had, "this is the second hour of the first work day under Interior. I hope you will understand that other members of my staff and I need some time to study the pay matter. We will need to look at how much we pay now for each kind of work. We will need to learn what the other employers—Truk Trading Company and the Catholic and Protestant missions—pay their workers. We will have to talk with our office in Honolulu." There had to be some degree of uniformity in wage scales among the six districts, I was certain. "But we need you to help run the base in the meantime," I concluded. "I urge you to return to work. I hope that within two weeks we can say something definite to you about pay adjustments."

I didn't tell them I had been startled to learn about a week earlier, when Lieutenant Lininger, the Supply officer, gave Reck copies of Navy payroll sheets, that unskilled Trukese workers earned nine cents an hour. Even in these tropical islands so abundantly favored by nature, seventy-two cents a day seemed like thin inducement for our workers to leave their families five days a week. I wondered if it provided enough for a worker to purchase even the barest necessities for himself while here on Moen Island.

I was dismayed to learn later in the morning that none of the workers except the Constabulary and key hospital workers, who didn't attend this meeting, had heeded my request to stay on the job. They indeed struck and went back to their villages.

After the meeting, I sent a radio message to the High Commissioner's office (HICOM) reporting the strike. In the afternoon I walked and drove around the base. I felt better when I saw the generator plant humming smoothly, and Dr. Hagentornas told me he had things under control so far. But he and Nick, the administrative officer, and the six remaining Trukese were going to have to put in some long hours. At the dock I watched the first small freighter arrive and get serviced by the Americans in Public Works. Ray Hann, the heavy equipment mechanic, who was also the boat pool foreman, handled the lines on the pier. Then he and Pete Becker began refueling and putting the fresh water hose aboard. The ship's refrigeration system had broken down. Our refrigeration man, whose nickname was "Deep-freeze," went aboard and worked on it through the night. The next morning he had it operating again.

Monday evening, after Frank and I talked further, we agreed that he should sound out Chief Petrus regarding his views on the strike. Whatever attitudes he held and made known to the workers, Frank pointed out, could importantly affect the duration and outcome of the strike. Lieutenant Bob Beck, who was one of Frank's closest friends and well-liked by the Trukese, went along. During their talk, Chief Petrus suggested a meeting in my office the next morning.

When I greeted the chief at the administration building entrance Tuesday morning, his expressive face flowed into a big smile. As we sat down and began to discuss the strike, his smiled faded.

"He favors the strike aims," Frank interpreted, "but not the strike."

I pointed out the difficulty being created for Trukese patients in the hospital. There were about sixty bed patients and daily out-patient lines of twenty to thirty.

Chief Petrus said he shared my concern about the hospital, and he agreed to talk right away with the strike spokesmen, who remained on Moen, about his views. The next morning all the striking hospital employees returned to work.

On Wednesday night about ten o'clock, after reading files and documents I hadn't previously studied, I turned out the office lights and drove down toward the dock area. Lights shone and I heard a pounding noise at the garage, about half-way between the administration building and the waterfront. Orrin Shelvock, the American garage foreman, was working alone on a heavy-duty truck. Normally, more than a half-dozen Trukese mechanics worked there. He looked tired and was unshaven. "With luck, I'll keep 'em all on the road for the next week or two," he said.

Driving on to the waterfront, I saw more lights on the pier. The self-propelled barge was tied up to a float behind the pier head. Looking down, I saw Ray Hann and Pete Becker kneeling by the engine hatch. They looked up as I climbed down the ladder and jumped aboard. Both were sweaty and their hands grease-stained. "We're trying to free up this frozen engine before the *Chicot* comes in," Pete explained. The *Chicot* was one of the two big freighters, operated under contract with the Interior Department, that would bring in trade goods from time to time and pick up copra for Japan and other markets. Captain Anderson had told me that first afternoon in the hotel that it had too deep a draft to come alongside the dock, so it had to anchor out a quarter-mile. We'd need to unload and load it by barge.

The next morning I sent a second radio message to HICOM, this time reporting that we were carrying out all basic operations and that all Trukese hospital employees were back at work. In the afternoon I received a telephone call from Captain Anderson's residence. He and most of the other Naval officers remaining on Moen were waiting for a Navy transport plane to fly in on July 7 and take them to Guam. His house had become a gathering place for the officers, since they no longer had duties on Truk. The captain's secretary was on the phone.

"Captain Anderson wants to see you at his quarters immediately," she said, and hung up.

For a few seconds my hackles went up. Why did any request have to be delivered to me that curtly? I decided I was again being too touchy. Furthermore, besides all the valid reasons, I had one narrow, selfish interest in trying to maintain good relations with the Captain. His personal vehicle was a nearly new jeep in mint condition. It was painted a shining black, in contrast with all other jeeps, which were much older and painted Navy gray. It also had tires that looked new. I had asked Bob Law if the captain's jeep would be transferred to the district.

"I don't know," he said. "It isn't district equipment. The decision's Captain Anderson's."

The secretary met me at the door of the captain's spacious house, unsmiling, and ushered me into his presence. He turned in a swivel chair from his personal ham radio set in the living room and looked up at me.

"Here, read this," he said gruffly. "You might want to send it right away." He thrust into my hand a freshly typed radio message in multiple copies, then turned back to the radio.

As the captain had faced me, so did a half-dozen other Navy officers in the big living room, and the secretary. I didn't save a copy of the message, but I recall that it went about like this:

```
TO:          COMNAVMARIANAS
             (Commander Naval Forces Marianas Islands)
FROM:        DISTRICT ADMINISTRATOR/TRUK
INFO:        CINCPAC (Commander-in-Chief, Pacific)
             COMMARFORPAC (Commander, Marine Forces, Pacific)
             HICOMTERPACIS (High Commissioner, Trust Territory
             the Pacific Islands)
```

TRUK BASE COMPLETELY PARALYZED BY LABOR STRIKE. ALL NA-
TIVE WORKERS STRUCK 0730 HOURS JULY 2. SITUATION TENSE. NO
VIOLENCE YET. URGENTLY REQUEST AIR- LIFT TWO PLATOON MA-
RINES TRUK SOONEST TO INSURE SAFETY AMERICAN STAFF AND
GOVERNMENT PROPERTY.

I was dumbfounded. I felt my face reddening. All eyes except the captain's
were steadily on me.

Captain Anderson again swung around in his swivel chair and looked up
at me quizzically. I felt certain everyone present knew the contents of the message.

"I'm not going to send this!" I said, probably too emphatically.

A trace of a smile moved at the corners of the captain's mouth. He
shrugged and turned back to his radio gear.

"Is there anything else you want to discuss?" I asked.

"Nothing else," he said without turning.

I tore the telegram in two, dropped it on the table, left the house and returned to the office.

Despite experiences like this, I found myself beginning to like the captain.
Several times after my first four or five days on the island, we met in the hallway of the administration building or at the hotel, and he made pleasant small
talk with me. Once, during my first week in charge, I went to his house to see
him about something other than that telegram. He was at his ham radio, and
I heard him call several people in other parts of the Pacific. They were, I gathered, other hobby ham operators. He simply identified himself as "Andy." I
asked him to check me out on operation of the picket boat, and he readily
agreed. He was a good man, but he didn't want to leave his little island para-
dise.

On the fourth of July, several members of my staff and I had lunch together at the hotel. Frank predicted the strike would be over within a week. The same day a special flight enroute from Guam to the Ponape District (eastern Carolines) and the Marshall Islands, both hundreds of miles to the east of us, dropped off three more new American civilian employees.

The next day, Thursday, Chief Upuini from Tol, largest and most populous island in Truk Lagoon, traveled to Moen on his boat, a former Japanese motor launch, and came up to my office. It was my first meeting with him. Next to Chief Petrus, Frank had told me earlier, Upuini was the most powerful chief in the lagoon. Perhaps in his mid-fifties at the time, he was, I guessed, more than five years older than Chief Petrus. His face had some creases and his thinning hair was curly and gray. All his movements were energetic.

After greetings and small talk over coffee, he got to the point of his visit. "I will send you workers—many good workers from my island." I was absolutely delighted to hear those words.

"I appreciate very much your offer of help, Chief Upuini," I told him, and Frank translated, his face registering concern. "If our regular workers don't return soon, I may call on you."

Minutes after Chief Upuini and Frank left, I got in touch with Dr. Hagentornas and Warrant Officer Reed. I asked them to pass the word quietly and off-handedly to their Trukese employees on the job that Upuini had been in. When Frank heard later what I'd done, he told me, grinning, that it wasn't really necessary.

"Word of Chief Upuini's visit has already reached the farthest village of Moen," he said. "By nightfall it'll be all over the lagoon!"

The next day the majority of striking workers returned, and by the following Monday all were back on the job. Now we could settle down as the new civilian team, I hoped, and move beyond a bare-bones operation.

On Friday evening a Navy transport plane flew in and the crew stayed overnight at the hotel. The next morning they airlifted Captain Anderson, Bob Law and all their remaining staff, except Lieutenant Beck and ten enlisted men to Guam. The latter had orders to stay on and complete improvements on the fresh water supply system above Telegraph Hill.

Reck came up to me at the edge of the airfield as I watched the plane make a sweeping half-circle and take a northwest heading. "I do believe the captain has abandoned some Navy equipment," he said, grinning. He nodded toward the parking area. I turned to look. There sat the black jeep with the keys in it.

Three weeks after the takeover, I drove the black jeep back down to the airfield with mounting excitement. A radio message from Washington two days earlier stated that my wife, Carolyn, and our girls—Marolyn, almost two, and ten-weeks-old Barbara—were enroute to Truk. Interior had booked them straight through to Guam—about 9,000 miles and more than seventy hours elapsed time, with only stops of a few hours at San Francisco and Honolulu airports. In those days Pan Am's four-engine, propellor-driven Stratocruisers flew about 300 miles an hour. After reaching Guam, my family would still have another four-hour flight on a little PBY plane to Truk. It was a gruelling schedule, even for a healthy young lady like Carolyn, with two tiny children.

When the amphibian landed and rolled to the parking area, I was up the ramp in seconds. Carolyn, beaming, looked beautiful and surprisingly fresh. Many people had driven to the airfield to meet the newcomers. After introducing her around, I drove my little family to our new home—Captain Anderson's former house. Keti, the middle-aged housemaid I had hired on Frank's recommendation, immediately took charge of the girls. An instinctive loving relationship seemed to form between Keti and the girls surprisingly fast. Having her—and later, Bertelina, as part of our family for five years was a very happy part of our lives on Truk.

Carolyn took a quick walk through the house. I followed, watching and listening to her delight at what she saw. We both had expected our home would be simpler. In constructing Captain Anderson's house, Public Works or the SeaBees had used a quonset for the central core, then added throughout those hardwood cherry walls, which we really liked, along with plenty of windows to create a light, cheerful look for the whole house. They had built generous-sized additions for the living room, two other bedrooms and a utility room. There were two bathrooms and plenty of closet space. The kitchen was equipped with both a big refrigerator and a freezer.

By the time we got to the girls' room, Keti, who had taken them in tow as soon as we entered the house, was bedding them down. Before nearly falling asleep during a nice dinner Keti had prepared, Carolyn told me that on the overnight flight from Washington to San Francisco, the stewardess gave both girls' seats to overbooked passengers, although she had tickets for both girls and herself. She held baby Barbara throughout the night, and Meme also shared their one seat. In the first hour of the San Francisco-Honolulu flight, which took eight hours, Barbara developed colic and cried all the way to Hawaii. Carolyn stood with her and patted her back. They stayed up near the engines so her crying wouldn't disturb people trying to sleep.

On Guam, Carolyn and the children had been met at one o'clock in the morning by a Trust Territory liaison officer, who drove them to comfortable transient quarters. About the time she got the girls in bed and she was at last ready for her first night's sleep on the trip, her eyes caught a movement on the ceiling.

"I was horrified!" she said. "Little crawly things that looked like tiny lizards were walking around upside down on the ceiling!"

Before I could say anything she went on.

"I was afraid they might crawl on the girls and me—maybe bite us while we slept. So I stayed awake the rest of the night with a light on and kept an eye on them."

One of the first things she learned on Truk was that *gekkos* are completely harmless. They inhabit virtually every tropical home and office, never bother anyone, and are welcome guests because they keep the rooms free of flies and mosquitos.

Carolyn was in bed minutes after dinner. She and the girls awoke the next morning, apparently fully recovered. It was hard to tell whether Carolyn or Marolyn began more eagerly to explore the new world around them. It was the first full day of their five-year stay in the islands.

Learning Trukese

In the weeks following the end of the strike and the Navy's departure for Guam, I continued to watch and listened with admiration as Frank Mahony talked with Trukese around headquarters in their own language. On each trip to other islands in the Truk Lagoon, as I was beginning to get acquainted with the chiefs, other leaders, and the villagers, I often had to use an interpreter.

I started carrying out my plan to visit every island in the district, to meet the people and begin to develop an understanding of the situation on each island. *If I could just talk their language*, I thought with every visit. During my work in West Germany on my first overseas assignment, what a difference it had made when I learned to speak even a little of that language.

During the first five years of civilian administration, the High Commissioner's staff—with the exception of Mr. Frank Midkiff, who was the second official to hold that position, gave only mild encouragement to us workers in the vineyards to learn the local language. I recall few memoranda from headquarters on the subject. There was no requirement to demonstrate language proficiency as a condition for advancement to the next higher grade, or for within-grade pay increases. But thanks to a Navy contract which carried over into the first months of Interior operations, Fred was there to help us start to learn Trukese.

Alfred "Fred" Smith was a young, down-to-earth anthropologist from Wisconsin, with a strong background in linguistics. His Navy contract had involved setting up an experimental program to provide special instruction in map reading, the three R's and other subjects to a small, hand-picked group of young Trukese from the district's most western islands and from the Woleai area of the Yap District. Those were some of the most remote islands in the entire Trust Territory. While he was winding down his work on that program for several months after the Navy left, I asked him if he could find time to teach a Trukese language class to our new civilian employees. Fred readily agreed, with one proviso.

"You'll have to move fast, though," he told me, "because I'll be leaving Truk in about another month."

"We'll start tomorrow afternoon, if that'll fit your schedule," I responded. We managed to assemble a group of about a dozen employees for the first class, held in a partially vacant quonset behind the administration building.

"First," Fred announced, standing before his class, "while I propose to teach Trukese by having you listen, then speak, I do want to introduce you to Elbert." He picked up a copy of a small, soft-covered book from a chair beside him. It was a Trukese-English dictionary, developed for the Navy Military Government staff on Truk by Lieutenant-Commander Samuel H. Elbert, USNR. A linguist in uniform, he had arrived only four months after the Japanese surrender and spent the next eight months doing field research.

During my first month on Truk I had told Frank I wanted to learn Trukese and intended to encourage all staff members who thought they had any language aptitude at all to study it. He showed me his copy of Elbert's dictionary—one of only two or three at the district center—and I promptly sent off a letter to Honolulu, asking for several more. Back came a brief note informing me their supply was exhausted, but steps were being taken to acquire more. We'd get them in due course.

Fred pointed out to his new class that the Trukese language is unwritten. Almost before he got the last words out of his mouth, one of our intermediate school teacher trainers who had been a member of Bob Law's staff, cleared her throat and held her hand up.

"Protestant missionaries from Ponape went into the Mortlocks (islands in the southeast part of the Truk District) in the early 1870s and translated the New Testament into Mortlockese. Reverend Robert Logan and other early Western missionaries wrote several simple elementary school textbooks in Trukese in the 1880s and later. We've had Elbert four years now. Why do you say it is an unwritten language?"

Fred explained that "unwritten" is a linguist's term which simply means that no standard system of spelling or pronunciation guides were developed and adopted. He went on to point out that Trukese is an *agglutinative* language: richly laced with two or more syllables glued together to make a new meaning. Many of those glued words, also common in Polynesian languages, have a syllable repeated: like *pwochopwoch* (white), *parapar* (red), *achengicheng* (dear), and *kiskis* (little).

"You will also soon learn," Fred continued, "that many Trukese words have been adopted from the three previous colonial powers—especially from German and Japanese. The Spanish, I understand, didn't get over this way very much from Ponape. Examples of German words are *zeppenin* (airplane), *mak* (mark), *nadeln* (needle). The Japanese contributed many words, including such common ones as *tenki* (electricity), *pencho* (toilet), *chitosa* (car), and *skogi* (airplane)."

My first Trukese lesson was a disaster. After these preliminary observations, and a little guidance on how to read the pronunciation marks, Fred said, "Now we'll practice speaking a few words. I'll pronounce them in English, then in Trukese. You will take turns repeating them. Margaret, the Trukese word for banana is *uch*."

"*Uch*," she replied flawlessly. "*Uch!*"

"Very good. Reck, the word for sailboat: *wa seres. Wa seres*."

"*Wa seres*," Reck intoned, and again the reply sounded to me like a perfect echo.

"Fine," Fred approved. "Will, the word which means 'to': *ngeni. Ngeni*."

"*Ngneni*," I sounded the word confidently. After all, I had been a good student of Spanish and did all right in the State Department's spoken German courses in Frankfurt.

"*Ngeni*," he repeated. "*Ngeni*. Try again."

"*Ngneni*."

"No." His voice was very patient. "*Ngeni*. Ngeni. *Ngeni*," he repeated slowly, carefully.

"*Ngneni,*" I tried again, by this time red-faced and shaken by my display of an apparent lack of ear for Trukese language study. The sensitive young instructor simply acknowledged my response with a nod and moved on to the person next to me.

Walking out of the classroom after the lesson ended, I suddenly realized that I kept mispronouncing *ngeni* because each time I added an extra n after the first two letters. I turned and walked back into the room.

"*Ngeni,*" I said tentatively to Fred. "*Ngeni!*" He gave me a slightly puzzled smile. "You had me worried," he said.

While I can't recall again complicating my language study by adding a letter, I encountered other problems, several of which embarrassed me and provided howls of laughter for my Trukese listeners.

When Fred left Truk, Frank said he thought I should get a Trukese tutor to work with me an hour a day. He suggested that I ask Napo DeFang, who was the Superintendent of elementary schools, and the top Trukese employee in the Education department. Napo agreed, and I soon found him both a fine tutor and a delightful companion. I worked fairly diligently at language study during the next year. Too often, though, my lessons were interrupted by meetings, visiting officials, a trip to Hawaii for a conference of district administrators, and because I often put a higher priority on other immediate tasks.

Napo began by having me learn a few hundred words of basic vocabulary. He followed this up by speaking to me in short sentences, drawing upon my small but slowly growing list of words mastered. After a month or so, he urged me to start putting this beginning knowledge to work, even if I made mistakes. With his assurance that the Trukese people would not only understand but also appreciate that Americans were trying to learn their language, I waded in.

Sometimes in the evenings Carolyn and I would drive in the jeep with Marolyn and baby Barbara, to Mechetiu or Iras village, each about a mile away. We'd park and walk slowly along the graveled beach road, past little wooden houses with rusting tin roofs and nice grassy yards, partly covered with a profusion of bright, tropical flowering plants, banana, papaya, breadfruit and coconut trees. One of us would carry Barbara, still too young to walk, while Marolyn, now more than two years old, walked or trotted along near us. On these evening strolls I first tested my language ability on some villagers, using the simplest greetings and pleasantries.

When a man or woman came walking toward us along the road, I'd call out, "*nepuin anim* (good evening.) *Ifa usum non ei pwin?*" (How are you this evening?) When the villagers didn't beat me to it by calling out the greetings first, they always smiled pleasantly and returned them. We'd walk on and see others sitting together on lawns or steps and porches, visiting in the cool evening hours. Again I'd call out in my best Trukese, "Good evening. The sunset is very pretty this evening," or "My wife and I think the night air is very nice."

Some villagers on Moen Island seemed to know through the bamboo telegraph that the new *kepina* was trying to learn their language but was not yet ready to engage in more than the simplest exchanges. In their gracious ways, they responded so that my sketchy knowledge was not over-taxed.

"Good evening, all of you," they would say in Trukese." "Yes, it is a good hour at sunset." Then they might add a couple of simple sentences in Trukese and, if they spoke English, switch at that point and continue the conversation. Often they fussed with our girls, and sometimes a lady or young girl would take a frangipani or hibiscus blossom and put it in Marolyn's very blonde hair. Barbara still had too little hair to accommodate flowers.

During one evening stroll the usual baby-fussing routine was reversed. We approached cluster of young women with babies, and a couple of older ladies, while men sat on a nearby porch and steps, smoking and talking. The villagers sang out greetings. Carolyn and I replied in Trukese with the traditional "Good evening to all of you."

We stopped to visit for a moment. With the group was a little girl who was, I judged, between two and three. She was dressed in a gay calico and wore a garland of fragrant frangipani around her head. Bending over the child, I smiled appreciatively at the women. "*Ei nengi mei fakkun murinno,*" I said in a voice warm with praise. The women turned to each other, trying to suppress giggles. From the nearby porch the men, who had stopped to join in the initial greetings and conversation, shook silently. Carolyn looked at me, smiling, but her eyes asked what I'd said wrong. I didn't know.

Back home that evening, I went immediately to the Trukese dictionary. What I found sent Carolyn into peals of laughter. By using the word *nengi* instead of the intended word *nengin* (small girl), I had said, "This is a pretty little onion."

Napo continued to work patiently with me as I tried to master tricky suffixes and improve my pronunciation. He explained carefully shades of meaning of words and one day emphasized with a little smile—he'd doubtless heard of the onion incident—that many Trukese words looked and sounded very much alike, but have a world of difference in meaning. Sadly for me, the truth of that statement was underscored several months later, during my most humbling language experience, while at Pis Island in the Mortlocks.

It was our regular field trip, made every two months, to those eleven islands strung out for 160 miles south and southeast from Truk Lagoon. That evening, with our work and dinner behind us, Chief Orlando called the community together at the island meeting house. Similar to many such meeting houses, the thatched building was partly open on the sides, so cool trade winds could blow through it. Several members of our field trip party had been invited to sit with the chief at or near a little wooden table in the front.

Community meetings like this provided our opportunity to talk with the people about conditions on their islands: their food situation, health problems, the school, and similar matters. It also offered, especially for people living far from the district center, a diversion—the best show in town that evening. The chief introduced us to the nearly two hundred men, women and children sitting on the sand floor, facing us. Then he spoke to the assembled islanders for a few minutes. Hard as I tried to follow his remarks, I picked up only fragments. My efforts were not made easier by the rapidity of his speech or the fact that in the Mortlocks they use an "l," where the people in Truk lagoon used an "n."

Finishing, he turned to me and said in Trukese, "*Kepina*, you will speak now?"

Despite my difficulty in following Orlando's talk to his people, I felt confident that evening. I had demonstrated to my own satisfaction on a dozen previous occasions that I could manage a greeting, followed by a few short, uncomplicated sentences, then sit down. On these trips I often asked Frank to interpret for me—especially anything more than simple exchanges. Now I motioned to him, sitting beside me, to remain seated. I stood and looked into a sea of friendly, expectant faces. Smiling back, I offered in a clear, confident voice, the traditional greeting.

"*Nepuin anim, kepina!*" the animated voices chorused back.

"I am very happy to see all of you here on your island this evening," I said in Trukese.

"*Kinisou chapur!*" (Thank you very much) the voices returned.

"We Americans and Trukese from the '*Ofis*' (headquarters) like to come here and visit with you," I went on. "We are happy that not many people are sick. We are happy to see you made so much copra. You took it to the ship fast." This was going swimmingly. Now I became a bit expansive.

Chief Orlando, moon-faced, past middle-age, was, even by Trukese standards, an unusually warm, good-natured man. I decided to drop a little praise on him for this pleasing quality. Quickly lining up the string of words that were to be the compliment, I spoke them. A look of sharp surprise swept away the chief's big smile; his countenance clouded. The instant change of expressions in the audience told me I had ripped it again. I glanced to my right and left. Trukese members of the field trip party were trying to suppress laughter. Frank grinned broadly. Leaning over in front of me, he spoke to the Chief in a voice which, in the hush that descended upon the audience immediately following my pronouncement about him gone-astray, echoed loudly off the farthest walls.

"Mr. Muller wanted to say that Chief Orlando is *focheoch*" (has a cheerful disposition). Instead, I had said "*fochefoch*" (sullen-faced). The chief's head went back, and he convulsed in laughter, joined by the audience. Wave followed wave. It sounded roof-shaking to me. I tried to laugh with them, while I felt my face burning. When the meeting ended, the chief, still chortling, walked over beside me, shook my hand heartily, and we walked out together.

Back on Moen I related the incident to Napo, though he doubtless heard of it the day our freighter returned. "Oh, that's all right, Mr. Muller," he said gently. "You're the first American *kepina* ever to learn Trukese. We had a Navy Education officer here once who began to study it. After he learned a little of our language, he liked to let us know about his progress. His little dog followed him around the base, so the officer sometimes pointed to his dog and said to us, '*Ngang konak!*' He wanted to say, 'This is my dog.' He didn't know he was telling us, 'I am a dog.'"

Wherever American wives gathered on Moen, they regaled each other with stories of completely misunderstood orders given in faltering Trukese to housemaids. This sometimes resulted in amazing happenings. Staff members who didn't learn the language had their own favorite stories of communications failures. Some island officials, especially those far from the District center, appeared to understand more English than they in fact did.

Using Trukese interpreters, although some were very capable, was by no means a sure-fire solution. Sam Mukaida, one of our teacher trainers, born and raised in Hawaii, was a man with a serious countenance behind black-rimmed glasses, but a strong sense of humor bubbled away just below the surface. He had an experience that illustrates the perils of channeling one's words through an islander with limited interpreter skills.

On this particular field trip to the western islands, Sam was field trip officer—the staff member in charge. The ship was at Pulusuk Island in the far western part of the District. After the day's work, Chief Fatan had called to order the customary community meeting. Sam thus was asked by the chief to be the lead-off visiting speaker.

Using one of our office employees as interpreter, Sam expressed the field trip party's pleasure in being on Pulusuk. "As field trip officer," he said, "I wish to thank you, Chief Fatan, and your people for your warm hospitality."

Our young office worker translated. Sam saw Napo DeFang, sitting nearby, begin to shake with mirth. After the meeting, Sam asked Napo what he found so amusing in the remarks.

"When your interpreter translated your words," Napo explained, "instead of saying you thank the people for their warm hospitality, he said: 'Dr. Mukaida thanks you and says you have a hot hospital.'"

"That was the day," Sam told me later, "I decided to seriously study Trukese."

Although perhaps twenty American employees and a few wives began to study Trukese, less than half of us stuck with it to the point where it was usable in our daily work. It opened a whole new world for us when we were able to talk directly with the people throughout the islands, the majority of whom did not speak English.

Life At the Taro Hilton

I had seen in the Navy that whether a ship was well-run and happy depended heavily upon the captain. I wanted our Truk headquarters to operate very effectively. I wanted, too, that both it and our little community there, with islanders and Americans, would be pleasant places to work and live, and for all of us to be good neighbors. Part of achieving this, I felt certain, would be for us Americans, including our wives and children, to reach out and become friends with Trukese families in Moen Island's villages and, hopefully, with people on islands beyond Moen.

Mr. McConnell had made clear to me, during my Honolulu briefings, that among my responsibilities as district administrator was to provide logistics support for all U.S. Government personnel on the island and their families. That included the High Court judges and certain headquarters staff living there because it was near the center of the Territory, and their work took them to all districts. It also included U.S. Weather Bureau staff, and special study teams such as from the U.S. Geological Survey. Those support services included housing, furnishings, water, electricity, fire protection and personal safety, medical and commissary services. I'd also be responsible for their morale, and to see that all Americans conducted themselves with decorum. It didn't take me long to realize that this latter part of my job was going to add considerably to my education in human relations.

Our frailties are harder to hide on little tropical islands than at home. When they did surface, they were more jarring to neighbors because we all lived close together and depended more upon each other. During my island years, I was to deal with some startling human foibles. When I was confronted with unacceptable kinds of conduct by American employees, and at least once by a wife, they came as a surprise in most cases. My reactions ranged, over the years, from frustration in a few incidents, and disappointment in others, to anger at the actions of two or three.

At least three couples arrived on Truk with their marriages in trouble. Those husbands and wives must have thought that, somehow, things would get better on a beautiful tropical island. But whatever it was that bothered them at home, they seemed to have brought with them. Twice I had to deal with alcoholics. Then there was the case of a man abusing his wife by constant physical threats. While verbally assaulting her in their home, I learned, he would terrify her by ordering her to sit on a chair near a wall, then throw his open pocket knife into the wall beside her head. Herb Wilson, head of our Education Department, and I once had to deal with a verified report that an American teacher tried to involve one or more intermediate boarding school male students in homosexual acts. Then there was the fascinating but troublesome case of the wife with nymphomania.

In carrying out my responsibilities for the conduct of Americans, I learned quickly that I could get in trouble with islanders by supporting the action of an American when, in the eyes of at least some Trukese, the American worker had acted improperly. One memorable incident took place aboard the freighter *Chicot.*

Public Works was responsible for loading and unloading freighters. One day, an American shop foreman was supervising a pickup group of islander stevedores in stowing 100-pound jute bags of copra below decks. The temperature was around eighty degrees, and at least ten degrees hotter in the ship's several holds. One young Trukese working on deck kept going over to the "scuttlebutt" (drinking fountain) below the front of the wheelhouse. Each time after taking a drink, he would moisten his hands in the water, then wash his face and under his arms, with some of that water flowing back into the scuttlebutt's sink.

The foreman told him on two separate occasions to stop washing himself in the drinking fountain. When the man did it a third time, the foreman came up to him, told him in a forceful voice, though not swearing at him, to stop it. At the same time he shoved him away from the scuttlebutt.

The Trukese man immediately responded with anger. He left the ship with a couple of his sympathetic friends, went directly to the Constabulary headquarters and asked to have the foreman arrested and brought to trial in the district court. Shortly thereafter, Sergeant Keiko, in charge of the Constabulary, came to my office and asked how he should handle the case.

My first thought was that if this had happened in similar circumstances at home, the foreman might have acted in the same way. He had performed creditably in Public Works, was well regarded by other Americans, seemed to get along well with his own shop employees, (stevedores were not regular staff) and had not previously created any trouble. If I started permitting Americans to be subject to court trials and possible fines or jail sentences for such a small offense, I thought, we may have a hard time getting American employees to return for a second tour, or even recruit to fill vacancies. I told the sheriff not to prosecute; I'd handle the matter.

Several Trukese on my staff, I soon learned, expressed their displeasure that I had not let the foreman be brought to trial. Neither Frank Mahony nor Chief Justice Furber was around headquarters at the time. When they returned, I reviewed the matter first with Frank, then with Judge Furber. Both thought I should have let the matter go to court. Frank said the American foreman's action did conflict with the culture. Trukese don't even like to have others slap them on the back in a friendly way. I acknowledged I had made a mistake. A directive went to all U.S. staff that we will take fully into account this part of the culture. I called in Pete Becker and the other department heads and told them that in the future no American was to lay a hand on any islander under any circumstance. I was learning—but sometimes too slowly.

Once I encountered a situation where, when the decision was made to send a social offender home, he refused to go. We had begun our second month on Truk with no electrician. Two other Public Works men who knew something about electrical work pitched in and helped, but they were busy with their own jobs. One day Pete Becker, head of Public Works during the first two years, heard that the electrician in the Ponape District had quit and was on the weekly flight that would land at Truk enroute to Guam. He wanted to offer the man temporary duty for two or three weeks. I asked why the man quit at Ponape. Pete didn't know. The plane was due in an hour later. I agreed. Pete met the plane and the man accepted the temporary assignment.

Several evenings later Carolyn and I were guests at a dinner, when the electrician's name came up. "You may regret taking that guy—even temporarily," said another guest, who once had worked for a contractor on Guam. "He's a tough, tough bird! I saw him get in a fight at a bar. He reached over, bashed the head off a beer bottle and started for the other guy, swinging the jagged end...."

Four days later, the temporary electrician, Jake, (not his real name) began drinking heavily. He stopped reporting for work. Pete and I agreed the man would be on the Friday plane to Guam.

I was at home shaving that Friday morning when the phone rang. It was Pete. His wife hadn't yet arrived on Truk, so he had agreed to let Jake stay with him. "We got a problem," he said. "Jake says he's not leavin'. He won't get up."

"I'll come right over," I said.

"Be careful, Mr. Muller," Pete warned. "He's a former prizefighter."

I had a reassuring idea. "I'll pick up Harry Reed on the way," I said.

Marine Warrant Officer Reed, battle-hardened in WWII Pacific campaigns had, among his skills, experience as a judo instructor. When we walked into Pete's house, Harry, dressed in khaki shorts, blouse, and overseas cap, asked, "Where is he?"

Pete pointed to a bedroom. We walked in. Jake was still in bed. He was of medium height, but his tattooed muscles rippled, and he had a chest like a draft horse. Even with his hangover, he looked mighty rugged and younger than forty.

"Get up! Get dressed!" Harry said in a commanding voice, with no preliminaries. You could tell he had faced greater dangers than this. Jake stared back at him coldly for fifteen seconds. He finally spoke.

"Is that an order or a request?"

"That's an order."

"What ya tryin' to do, frig me?"

"Get up!" Harry repeated. "Now!" He still looked and sounded perfectly calm as he took two steps toward the man.

Jake pushed back the blankets, swung his feet to the floor and reached for his socks. He was on the noon flight out.

Relating these problems may give the impression that our American community was a scruffy lot. Actually, we had a fine group of people. What I described above were isolated cases, spread out over five years. We had about 125 American adults—including my staff and about a dozen headquarters employees and our wives, plus around twenty-five young children.

The U.S. Weather Bureau maintained a station on Moen, manned by two Americans. Their wives were with them at Truk. The U.S. Post Office Department had one postmistress there. From time to time we had special contractors or other teams living in our headquarters area. Those who caused problems never represented more than two or three percent. The rest were very decent, pleasant, well-adjusted people.

A couple of times during my island years, when two kinds of documents prepared by the staff landed on my desk I was privileged to read some of the most soaring creative writing, in draft form, to be seen in the islands. One of those literary flights was in response to a request from headquarters for background material for use in updating the recruiting brochure. The other draft document was justification for our special "hardship" allowance—paid to personnel living overseas in isolation, difficult climates, and other forms of deprivation. This latter kind of allowance, given also to Foreign Service officers and some military people overseas, was not looked upon with a strong measure of kindness by some Congressional appropriations committee members.

The draft recruiting document, sent to me for review and clearance to mail to our headquarters, described lyrically for prospective employees the joys of living in the tropics. It painted word pictures of palm trees rustling gently in trade winds, white sandy beaches, laughing islanders. It told of happy, free times when one could indulge in swimming, shell collecting, fishing expeditions, snorkeling, a seemingly endless round of picnics and parties with Trukese on neighboring islands, socializing at the hotel and in our homes. One could have reasonably concluded from reading it that there wasn't much time left for work.

The hardship allowance document, drafted by the same creative staff scriveners but aimed at that entirely different readership, emphasized in the most negative terms conceivable the battles one had to fight daily to stay alive: extreme isolation, a catalogue of frightening diseases, the long dry season, with attendant water rationing, a description of the food situation that would make a reader eager to see the next instalment to learn whether we made it until the supply ship arrived. It reported almost non-existent recreational opportunities, dulling monotony for wives, further burdened by living in left-over World War II quonsets, and leather goods and clothing being damaged, along with their wearers, in stifling heat.

Happily, the truth of the matter lay far above middle ground. Each time, after some headshakes and rueful smiles, I picked up my editing pencil. I laughed, though, as I stopped to picture what might happen if such unedited *recruitment* material inadvertently landed on the desks of Congressional appropriations committee members reviewing *hardship* justifications.

Before we got to Truk, Carolyn and I thought we'd have lots of time in the islands for reading. It didn't work out that way. At first we missed the daily newspaper and radio broadcasts. We hadn't known TV in Germany, and we saw little of it during the short time at home between assignments. Once every two or three months the *Gunner's Knot* or *Chicot*, which carried freight to the six district headquarters and picked up copra, brought us cargo and mail. Dozens of big canvas mail bags were barged in from the ship a quarter-mile off the dock and trucked to our little post office, where a crowd of American women and children already were gathered. These were social occasions. Women talked about what they had ordered from Sears or Ward's and about what shopping treats the commissary might offer tomorrow.

The first time Carolyn and I were the happy recipients of a mountain of "surface" mail (all first class came by plane) postmistress Frankie Mayo stuffed it into two of those big canvas bags for us. We dumped it all onto the middle of the living room floor. It was like Christmas in September. After stacking, like fireplace logs, a dozen fat copies of the Sunday *Washington Post*, we decided to set up a system of opening one paper every Sunday morning until they were gone. By then, we figured, the next batch would have arrived. We were getting our current news mainly from air-mailed copies of *Time* and *Newsweek*. We liked our Sunday paper system and stayed with it all the time we were at Truk.

Every American family had a radio. We soon learned they had sharp limitations on a remote Pacific Island. When we were lucky, we picked up the Armed Forces Network broadcasts from Guam. They were mostly recorded. Occasionally, when there was a fortunate bounce of radio waves off a cloud, we'd hear the crisp British accents of a BBC announcer, relayed from Hong Kong. The only radio programs we could be sure of receiving were from "The Voice of Del Rio" on the southern Texas border. It was a very high-watt station, and its western music and news came in strongly all across the Pacific.

What our quonset homes lacked in outer appearance, they made up in comfort and great views out over the lagoon. Their high ceilings, louvred and screened windows provided good air circulation. Smooth painted cement floors, except in our house and several others which had wooden floors, helped keep the rooms cool. Most families covered their floors with hibiscus fibre or pandanus mats, finely woven by Trukese women. Others imported "Philippine squares"—attractive fiber mats shaped into tightly-woven squares. We inherited our nice mats from Captain Anderson. Some neighbors preferred the feel of the bare floors on their feet. Most of us adopted the habit, because it made sense in the tropics, of removing our shoes or *zoris* (Japanese rubber sandals) just inside the doorway.

Headquarters began a program of replacing, in increments, our worn furniture. The first shipment consisted of rattan living room couches and chairs—each with identical fabric colors and designs, from the Philippines. The ladies got together and appealed, with limited success, for some variety in fabrics. For a furnished home and utilities, we were charged thirty to forty dollars a month (around $250-$320 in today's inflated dollars). Even then, when an American craftsmen in the our Public Works department earned a base pay of around $2.50 an hour, and our American teacher trainers earned little more, it was a real bargain.

Carolyn picked up some useful tricks from other women that first year: like keeping her cake mixes and anything else made of flour in the freezer part of the refrigerator for two weeks. This prevented weevils from hatching. The same treatment also kept film from mold damage and nylons from rotting. Women didn't wear nylons on Truk. It was too warm. But they kept them in good condition for a vacation trip or home leave in a colder climate. It was very dangerous for anyone to hang clothing directly over a hot locker (Navy jargon for a clothes closet) light bulb installed about a foot off the floor—even though it was covered with heavy mesh wire. We had several close calls in the community when women hung rayon dresses or nylons over a light to protect them from mold, and the bottoms of the cloth touched the screen wire and began to smolder. We heard from the headquarters' roving safety officer about how a quonset home in another district caught fire and was consumed in minutes. My greatest single worry about district center operations was fire danger.

Daytime temperatures stayed around eighty-five degrees and dropped five to ten degrees at night. Humidity is high all over that part of the Pacific. Steady trade winds, which change directions twice a year, helped make us feel comfortable. So did the fact that people's blood thins out in the tropics.

But we did experience very noticeable weather changes there near the equator. In that region, July through November is known as the typhoon season. Americans working at our U.S. Weather Bureau station on Truk often reminded us that typhoons can and do occur, however, any time of the year. When a typhoon passed within a hundred miles of Truk in its great half-circle sweep westward toward Japan's islands, then curved north and eastward, we felt its backlash in the form of torrential rains and strong winds, cold enough so that a woolen sweater or jacket felt good.

"How did you happen to come to the islands?" visitors inevitably asked us. We asked each other the same question. "Dr. Mac," McDonald, Chief Medical Officer for the Trust Territory, was a man everyone loved. Someone asked the lanky, droll brain surgeon from New England what brought him to the Tropics.

"Why—I was cold up there in Maine," he said.

We heard all kinds of answers, the most common of which were, "It sounded like interesting and challenging work." A few said it seemed like a good place to work for a few years and save some money. Others explained that they always wanted to live in the South Seas Islands. Sometimes people said, "I wanted to help the natives." This latter response regularly brought one of our local wags from Public Works to his feet to mimic a soulful violin player.

The two focal points of American social life were our homes, where we had dinners, "firesides," card parties and cocktail parties, and the hotel, where the Community Club met and held many of its activities. Besides American and Trukese neighbors, we entertained visiting headquarters staff, Transocean Airlines (TALOA) crews on their weekly logistics flights, military plane crews, and ship officers and crews. Some winters, about the time snow began to fly back home, a Congressional party would arrive to look us over for a few days.

In our small community there was time for visiting—like in the America of a few generations earlier. Sometimes on a stormy Saturday morning, a nearby neighbor, "Teddy" Ott, whose husband, Wellington, succeeded Pete Becker as head of Public Works after the first two years, would phone Carolyn and me and say, "The coffee pot's on. I just took a pan of cinnamon rolls out of the oven. Come on down!"

Sitting at a table near their kitchen, made warm by the open oven door, savoring the coffee and hot rolls, listening to the wind buffeting the house and rain pouring down, and exchanging small talk, was a simple, enjoyable island pleasure.

Most families did quite a bit of informal socializing like that, and there were no cliques. Family visiting back and forth was based on the enjoyment of each other's company, and sometimes also on mutual interest in a hobby. No family or single person was left out of community social life. Guests at a dinner party might include the electrician and a teacher, the carpenter, doctor, and the Chief Justice. Any one of the guests and his wife, or a bachelor, might be host for a similar group at the next party.

Even by the early 1950s, most islanders in Truk Lagoon had, with few exceptions, experienced much more cultural change than their friends and relatives on the outer islands of the district. This was due to their contacts over past decades with, in turn, Germans and, especially, Japanese and Americans in these islands. The proud, highly self-confident people from the far western islands of the district were quite another matter. Being most isolated from touches of modernity around the district center, they stayed more with the old ways, which they considered best.

One morning word reached me that a big Puluwat Island sailing canoe from the western part of the district, with six men aboard, including Chief Romelo, had just arrived. This was during my second year in the islands. By then he and I had become good friends. I drove to the waterfront, located them at Truk Trading Company (TTC) and invited the chief and his sailor companions to dinner at our house the following evening. Carolyn was accustomed to cooking food the Trukese seemed to like best. But preparing dinner for a crew of western islanders was a new experience for her. They didn't come to Moen often, and this was our first time to invite them to our home.

"What'll I feed them?" she asked. We had learned in the first year that, at least for Truk Lagoon guests and Mortlockese from the southeast part of the district, we couldn't go wrong serving rice with hamburger, tinned beef or fresh tuna. They liked chicken, but because of a shortage of them in all the islands, we seldom bought any. An American hostess was on solid ground serving breadfruit and taro and any of the wonderful fresh fruits. Most Trukese liked coffee and found it hard to turn down home-made ice cream.

"How about serving rice mixed with tomato sauce and hamburger or tuna?" I suggested. "Better make plenty. They're good eaters. And they've just finished sailing 160 miles on tight rations."

The next evening one of the Americans I had invited to join us and I went down in two jeeps to pick them up near the dock. For the occasion Chief Romelo and one of his five companions wore open khaki shirts in addition to their loin cloths. The rest wore only loin cloths. When dinner was ready, Carolyn set it up buffet style, so each man could file past the kitchen counter and help himself. I noted with satisfaction that she had made three big, heaping bowls of the rice casserole. I greatly underestimated their capacity. Before the third guest had served himself, she realized she would have to do some fast improvising. While Keti, our housemaid, put more water on to boil, Carolyn opened packages of macaroni and more tins of tomato sauce and mixed them together with tinned corned beef.

The Puluwat men were a delight to entertain. As we ate, they sat on the living room floor mats in a big semi-circle with several American men. After dinner, the Puluwat men rearranged themselves slightly, ready to enjoy one of the forms of entertainment Trukese from all parts of the District seemed to like best: looking at slide pictures, taken on field trips, of themselves and others on the different islands. Throughout the evening they were as at ease as an ambassador at a formal dinner. The freshness of their enjoyment was a pleasure to see.

The next time I invited western island sailors for dinner, nearly a year later, Carolyn groaned when I mentioned food. "This time," she said, "I'm not going to get caught short! I'll make it in a washtub." And she did. It worked fine.

The Chief Justice's wife, Ruth Furber, along with Carolyn and other American women, often were called upon to organize dinners and receptions for visitors: island leaders and officials coming through from Honolulu and Washington. Military planes came in once in a while from Guam. Twice we had U.S. submarines, enroute from Hawaii to Guam or beyond, stop by for a day or two. And the two big freighters, *Chicot* and *Gunner's Knot*, were in our harbor for a few days on each trip through the districts. Those were incentive enough, and opportunities, to have a party.

Some wives did things like start a thrift shop and gave the proceeds for intermediate (boarding) school student welfare or some other worthy cause. Most mothers taught their own children from Calvert Courses—an American home-study program—until parents organized an American primary school. Several women started little gardens. By the time we left Truk, Carolyn had a pineapple plantation out behind our house with 300 plants.

Someone suggested early in the first year that we ought to start a little newspaper for the American community. I liked the idea and encouraged it. Nearly a dozen people, including my wife and me, volunteered to help produce the first issue. We put out word that we were going to press in the administration building on a Friday evening, and called for stories. We received enough to fill several issues.

Our first edition turned out to be six mimeographed pages. Readers liked it so well that we put together another issue a week later. In it, the editor announced a contest to name the paper. The prize: a free subscription to this give-away paper. Eight or ten names were submitted, with no contestant's name showing, and Carolyn's won. From then on it was known as the *Truk Tide*. The paper continued for the next twenty years.

The *Tide* offered its readers a pretty well-rounded picture of life in our community. The Navy had started a small mimeographed monthly paper called *Met Poraus* (What's New?) which we continued, for our Trukese employees, island chiefs, and others interested. Most *Tide* stories were written with American readers in mind.

Writing for the *Tide* wasn't limited to English majors. Over a year's time, almost every adult in the community and some children were contributors. The flavor of the "press room" on Friday night was reflected in a story it carried in the first anniversary issue:

Tide has a Birthday!

The constantly changing tone of the *Tide* is due in large part to the fact that there is a new editor each month, and each editor is completely free to change the makeup, tone of stories and story headings to his own taste...

The staff meets at the *Tide* office each Friday evening and the editor begins to parcel out to journalists on hand, and then to the "printer master," stories submitted during the week by community members. Sometimes during the evening some wonderful person will stop in with a batch of cookies, a plate of doughnuts, or even a pie. There usually is a pot of coffee brewing, and the call, "Copy! Copy!" drowns out the laughter of a staffer breaking up over his or her own humorous prose.

Stories ranged from visitors coming and going, plane day—"holiday mood...new faces...mail..."—and social activities, to special events like United Nations Day, held jointly with the Trukese. The latter featured outrigger paddling canoe races, track events and feasts. Everyone knew when a long-awaited shipment of spare parts arrived, which were needed to put one more jeep back into motor pool service, and about water rationing hours in the dry season. And the *Tide* printed some of the more colorful quotes relating to those water restrictions.

Reporters wrote about happy events: a wedding, the birth of a child, the time Ardis Christensen, one of the young wives, started a home bakery where we could purchase her great pies and cakes, cookies and doughnuts, and about the time a weathered trading schooner from Australia brought in real butter, cheese and ice cream.

Tide readers were kept informed on such happenings as a Navy demolition team coming in to explode a Japanese floating WWII mine with long prongs, which Trukese had sighted in nearby waters, and how parents got together and organized a primary school for the seven American elementary age children. Then there were stories on what was the latest with several hobby clubs built around interests in short-wave radio, photography, great books study, and the drama group.

The more imaginative *Tide* reporters outdid themselves dreaming up publicity for upcoming parties at the Community Club. In such stories, the hotel was referred to as "Harry's Barn," "Halfway House—featuring the beautiful Lagoon Room," "The Taro Hilton," "Breadfruit Palace," or "The Last Resort."

Nearly every weekend the Community Club's program committee had some activity at the hotel: little theatre presentations, bingo, card games, and—most often—informal dancing to recorded music. At the latter type gatherings, there were inevitably advance calls by the committee for volunteers to provide intermission entertainment. This usually took the form of solos, duets, hula dancing and piano playing.

Russ Curtis, who came out as my Administrative Assistant, later was promoted to Deputy District Administrator and, at the same time, head of Island Affairs. He and his wife, Verna, added in so many ways to a good spirit among the Americans, and had a wonderful way of working and being friends and neighbors with the Trukese people, and helped make the Truk Tide popular. Russ and Verna spent nearly all the rest of his working career in Micronesia in a number of different roles. Verna volunteered to spend time at Nama Island in the Mortlocks showing women how to make aloha shirts as a cottage industry project. She held many other volunteer roles in helping the islander people. Russ and Verna years later helped the Trukese start a hotel. Russ helped develop a very successful cooperative in the Yap District, and was a mover and shaker in helping to get Micronesian Airlines going.

Probably the two worst singing voices on Truk belonged to Chief Justice Furber and me. I never was certain whether he was aware of the quality of his vocalizing. With only mild encouragement at hotel parties, he would break into a few lines of *"Lord Geoffrey Amhherst,"* who was, we all learned, "...a soldier of the king, and he fought in that wild countree..."

Several times, when the call went out for hotel talent night acts, I thought of suggesting to the Judge, a man with all the dignity of his Boston area-Harvard upbringing but also with a lighter side we all enjoyed, that he and I offer an act. We could, I visualized, memorize the words to *You Can't Sew A Button On A Heart,"* which Sophie Tucker had made famous years earlier. Dressed in Gay 90s clothes, and with our faces set in solemn expressions, we'd sing a verse or two, then break into a few soft-shoe shuffle steps between verses, like Harry Kelly did. The main reason I never quite got around to suggesting the idea to the Judge was my fear that the audience might believe we really thought we could sing.

Trukese Medicine Man

Frank Mahony was fascinated by the important parts ghosts, sorcerers and medicine men played in the daily lives of the people. Listening to him, Dr. Clark Richardson, the new head of our Medical department, became interested, and I did, too. We tried to learn as much as we could about them, mainly through Dr. Michi Kolios, Dr. Ngas Kansau, when he returned from the Fiji medical school, from other Trukese members of our hospital staff, and from Frank.

Practitioners of an esoteric craft, the medicine men, *soun safei*, were widely respected by the Trukese people. Inheritors of arcane knowledge handed down through the centuries, in each generation one or more worthies on an island were so anointed. They were believed to possess special capabilities to intervene with spirits which inhabited sea or air or lurked in parts of an island, waiting to nip or climb upon those who displeased them.

Before the first foreigners came to live in these islands in the 1870s, calling for a medicine man was the only way known to a family to stretch forth a helping hand to a loved one who had crossed a spirit power and was ailing with anything from a sore foot to a hurting stomach or a raging fever.

Trukese rarely volunteered information to us about their island spirits, capable of both good and evil. The main exception was their willingness to talk more freely to an anthropologist. But this took place only after the latter was in the islands for some time, convinced them that he or she was trying to be a bridge between two cultures, and that any information given to him or her would not be used to their detriment. When an islander did venture upon the subject with other respectful foreign listeners such as Clark or me, he was more guarded—uncertain of the responses his lifting of the curtain for even a slight peek might evoke. The Trukese were conditioned, in part, to this attitude by some scoffing foreigners, including at least a few missionaries who openly ridiculed such beliefs and warned of the terrible consequences if the practices were continued.

We were in the islands at a time when the old ways were being challenged. From my first months there, I started to become fascinated by different aspects of the Trukese culture. As my understanding of their ways slowly grew, I became increasingly concerned that my staff and I might, with the best of intentions, inadvertently help bring about undesirable changes. In our ignorance or lack of clear understanding, we might help weaken or even destroy some soundly based part of their culture, which had helped them for untold centuries to survive, living through good and bad times. I talked many time through the years with Frank about this. He sometimes grinned, sometimes frowned, but he always said he'd be there to send up warning signals to us.

Some of the strongest challenges to the old ways were in the area of modern medicine, represented by our district hospital on Moen and, to a much lesser extent, dispensaries on each island, presided over by young health aides with medical knowledge going little beyond boy scout first aid.

The story which follows relates not to sorcerers but to one of that more widespread and generally benign group of Trukese medicine men, *soun safei,* who believed in the efficacy of their work and earnestly sought to help people get well. Some even tried to help a patient who had wronged a family member or neighbor to mend the damaged relationship. Doing so could be an important part of the cure. This story is based on facts. It telescopes a number of separate, limited pieces into a single mosaic. Just as a painting often can catch the essence of a scene better than a photograph, this sketch, I believe, may better capture the role of a traditional Trukese medicine man than would straight exposition. Much of the factual information here was given to me by

Frank, who made an in-depth study of the subject. Some years after leaving Truk, he wrote his Doctoral thesis at Stanford University on the work of Trukese medicine men. He told me he was helped in his research by Jack Fischer, Tom Gladwin, and other anthropologists who had spent time at Truk during Navy years.

Anter lay ill in his home on Tol Island. Both inside and out, the house was typical of most in the village: rectangular, with weathered wooden siding and rusting tin roof. The sagging, unscreened wooden porch facing the lagoon braced its shoulders into the prevailing trade winds, as if nature had given it the ability to make this accommodation. The porch led directly through the only door to a single large room.

In that part of the house where he lay, the breadfruit wood floor was partly covered by a tightly-woven, bleached pandanus mat. Other sleeping mats were at the opposite end of the room, and near them light blankets were rolled up; mosquito nets, secured to the ceiling, were tucked up out of the way in the daytime.

A scarred wooden table, remnant of the prewar Japanese civilian years, stood along one wall. The room was otherwise unadorned, except for a wooden packing case once used to ship groceries from Japan to Truk. The box, nailed to the wall, now served as a cupboard. In it were some plastic dishes, two empty tin cans, used to hold needles, safety pins, buttons and a pencil. Two larger opened tins contained small amounts of sugar and tea.

An oil lamp sat on top of the cupboard. Between two rough-hewn bread-fruit wood rafters someone had placed a couple of boards to serve as storage shelves for pots and pans. On another such shelf were stored an extra blanket, several dresses and a coffee can holding nails.

Anter's head rested on a white pillowcase his wife had decorated with flowers scattered across it, sewn with bright colors of embroidery yarn. The rest of his body, covered only by a pair of Truk Trading Company shorts, was stretched out on top of a lightweight blanket. He lifted his right arm and moved his palm slowly across his forehead.

"*Pwich*" (hot) he mumbled to himself in the empty room. "*Terepwich*" (very hot). He rolled his body so he could rest on his left side. Soon he shifted to the right. Unable to find comfort in that position either, he returned to lying on his back.

Anter gave a tentative low groan. After some seconds he raised his voice to a loud quiver and called, "Seen-opya!" Seen-opya!" That effort was followed by more groans.

His wife sat on the grass in the shade of the big mango tree at the side of the house, visiting with a younger sister while they sewed. Sinopia and Anter shared the home with this sister and her husband and small children. A still younger married sister and her husband lived next door with their small children. The young women's mother possessed the tribal land on which both houses sat, and their nearby garden land. Sinopia looked toward the screened window at the side of the house, then put her sewing on the grass and both women walked over to their home and stood inside the doorway.

"My head is hot," Anter told his wife fretfully. "My bones ache." He coughed for several seconds, his lean body shaking.

Sinopia went over and knelt beside him on the blanket. She placed her hand on his forehead and suppressed an exclamation of concern. After a brief exchange of words with him, she said, "I go now to talk with Iosi." Without waiting for his protest, she stood and walked out the door.

In the next few minutes she gathered from within hailing distance a grown sister and that sister's small son, two aunts, an uncle, and one of her sons-in-law. Leading them across other yards in that part of the village where much of her extended family lived, they came to the beach. Here Iosi, her oldest brother, by tradition and temperament the strongest male voice in the family, worked with a friend of his repairing a wooden outboard motorboat turned bottom up.

"Anter is very sick!" Sinopia said, breathing hard after her fast walk. "His head is very hot!" The brother and sister talked briefly, then Iosi began to set in motion the first of a series of events very much like those that took place, with minor variations, wherever a Trukese man, woman or child was considered ill enough to merit such attention.

Sinopia and her relatives trailed Iosi back up from the beach and over to her mother's house. They all stood barefooted, on the cool woven mat while Iosi and Sinopia knelt and talked with Anter to fix more precisely the nature of his ailments.

Iosi and other family members knew, because it was fairly common knowledge among adult Trukese, that there were nearly a hundred different medical formulas, each associated with a different spirit power. But the only way to choose from among them the right one for Anter's illness was to identify the spirit power who had "nipped" him. Each spirit power, when attacking a person, left his own particular marks upon the victim in the form of a symptom or combination of symptoms; thus, reading Anter's own ailments accurately was a key to putting the finger on the one spirit power involved.

But identifying a patient's symptoms was not enough. Trukese believed implicitly that their system of medicine always worked successfully if the diagnosis was properly made. When a patient was treated and didn't get well quickly, the fault was never with the medicine. It had to be improper diagnosis.

If a medicine man's diagnosis were limited only to identifying two or three symptoms, after which he would match these to the attacking spirit power, the efficacy of the entire system could be brought into question when the patient didn't recover quickly. Thus there had to be built into the system elements of uncertainty in the diagnosis. This was accomplished mainly by adding another dimension even more important than the symptoms: probing into the sick person's recent behavior. In situations like this, bad behavior is much less meaningful if no punishment follows. Thus, the Trukese believed that if they broke a taboo, they could expect punishment: a typhoon, hunger, sickness, drowning. Now, by combining symptoms and behavior, the possibilities for a mistaken diagnosis were greatly increased.

Regarding recent behavior, one taboo, for example, was that a person should never bother the area near where an island's reef spirit was known to dwell. Already Iosi's and other family members' minds were at work on the sifting process.

After an extended interrogation, during which Iosi asked all the questions and Anter responded with coughs, groans and weak-voiced replies, it was confirmed that the patient was feverish, had a headache, his stomach hurt and he ached in his chest and in his bones. Satisfied that he had enough information on symptoms, Iosi's questioning now took a new turn. He motioned Sinopia and the other women back.

"When did you go fishing the last time?" he asked Anter. He was almost certain he knew the answer. After all, they were members of the same family; everyone in the village pretty much knew what was going on all the time.

Anter coughed and stirred restlessly. He took more than a minute to reconstruct, half to himself, his recent activities. "Five days ago," he finally said.

Iosi lowered his voice for Anter's hearing only. "When were you with your wife the last time?"

Anter smiled wanly. Every Trukese knew that only a stupid man would have intercourse with his wife or lover the night before he went out to the reef to fish. That was certain to bring down upon him the reef spirit's wrath.

"No problem there," he assured his brother-in-law.

Iosi now began to question Anter in detail about his experiences that day on the reef. There were many other ways to upset reef spirits. This line of inquiry brought no suggestion of offensive action on Anter's part.

"You eat fish before you went to that reef?" the brother-in-law asked.

Anter fell silent again for a few seconds; then his dramatic groan signalled that significant information could be expected. He recalled for Iosi that he had been visiting with friends in the next village the very night before the fishing expedition to the reef. Some *achi* (fermented coconut milk) was brought out and he and his companions drank it from several old, recycled Japanese *sakau* bottles until they were empty. Later, the host had brought out cold pieces of red snapper, one of Anter's favorite foods. With his head slightly whirling from the *achi,* he had joined in the eating and had not given the matter another thought until this second. To make matters worse, Iosi learned with more probing, the fish, caught two days earlier, had become ripe—nearly spoiled. Reef spirits were especially affronted by anyone eating spoiled fish.

Iosi turned away from the sick man and motioned to the other family members, who followed him outside. "The reef spirit punishes Anter," he announced with no trace of uncertainty. A less confident family leader would at this point have called for a *soun pwe* (diviner) to come in and confirm Iosi's conclusion, undisputed by other family members. If a diviner had been called and Iosi was wrong, the diviner would have named the real culprit.

"We need the *soun safei,*" he told Sinopia and the others.

One man in Iosi's and Sinopia's own village was regarded as highly skilled in Trukese medicine, but he worked on Moen and came home only on weekends. Teruo, husband of Iosi's and Sinopia's youngest sister, now spoke for the first time.

"That man Saak still lives in my mother's village."

Teruo's reminder brought animated murmurs and nodding of heads from the ladies, and monosyllabic expressions of approval from the men. Saak not only enjoyed a fine reputation as a medicine man, but was especially respected for his many successes in treating attacks by reef spirits.

"If you want," Teruo addressed Iosi, "I will go now to his village. I will ask him to come." With the family's agreement, he turned at once, walked to the beach, got into a small outrigger canoe and paddled along the shoreline for more than a half-mile to Saak's village. Upon reaching his destination, he found Saak at home with several other members of his wife's family, finishing their evening meal. Politely refusing food offered him, Teruo waited until they finished, then explained his mission.

After asking questions about the patient's condition, any tell-tale recent conduct, how long he had been sick, and particularly about the spirit power or powers believed to be involved, Saak agreed to the undertaking and said he'd be there the next morning.

Before Teruo left, however, Saak instructed him carefully that he and his family must have ready on his arrival a number of bunches of green (drinking) coconuts, other bunches of ripe ones, and firewood. The wood must be very dry. If it was even a little damp and caused the fire to hiss or "cry" while burning, that would risk the possibility that the patient might die, for the sound would be like that of people crying for a dead person. He further instructed that the coconut bunches should be lowered to the ground by a rope, rather than the usual method of cutting them loose and letting them fall. If a nut should split apart from the bunch, the patient would be unlikely to recover.

The next morning the medicine man was up early, before most people in his village were awake. Leaving unobtrusively, Saak took a circuitous route to minimize chance encounters and walked toward his favorite herbs collecting place, a quarter-mile away. Knowledge of herbs was secret—something carefully guarded within his own extended family. Furthermore, for someone to stumble upon him while he was in the act of gathering them could be dangerous for that person, for the patient, and even for the *soun safei*. Should Saak's particular herbal medicine combination be discovered by some unfriendly person, it could cause the patient to take a turn for the worse, and even make the medicine man sick.

When he arrived at the herb gathering place, Saak looked around again to insure he was alone; then he went quickly to work. Approaching each plant, he spoke aloud and softly to it.

"I am sorry but I must take a little from you, o plant," he explained in earnest tones, "to heal that sick man, Anter. I will use it as medicine against that reef spirit that attacks him."

Only after completing this explanation to each kind of herb he planned to use, did Saak begin to remove gently each cutting needed. This ritual helped insure that the herbs were a specific remedy for that particular spirit power.

Quickly, almost tenderly, he put the cuttings into a jute sack of the kind used for copra, then carried them down to his canoe in the village. Again he was careful to avoid people. Placing them in a dry part of the canoe's bottom, he paddled quickly toward Anter's village. The morning was still pleasantly cool when he arrived.

Sinopia was the first to see the *soun safei*'s outrigger approaching. Immediately the air echoed with high-pitched calls of women's voices and the deeper echoes of male relatives. By the time the canoe arrived, most family members were gathered. Saak beached the canoe in the soft sand and, taking his jute bag, walked barefooted up toward the delegation in the yard.

They greeted respectfully the thickset man with graying, close-cropped hair and blue tattoo designs on both forearms, and took him to the house. Making a semi-circle around where Anter lay, they watched and listened intently while the *soun safei* squatted on his haunches beside the sick man and exchanged short greetings. He stayed only long enough to observe Anter's condition and verify his recent behavior.

When the medicine man went back outside, they followed. Iosi led him over to a patch of bare ground behind the house and a few yards to one side of the cookhouse. The latter was little more than a lean-to made with poles, while rusted tin covered the sloping roof and weather side. Here they had deposited firewood and bunches of coconuts. Saak inspected them carefully. He further noted that someone had the foresight to anchor solidly into the ground a coconut husking stick, with the sharpened end protruding outward at an angle.

"You prepared well," he told the older brother.

Already he had decided to treat Anter first with ungupat (cool squeeze), one of more than a dozen main ways to administer medicine. Carefully studying the bunches of ripe brown nuts and matching them, he selected two. Carrying them over to the husking stick, he took one and with a few fast downward chops, split the husk enough to remove it carefully and set the pieces of fibrous husk to one side. He repeated the motions with the second nut.

Next, he studiously paired the bunches of green nuts, selected two, slashed a piece off their tops and poured the clear liquid into a white soup bowl which he had brought along in his sack. The thick ceramic bowl had been a gift from an American sailor stationed on Moen. The *soun safei* peered over his shoulders toward the family in the distance. Satisfied, he again turned his back to them and carefully removed from the gunnysack several of his herbs. He reached deeper into the bag and brought forth a small, scarred breadfruit wood pounding board and a coral stone pestle. He placed the herbs one at a time on the board and pounded them into small piles of pulp. Two of them gave off a light, agreeable fragrance.

Picking up several chunks of coconut husk fibre he had cut away earlier, he fashioned them into three small pouches. Into each he stuffed some of the herb pulp, then tied the pouches shut.

"*Iwe!*" (Well!) he called loudly, announcing to the family that he was ready to give the medicine. One of Sinopia's sisters ran ahead and opened the door, while the rest of them trailed him inside. The medicine man walked over and knelt beside Anter. He spoke solemnly to his patient, while placing the bowl and pouches on the mat within reach.

Beginning final preparations, he picked up one fiber pouch. With each movement slow, deliberate, ritualistic, he dipped it into the coconut fluid and let it soak there for a few seconds. Then he held it directly above the bowl and squeezed hard with his thumb and forefinger until a thick, cloudy fluid trickled back into the bowl. He repeated the process with the other two pouches.

Ceremonially lifting the bowl with both hands, he faced Anter. "Sit up," he said. When Anter, glistening with sweat, did so, the medicine man placed the bowl carefully into his two hands. "Drink slowly, slowly, slowly," he requested, almost pleading. After the sick man emptied its contents, the *soun safei* took the bowl again, while his patient lay down and closed his eyes.

The medicine man stood and mingled for a few minutes with family members, all the time carefully watching Anter's reaction to the medicine. When the sick man clearly was seen to relax and appear more comfortable, Saak was pleased. This was a good sign the reef spirit had caused Anter's sickness. The medicine associated with that spirit seemed to be helping.

"I will come tomorrow before dark," Saak told Iosi before paddling back toward his own village.

He arrived the second evening before sunset with his jute bag and went directly to observe his patient. Neither his brief conversation with Anter nor his careful observation revealed any signs of improvement. After a few words with Iosi and Sinopia, the medicine man announced to family members gathered around, "Tonight I use a different medicine. I will give him *safeiso* ("steam and drink").

Heads nodded appreciatively. In Trukese medicine, what counted was not only the substance—the particular combination of herbs, coconut milk and other materials—but also the *form* in which these were prepared and administered. "Steam and drink" was widely regarded as the strongest way to give Trukese medicine.

Walking over to where the family had deposited the bunches of nuts and firewood the previous day, he set to work. Following his instructions, they built a fire a short distance away.

Alone now, he took from his jute sack some herbs, different from those used the previous evening. He pounded and blended them until they were a pulp. This finished, he fashioned, as he also had the day before, three pouches from the coconut husks, and filled them with the pulp and tied them shut. In the gathering darkness, he called to the family members by the fire they had built. "Bring a big bowl. And I need four rocks."

"How big you want those rocks?" someone called back.

"Half as big as a mango."

When these were brought, the medicine man set the dishpan on the ground near the fire and inspected each rock. Satisfied, he placed them carefully into the growing bed of embers. After throwing more dry mangrove wood onto the fire, he opened four green coconuts and poured their liquid into the dishpan until it was two-thirds full.

Picking up the pouches, he soaked them briefly in the dishpan. Then he lifted them one at a time and squeezed hard until creamy white fluid and a darker fluid dripped into the dishpan.

When he saw the stones glow red hot, he used two pieces of mangrove firewood as tongs to lift the little rocks and drop them into the dishpan, where they hissed loudly for a few seconds. Finally, he picked up the steaming pan in both hands and hurried with it to the house. Family members trailed him.

Again the *soun safei* requested his patient to sit up on the mat. When Anter did so with much groaning, the medicine man motioned for him to move his feet apart far enough to position the dishpan between them. Steaming fumes enveloped Anter's face and upper body and invaded his nostrils. Saak asked Sinopia to hand him the lightweight blanket which had covered Anter. He draped it around the sick man's shoulders and over his knees so that it enclosed the dishpan and helped to better channel the fumes. Anter coughed several times and his body shook. In the gathering darkness Sinopia lit an oil lamp.

Trukese considered it a protective act for themselves to inhale some of a patient's steam-and-drink fumes. The semi-circle of relatives edged closer to Anter and leaned inward above his head, so they could absorb some of the vapors which flowed upward, past Anter's face. When the steam began to subside, the medicine man took a short stick from his pants pocket and turned the stones over so the hot parts which had protruded above the water went under, causing more strong hissing and steam to rise.

The blanket was removed after steam no longer rose. The medicine man turned to Sinopia. "Can you bring me a cup?" She produced a tin cup, which he dipped into the dishpan and handed it full to Anter to drink. Trukese people believed it was healthful for them also to drink some of the medicine. Accordingly, later the cup was refilled a number of times and passed around to family members. The medicine man drank, too. Soon the pan was empty. Anter lay back upon his mat and his wife covered him with the blanket. Closing his eyes, he wiped sweat from his face with the back of his hand. He coughed some more and still looked feverish.

Preparing to leave, the *soun safei* announced that he would return the next evening. Before he left, Iosi went over to his own house and returned with a jute fifty-pound rice bag in which about a third of the rice remained, and offered it to the man. At first the medicine man magnanimously refused the gift, but when Iosi continued to press it upon him, he accepted it with feigned reluctance. All present were familiar with this little act; they knew that to refuse the gift could have weakened the medicine.

On his third visit, the medicine man repeated the identical steam-and-drink treatment with still no good effect. Now it was certain that the reef spirit wasn't the guilty one after all. At this point the oldest brother called in a proper diviner. His task would be only to determine the offending spirit.

The *soun pwe* identified from his fresh review of Anter's recent behavior and symptoms, two other spirits, one of which might have bitten him. By a slow process he eliminated one, leaving to his satisfaction the attacking spirit. Now another medicine man was summoned and more courses of medicine followed, but in the end none of them worked.

Another family conference was held, during which an entirely different course of action was agreed upon: they would try *safei imwen tokache* (hospital medicine). Early the next morning the outboard motorboat was fueled, and a makeshift litter placed aboard. Anter, wearing Sinopia's warm sweater and a man's double-breasted coat which Truk Trading Company (TTC) had brought in as part of a shipment of old clothes, was helped into the boat and onto the litter. After a blanket was tucked around him, the boat sped northward to the Moen Island dock, more than a dozen miles away. There a passing Constabulary vehicle about to head for the district center, gave Anter and the three accompanying family members a ride to the hospital. He was quickly diagnosed as having a moderately severe respiratory ailment. Medication, rest, and nourishing food contributed to his uneventful recovery ten days later.

The experience did not shake Anter's or any of his family's strong faith in Trukese medicine. They simply had not been able to identify the right spirit power. The family felt they had done the sensible thing. They hedged their bets by calling upon both the old and new ways of medicine. When the old way didn't work, they shifted to the new way. It was a pattern we saw and heard about often in the district.

Anter's case had a happy ending, and so did most others where a family first tried the local medicine man but later brought the patient to the hospital. Too often, though, a sick person was brought to the hospital and began to recover, but not fast enough to suit the family. An important part of traditional Trukese medicine was that it was expected to get fast results. In those circumstances, they might take the patient back home for more treatment by a *soun safei*. Sometimes this worked out all right, but more often, it seemed, it didn't.

Fairly typical of the latter was the case in which the hospital had diagnosed a young woman as having tuberculosis—almost certainly curable by antibiotics, rest and nourishing food, though the cure might have taken many weeks. The patient and her family considered this too long a time. They took her home after a week, against strong advice of the hospital staff. Back on her home island a *soun safei* treated her by "smoking." In this form of treatment, the appropriate herb is laid on half of a scalloped tridacna shell, and a hot rock is placed on top of the herb to create smoke. As with Anter's steam-and-drink treatment, a blanket is wrapped around the patient. In this case, it is to help channel the smoke upward, sometimes for as long as the patient can stand it. The young lady was "smoked" at home for about a month, after which she died.

That experience made Clark and his staff—Trukese and American—all the more determined to help build stronger bridges between traditional and modern medicine. Some fascinating experiences followed as they pursued that goal.

Shark Bites, Hysterical Blindness and Other Problems

Clark's introduction to island medical problems had started out fast. Seven weeks after our takeover from the Navy, he arrived on one of the weekly flights out of Guam to Truk and the two districts east of us. I couldn't go down to meet him, but Carolyn and I sent him a dinner invitation. Answering the door that evening, I saw for the first time that boyish, sometimes impish grin that was to become so familiar. Trim and athletic, with blonde hair worn in a part, he looked younger than his thirty-five years.

Halfway through the meal, the phone rang. It was our only other doctor, Alex Hagentornas, surgeon and acting head of the Medical department until that afternoon. Our third doctor, Dick Lahr, who had been here as a Navy doctor, was on home leave. "Will, sorry to interrupt. Could I please speak with Dr. Richardson?"

Clark, surprised, talked briefly with Alex, then hung up and turned back to us apologetically.

"A shark bite case just came in," he said. "Dr. Hagentornas needs someone to handle the anesthesia. I said I'd go right down."

The hospital staff saw shark and barracuda bites fairly often. Spear fishing was common at Truk. It appealed to the people because it added a sporting element to their work. Over the years, Trukese, like islanders all over the Pacific, had developed a respectful relationship with sharks—ranging between casual and guarded—and often swam near them while fishing.

We began to hear about, and occasionally talk with, a few Americans scattered throughout the Territory who dared to swim among sharks. Quite safe, really, those derring-do American swimmers would tell us. Nothing to worry about. Then they'd begin a litany of qualifying statements: Shark attack could be triggered if the swimmer made too-quick movements or splashed too much. Naturally, they usually explained, the thrashing of a speared fish, with its blood oozing into the water, could bring sharks. Then there is the occasional rogue shark—crazy in the head. We heard a dozen other explanations from them—each further weakening, at least for me, their earlier strong assurances. Surprisingly few Trukese were killed or lost an entire arm or leg in such encounters. I wondered if somehow, through the centuries, this kind of swimming was another of mother nature's miracles of adaptation to help them swim and fish safely in an ocean region with lots of sharks, barracudas and sting rays.

When Clark walked into the quonset surgery, Alex already had scrubbed. Clark was happy and relieved to find that the gas anesthetic machine was a type he had trained on at Stanford Medical School.

"This shark had attacked by biting at the fish the man removed from his spear," Clark told me the next morning. "The bite ripped a deep gash into the fisherman's upper thigh and scrotum. The wounded man struggled to the surface, where his companion managed to get him back into the canoe and rushed him to us."

In situations like this, Trukese seemed to realize that the herbs and incantations of their local medicine men were not the way to go. Clark and the attending Trukese nurse watched Alex deftly suture the torn parts. When the patient returned to the hospital some weeks later for his final checkup, Dr. Hagentornas told him he'd made a full recovery. The man agreed. He repeated Alex's words and, grinning broadly, placed extra emphasis on the word full.

The Truk hospital in those days would have made some stateside doctors shake their heads in wonderment. The buildings were a collection of World War II quonsets, joined together and arranged with a long central corridor and three wings off either side: male and female wards, TB ward, surgery, dental office, and medical supply room. Offices were at one end and the kitchen was a small, detached building.

Almost every entering patient was accompanied by a procession. Relatives and friends often walked into the ward single file, carrying woven coconut leaf baskets of cooked breadfruit and taro. More often they brought those two staples of the Trukese diet, wrapped in banana leaves, in pounded and preserved form so it would last longer. They brought baskets of papayas, mangos and other fresh fruit—whatever was in season. And they brought drinking coconuts, stalks of bananas, and dried fish. Women balanced on their heads food wrapped in large kerchiefs. They strung the food from hooks in the ceiling over the patient's bed or at the head or foot of it. Female patients and children, particularly, wanted a relative within sight and call at all times.

Since the wards were crowded, only one relative was permitted to stay in the hospital—sleeping on a mat under the patient's metal cot. Within a few months, Clark made a rule that no accompanying family member or friend could stay overnight, unless the patient was a child or a critically ill adult. From then on relatives accompanying outer island patients were absorbed into villages on Moen and nearby islands for the duration of the patient's stay. Those from beyond Truk Lagoon had to wait up to two months for the next field trip ship home.

One day more than a year after Interior took over, a telegram from Honolulu alerted us that a U.S. Congressional delegation would visit Truk soon. As part of our preparation, we drafted a mimeographed briefing paper for the congressmen to read enroute. Clark wrote the medical section. After pointing out that in the previous year more than 1,000 bed patients were cared for in the hospital and 7,000 out-patients at the clinic, plus several thousands treated on field trips, he wrote:

"The daily average number of patients was 68. How do you get this number into a 64-bed hospital? Simple. You just squeeze in more beds and there is always the floor if necessary, as during the influenza epidemic."

Hiding his Medical Department staff's light under a bushel basket wasn't one of Clark's most ingrained habits. In the same briefing paper he added:

"For such a small hospital in a community of 16,000 people scattered over distances as far as from Washington, D. C. to Philadelphia, this is an incredibly good record. But the amazing part," he continued modestly, "is that this service was performed by a tiny professional staff."

American doctors	2-3
Trukese medical interns	2
Trukese Nurses	3-4
Korean dentist	1
Health aides and lab. men, nurses' aides	20

More often than not, it appeared that bringing someone to the *imwen tokache* (hospital) was a last resort—after Trukese medicine had been tried and failed. The Navy did a lot to pave the way for greater acceptance of modern medicine. In late 1945, U.S. Navy doctors were part of the military government occupation team that landed at Truk. With the treatment of one particular disease, they made the people sit up and take notice. They started treating yaws with penicillin.

Yaws takes the form of a lesion, which doesn't heal for years—often not at all. It is a spirally, undulating bacteria transmitted by insects. Once an islander has yaws, an insect will land on the open sore and transmit the disease to another person with a slight sore or a crack in the skin of the foot. Yaws then spreads to other parts of the body, often attacking the bridge of the nose and destroying it, causing a tragically disfiguring, sunken look to the islander's face.

The Navy medical staff passed the word through the islands about their miracle cure. "Look, " they told the Trukese, in effect, "we'll take your worst yaws cases and treat them with penicillin, and in three weeks your skin will be all healed up. It won't get back the bridge of your nose, but it will remove the disease from your bones."

Miraculously, in the eyes of the islanders, that is exactly what happened. That experience with yaws built into the Trukese people a little more faith in modern medicine, and our civilian administration inherited that legacy. Our doctors continued to treat yaws throughout the islands, always with the same dramatic results. By the time I left we weren't seeing many such cases.

Clark's fascination with Trukese medicine men—kinds of medicines they used and how they treated their patients—led him into discussions with Dr. Michi and other Trukese hospital staff on the subject. How could the Medical Department best relate to them? Clark understood that the medicine men had their roots deep in the culture. He also believed that their strong psychological effects on patients often could have value. Over centuries Trukese medicine men had developed herbal potions and more than a dozen main ways to administer them. Clark became convinced that some of these potions and at least a few of the ways of administering them could have salutary effects.

Our medical staff also had frequent reminders of island medicine's shortcomings.

High on such a list was the matter of pig dung. This involved the long-established and nearly always harmful practice by midwives of applying pig dung to the umbilical cord of a new-born child. They did this on those frequent occasions when the umbilical cord got a little wet and then infected. The dung was used as a poultice or blotter over the infected area.

"Pig manure is fairly rich in tetanus bacteria," Clark pointed out. "We Westerners can get tetanus bacteria into our intestinal tracts and it doesn't give us any difficulty. Put it on an open wound, however—say, an umbilical cord wound—and it will cause tetanus in the new-born."

Once the hospital had three cases of new-borns with lockjaw. "Each was the result of the pig dung practice," Clark reported afterward. "We were able to save two of the babies, but the third was too far gone. Right after that we began to provide the health aide on each island with little sterile gauze squares to cover the umbilical cord. Every health aide was asked to pass them along to midwives, with the message, repeated with each new batch handed out, that here was a much stronger and more effective way to protect the umbilical cord." The pig dung practice gradually died out.

I pressed headquarters hard and got enough money to install the first two short-wave radios in the outer islands: one at Lukunor in the center of the Mortlocks in the southeast part of the district, and the other at Ulul in the western islands. We wanted them for medical emergencies. After a very long wait, we got them. Too many people of all ages died needlessly from medical problems that any doctor could have handled successfully. The two worst problems of this nature were appendicitis and complications with childbirth.

The Trukese had a chilling expression for one common childbirth problem: "stuck baby." Too often a midwife tried to cope with delivery complications; by the time she realized she wasn't going to be successful, the expectant mother's life was in great danger.

Clark was sitting in his office at the hospital one day when Nellie Selifis, the chief nurse, came rushing in, highly excited. "Doctor! A woman is coming in! We must get her to the delivery room quick! Baby's head is hanging out!"

"I hurried down the hall," Clark recalled, "in time to see two Trukese men from one of the islands in the lagoon supporting a young woman between them. Her skirt was low, but she lifted it when she saw me, and showed the fetal head of a dead baby."

The baby, the doctors learned, had been out like that for forty-eight hours. It took that long for the young lady's family to reach the decision to try hospital medicine and bring her in by boat.

"I thought she was a goner," Clark told me. "While it was easy to turn the fetal body and get it out, there were signs that the young lady's whole uterus was infected. After cleaning it, I was dismayed to find that, whereas it should have contracted into a nice, hard-packed ball, it was as flabby as a deflated basketball bladder. I was really concerned during the next twelve hours that it would rupture from infection. But we loaded her up with antibiotics—penicillin. I'll be damned if by the next day that uterus hadn't contracted down! The infection was held under control and she survived and went home."

Our doctors rarely saw such cases on field trips. If the midwife couldn't handle delivery complications, both the mother and baby died. After short wave radios were installed in the outer islands, health aides on those islands called our district headquarters for help, and one of our doctors gave detailed instructions or we'd arrange an emergency trip. Sometimes we did both.

The main health problems that crowded our hospital wards and kept the outpatient clinic staff busy were respiratory ailments, TB, and gastro-intestinal problems—especially food poisoning. Others were infectious hepatitis and accidents. In most cases the patient had been treated first by a medicine man and came to the hospital only when ancient remedies failed.

Doctor Michi Kolios was the first Trukese to be sent by the Navy to the Pacific Islands medical school started by the British at Suva, Fiji. He was not there long, we learned later, when he began to catch the eye of the staff as one of their outstanding students. When he was graduated after four years of intensive study, they awarded him a prize for high scholastic achievement. He arrived back home not long after Clark came. From Dr. Michi's first day in the hospital, Clark and his entire staff found him very talented and a joy to work with. Trukese throughout the district were proud that one of their own young men was now a respected doctor at the hospital.

First, Dr. Michi and later Dr. Ngas Kansou and Dr. Kiosi, when they returned from Fiji, worked closely with the American doctors and made important contributions in helping to build a bridge between Trukese and modern medicine. This was not easy. Until Trukese throughout the islands could be taught the germ theory and accepted it, how could our hospital staff create in their minds the belief that for some ailments hospital medicine had much stronger curing power? And how could Clark and Alex and their Trukese hospital staff, thinking and planning together, bring all islanders to understand and believe that hospital medicine had infinitely stronger qualities than Trukese medicine?

Many villagers said to each other and occasionally to islander hospital employees or Americans on field trips: "We go to the *imwen tokache* (hospital) and they give us a little white pill, and it doesn't help. So why go?"

Clark and Michi put their heads together one day and decided to add a little implied touch of magic to the treatment of their most common outpatient complaint: low-grade respiratory ailments. The first step in such treatment usually was aspirin.

"By itself," Clark explained to me, "aspirin did little good. Coupled, however, with clear instructions to patients to rest, drink liquids and—most important—return to the out-patient clinic in a week or two if they didn't feel better, it gave the hospital staff a chance to add treatment. We could give penicillin and other medication if necessary before we had a case of pneumonia on our hands."

Dr. Michi was all for trying a new approach. He brought several other Trukese hospital employees in on the discussions. "At one early meeting," Clark said, "I suggested shifting to pink aspirin instead of white, because in America the pink color seemed to have a favorable psychological effect."

"No," Dr. Michi replied. "In Truk, orange or gold will be a much better color. Add a little orange flavor and it will be even better."

Getting into the spirit of the matter, another Trukese employee suggested, "Let's use our lucky number, three! Three tablets a day. Or three at a time. That will make people think it is strong medicine!"

Nick Gianutsis, our hospital business manager, immediately ordered orange colored aspirin tablets from the United States. Clark, Michi and the others in on the planning were disappointed to learn a few months later, when the tablets arrived, that they had no flavor. After all, the Trukese medicine man's herbal potions often had both flavor and fragrance.

"We got around this problem easily enough," Clark recalled. "Opening each jar of 1,000 tablets, we removed the cotton from the top, poured in essence of orange which we borrowed from several American wives, then resealed the jars. The flavor permeated the tablets nicely. We started giving them out and watched closely for reactions. Soon we saw that patients were quick to accept and read significance into the new tablets with the combination of color, fragrance, taste and the magic number three."

Out-patients' complaints about useless *imwen tokache* medicine dwindled. More islanders returned when their respiratory ailments didn't take a turn for the better, and they received follow-up treatment. The result: fewer deaths from pneumonia.

Another case where Clark and Michi used a little implied hospital magic began when Pwon, a young man in his twenties, was led into the hospital admitting area one day by two male relatives. He complained that he couldn't see. Dr. Michi did some testing and confirmed this. After further extensive examination, he went to Clark and said he thought something was wrong here.

Clark joined him in still more testing. They got a 300-watt light bulb and turned it on in front of Pwon's eyes. The young man said he still couldn't see. Clark and Michi concluded that here was a case of hysterical blindness. Now they faced the important question: what was Pwon's strong emotional problem that caused this reaction?

"This was a strange one," Clark recalled later. "I asked Michi to do a little psychological probing with the patient in an effort to learn what was troubling him. Michi, after talking sympathetically with him at considerable length, and gaining his confidence, learned that Pwon had "kited" a check—

added a number at the end of the figure, like raising it from ten dollars to a hundred. His dishonest act was bothering him so much that his outlet was this form of blindness.

"A person with hysterical blindness actually can't see," Clark explained. "The patient simply wills himself not to see."

"What happened?" I asked. "What did you and Dr. Michi do?"

"How to bring this thing out gracefully?" he went on. "Well, Michi and I talked it over again with Pwon. Later, we talked with the Constabulary about it. They agreed that if Pwon would make up for his theft of funds, they'd drop the charge.

"Then to make it work out so Pwon would have a good excuse to give his family and others, and at the same time to throw in for the benefit of his relatives a little inferred hospital magic, I agreed that we'd put a couple of cotton gauze squares on his eyes. While the relatives stood watching, I put several drops of alcohol on his eyes. That would gradually penetrate under the lids and burn like hell but do no real damage. It hurt him some; we intended it to hurt a little. He was gripping his knuckles. Then we announced in lofty tones to his relatives standing watching that when we removed those gauze squares, he was going to be able to see. And that's exactly what happened. We removed the gauze and he opened his eyes and said, 'I can see! I can see!' In the next month he took care of his raised check, and it was over."

Some months later a patient came in with a case of hysterical paralysis. Clark explained that this also is a situation where a person has performed some misdeed and is looking for a way out—a mental loophole to escape responsibility for the act. The patient suddenly invents a medical problem to divert attention; thus the causes are very similar to those for hysterical blindness, paralysis or lameness.

"Dr. Michi called me in the middle of the night," Clark recalled, "and said that the lady patient's arm was paralyzed from about the elbow down. She said she couldn't feel when he put pins in her arm. I went right down. I quickly suspected that something was unusual here and so did Michi. When she was pricked by a pin, the lack of pain sensation in her arm did not, as it should have, follow the nerve distribution down her arm.

"People perceive sensation in a very clearly diagrammed pattern. This girl didn't. She had so-called 'glove anesthesia'—as if she were wearing a long

71

glove that came to just below her elbow and everything was cut off from below it."

Clark sounded like he didn't plan to finish the story. "Well, then what?" I asked, eager to hear the outcome.

"The young lady was a member of the Catholic Church down at Tunnuk," he said, "so we took Father Hoek into our confidence on the case. He looked into it and it turned out that she was two-timing her husband. We felt that the only way she could get back to normal was by some understanding of the problem. We told Father Hoek how we proposed to proceed in this case. He grasped it immediately and agreed to talk it over with the young lady. When she understood it, including his assurance that her sin would be forgiven, her hysterical paralysis disappeared."

We had our failures with modern medicine, too. Sometimes the problem was the mistaken perception of the patient's family that hospital medicine had failed. If a hospital patient didn't show rapid improvement, the family might decide to take him or her home—even if that person was recovering well but was still weak, and bring in a medicine man.

One apparent failure of western medicine and successful takeover by Trukese medicine involved a patient in his forties, brought to the hospital with severe jaundice.

"It was a typical case of hepatitis," Clark said. "At the time we didn't know as much about infectious hepatitis as we did a few years later. We knew we had to get liquids into him, especially glucose solutions intravenously, to protect his liver and give him the necessary nourishment. The patient's condition kept deteriorating steadily. A day came when we held a conference and concluded that this patient wasn't going to make it.

"The dying man's family had been asking for days that he be allowed to go home. We decided to release him. Before doing so, however, the man's wife listened very carefully to instructions we gave her about feeding him by spoon certain foods in small amounts. The family took him back to his island, where his wife faithfully followed our feeding instructions. At the same time a Trukese medicine man who had been called in also administered his medicines, along with taboos and rituals. The man slowly began to improve. When we saw him some time later, he had regained good health."

Tsunami!

I was at the dock one morning when Amantap from the boat pool hurried over to me and said I was wanted on the phone. Walking into the nearby pier shed, I spoke into the hand-cranked phone.

"Mr. Muller," my secretary said. "an urgent radio message just arrived from Honolulu. I'll read it." Her voice sounded excited. The message went about like this:

TO: DISTAD TRUK URGENT
FROM: HICOMTERPACIS (HIGH COMMISSIONER
              TRUST TERRITORY OF PACIFIC ISLANDS)
TSUNAMI WITH HIGH WAVES POSSIBLE MAY REACH YOUR AREA
ABOUT 1015 HOURS TRUK LOCAL TIME. TAKE IMMEDIATE PRE-
CAUTIONARY MEASURES.

Tsunami! My God! I glanced at my wrist watch. It showed 8:45. Great waves might hit us within 90 minutes!

I looked toward the water behind the "T"-shaped pier. Our three main small craft—the cabin cruiser, thirty-eight foot motor whaleboat, and the WWII Navy landing craft used for loading and unloading ships out in the harbor—all rode in dead-calm water. Moored at the front of the pier was the

"YOGI"—our huge steel diesel fuel barge. The tremendous force of high waves could smash the wooden hull boats to pieces, and wreck the YOGI. It could sweep away the dock, our warehouses and Truk Trading Company's, a few hundred yards back from the beach.

What about people on all the other islands? There was no way we could warn more than a few of the nearest ones in Truk Lagoon. How could people on all those low outer islands beyond the lagoon protect themselves from such waves? Most low islands aren't over thirty or forty feet at their highest point. We hadn't yet installed the first short-wave radio out there. My palms felt sweaty.

Growing up on Washington State's Puget Sound, I had heard of this phenomenon. Like others around me, I referred to it incorrectly as a tidal wave. Tides have nothing to do with *tsunamis*, I learned after our Truk crisis. They can be much more serious than the terrors of a typhoon—especially for low island people and those living along coastal shelves of high islands.

Tsunami, from the Japanese language, literally means earthquake sea wave. It is not a single wave, but a series of them. One may be started by a volcanic eruption, a quake on the sea floor, or a shifting of sea-bottom tectonic plates, causing them to rise or fall substantially Thus waves are formed and move speedily through the ocean. Far out in the Pacific such waves may rise only a few feet above the surface. Oceanographers say a *tsunami* is a great wall of water which can reach from the ocean floor to surface wave crest, racing across the ocean at up to 500 miles an hour or more. They travel faster in deep than in shallow water. Following the ocean bottom contour as they approach shore they can rise like a fabled sea monster, thirty or fifty feet or more into the air. They will be much bigger on a shallow beach than on a steep one. The big waves often hit shore at fifteen to sixty minutes intervals. They occur mainly in the Pacific ocean.

Back in 1896 a *tsunami* smashed into the Japanese coast, drowning 27,000 people and ruined 10,000 houses. Early in the twentieth century a series of such big waves once hit the Hawaiian Islands and demolished the entire small town of Ponoluu. In 1946 a violent seaquake in the Aleutians Trench created powerful waves that swept away a lighthouse on Unimak Island, 100 miles distant, and the five U.S. Coast Guard men stationed there.

My secretary waited on the other end of the line. I gave her instructions.

74

"Please telephone Sheriff Kintoki immediately, or the senior man on duty. Explain the problem. Tell him I said to send Constabulary men out immediately to both ends of the island. If they need more jeeps, take them from the motor pool. They are to order all people to leave their villages, climb up at least two hundred feet and stay there until they receive an all clear signal."

"I'll call right away."

"Then notify all department heads, beginning with Public Works and Medical. And get word to all families to stay at home or in the upper headquarters area."

Since most of the district center was more than 100 feet above sea level, it wouldn't be necessary to evacuate the hospital, schools, offices and other groups. Only workers in the dock area, the Weather Bureau staff at the airfield, and the garage mechanics would have to move, and drive as many vehicles as possible to high ground. From the phone in the boat pool building at the end of the pier I called TTC to warn them.

Pete Becker and Ray Hann, the American foreman who supervised boat pool and heavy equipment operations, came racing down the beach road in a jeep, drove out onto the dock, skidded to a stop a few feet from me, and climbed out. Ray's face was flushed. Beads of sweat stood out on his forehead. "There isn't a damned thing we can do in the next forty-five minutes," he said in a tense voice, "to protect any small craft except the outboard boats from a tidal wave! If we just beach them at the water's edge it won't protect them in the least. Not from the kind o' waves we're talkin' about..."

I broke in and asked them to send our own small boat with an outboard immediately to the southwest part of the lagoon and spread the word to those high islands. The foreman exchanged a few words with two Trukese boat pool men who had come over from the outer end of the dock and stood listening. Now they hurried to the boat shed to get the motor, gas tank, and other gear.

———

Driving off the pier and into the TTC compound, I saw Reiong, one of their especially well-regarded employees, walking toward me. I knew he had a fast little boat powered by an outboard motor. He lived on an island in the southern part of the lagoon.

"Reiong," I said, after quickly explaining the crisis, "will you take your boat and go warn the people on Fefan Island? Ask them to tell the people on

Dublon Island and on Parem Island. Then take your boat on down to Uman Island and stay there until three o'clock." That would cover the southeast part of the atoll.

Reiong frowned as he considered my unusual request. "You pay me for this?" I wanted to tell him to get moving, but he didn't work for me.

"Yes."

"How much?"

I had no frame of reference for something like this. He normally earned perhaps twenty-five cents an hour, and he'd be using his own boat. "Ten dollars," I said.

"That is hazard duty," he said. "Pay should be more."

There was real risk involved—especially if the Honolulu office hadn't calculated precisely the arrival time of the big waves. If they were right, and if he hurried, he could make the trip safely.

"How much do you want?"

"Twenty dollars."

"Twenty dollars," I agreed. I glanced again at my watch. Forty-eight minutes left. Three minutes later I looked toward the beach road and saw a Constabulary jeep with two uniformed men in it fly past on the way toward the southeast end of the island to warn villagers.

Without returning to tell his supervisor, Reiong headed toward the building where he stored his outboard motor. Soon I saw his fiberglass boat speed away toward Fefan Island, about five miles away.

Wiping sweat from my forehead with the back of my arm, I got into my jeep and sped along the waterfront road to the Weather Bureau quonsets by the airfield. The American in charge and several Trukese had loaded some gear into the back of their jeep and were about to drive off. I waved them to go on.

After that, I drove to the garage, halfway to the headquarters area. The big yellow-colored avgas tanker truck, which we used to refuel planes, backed slowly toward me. Foreman Shelley told me several vehicles already had been driven to higher ground. The tanker and remaining trucks and jeeps in running shape would leave in a few minutes. I phoned the radio shack from the garage. No further message from HICOM.

I drove on up the road and turned right onto Telegraph Hill and parked at the radio shack. From there I could look down over the harbor. The American radioman on duty with a Trukese at the time, came out and stood with me for a few minutes. He looked and sounded calmer than I felt. Each minute dragged by.

The expected arrival time of the big waves—10:15— came and went. There was no sign of a sea disturbance. I went inside the radio shack and waited and watched for another half hour. The lagoon remained flat calm.

"We'll stay on alert two more hours," I said to two other staff members who had joined me there. Then I went down to my office. My secretary hurried in.

"The Constabulary called in a few minutes ago. They've gone out to all villages. Sheriff Kintoki asks what you want them to do next. Do you think there's still a danger?"

"No," I said. "I believe it's past. Tell them to call off the alert at 12:15."

No big waves came near the Truk District that day. Perhaps they spent themselves in the depths of the vast Pacific. It was the only *tsunami* alert we had during my years in the islands. One positive thing came out of the experience: it moved us to learn more about *tsunamis*. It also made us realize how very vulnerable the Trukese and other people on low islands all over the Pacific are to the terrors of a *tsunami*. Fortunately, they very seldom happen.

Educate Them—For What?

Learning "those old things" and "those new things"

Like Clark at the hospital, Herb Wilson, our new Truk District Education department head, arrived at Truk about two months after takeover from the Navy. I was startled when Bob Law told me during my first week on Moen Island that Herb was only twenty-eight, and had gone directly from college graduation into the Navy, where he became skipper of a small patrol ship. His practical experience in education was limited to about a year as an education specialist on Captain Anderson's Territory-wide staff at Truk. After the new civilian High Commissioner in Honolulu offered him this education job at Truk, he resigned and went on home leave shortly before the Navy left. At least, I thought, this guy has a degree in education, and he has lived and worked among the Trukese—more than most of us could say. Still, I was concerned about his very limited professional education work experience.

I drove to the airfield to meet him. When I saw the tall, pinkish, red-haired fellow coming down the ramp, I thought, *My God! He looks even younger than twenty-eight!* But he had a ready smile and a confident manner. I noticed, too, that many Trukese came up and greeted "Mr. Winson" with real warmth.

When a U.S. Navy military government team moved in to Truk in late

1945, they had to start nearly from scratch in building an educational system. All Japanese educators had been repatriated at war's end. They did leave behind a few good school buildings in Truk Lagoon and a small number of trained Trukese craftsmen. Assigning education a high priority, the Navy team searched out and hired a small group of Trukese who had received some of the best education at the Japanese schools in these islands.

Most Japanese schools for islander children had covered only the first three primary grades. Emphasis was on teaching the Japanese language. Other main subjects included arithmetic and geography. A few of the brightest students had been selected for an additional two or three years of schooling. The Japanese had created specialized training programs for a small number of Micronesians at the agricultural research station on Ponape, about 400 miles east of Truk. And they set up a carpentry school at Palau in the western Carolines, which proved very successful.

Some of the best islander craftsmen at Truk when our civilian administration took over from Navy, were graduates of that three-year carpentry school. By the time we American civilians took over, the Navy had created a whole new elementary program, with one or more schools on each populated island. They also had set up in Truk's headquarters area a boarding intermediate school. which included grades seven through nine, and the only Trust Territory-wide two-year high school: the Pacific Islands Central School. Everyone referred to it as "PICS."

Once a year each elementary school teacher recommended several of the brightest boys and girls to begin studies at the intermediate school. Our field trip freighter brought them from the more distant islands in to headquarters. Some came from islands up to 150 miles north and west of Moen; others from the Mortlocks, where the most remote islands are southeast about the same distance away.

Very few new intermediate school students from islands beyond Truk Lagoon who arrived at the district center had ever seen electric lights, running water, modern furniture, jeeps, trucks (there were no passenger cars in the district) or movies. They came carrying food in kerchiefs or pouches, rough-woven from coconut fronds. Some had brought woven sleeping mats. A few brought lanterns.

Here the new students found a strange, often puzzling and, in the beginning, lonely world. Suddenly they were surrounded by 130 other students—mostly strangers. Many even spoke different dialects. They found all teaching in English. Most of them had a poor grasp of that foreign language. So remedial English became a required class for them.

They were puzzled by the new ways of personal hygiene and indoor plumbing. In the first days, some squatted on top of toilet seats and, quite understandably, didn't comprehend flushing. Early in the first year of civilian administration, young male students, due to a sense of modesty, wore their undershorts while showering. This soon resulted in cases of fungus and rashes, which the Medical department was called upon to clear up.

The school staff consisted of Principal Lawton "Rip" Ripsom, several Trukese teachers, and four American teacher trainers. As a practical matter, the Americans had to do most of the teaching while they helped upgrade the Trukese teachers by on-the-job training.

Herb and his Education office people tried a number of innovations that first year. One of their earliest ideas for change, both to save on their tight budget and to make these youngsters feel more at home, was to throw out of the dormitory buildings, which were row upon row of gleaming white quonsets, all the metal GI cots and mattresses. The latter, WWII leftovers, were lumpy and worn after years of student use in Navy times.

They proposed to replace them with sleeping platforms—like those many Trukese used at home. But instead of using local materials, which would take much more time to gather and construct, our Public Works carpentry shop decided to make them of plywood. They would be built to a height of six inches above the quonset floor, and run the length of the building on both sides. This would leave an aisle down the middle. For those students who didn't bring their own woven sleeping mats, our Education office people arranged to obtain them from nearby villages. Rip and his staff discussed this proposed change with the students. They enthusiastically agreed. They preferred to sleep island style. It worked fine from the start.

Our Education department fed them and PICS students in a central dining room on a tight budget. The young manager, Raymond Setik, was a talented PICS graduate. Here Herb ran into a combined cultural and communications problem, regarding which he almost came a cropper.

Some enterprising young Australians sailed into Truk Lagoon one day on a big, old schooner, the *Mileeta*. They tied up alongside Baker dock, opened their hatches and announced cheerfully in their unmistakable accents they were ready to offer us a wide range of trade goods at attractive prices. They even had many gallons of rich ice cream aboard. As soon as word of the *Mileeta*'s arrival reached Herb, he drove down for a look.

"They had a large supply of canned Australian hare," he recalled later. "With our limited school budget, I thought of this as a tremendous source of protein. So I went ahead and purchased, at a very good price, cases and cases and cases of the meat. When stewed rabbit was served for the first time the next day, the students all threw it away. Napo came to me after lunch, looking grim. 'The students will not eat the hare,' he said in measured words.

"Well, I was stunned. I had already spent a large chunk of our food budget on all this canned rabbit meat. In desperation, I called the American teachers together and asked if they'd go down with me to the student dining room and at least pretend we just loved eating stewed hare. We faked it as much as we could. The students looked at us wide-eyed. But they continued to chuck it out. I asked Napo, 'Why won't they eat the meat?'

"He told me the Trukese word for rabbit is '*usangi*.' He said the students looked up the word rabbit in Webster's dictionary. On the page where a rabbit is described there is a picture of one. But on the same page there is also a picture of a rat. The rabbit looks like a rat and the Trukese do not eat rats."

Herb went to a dictionary, looked up the page, and found there was no scale to indicate the relative sizes of rabbits and rats. With both pictures on the same page, and no apparent difference in size, the students, hardly able to read English, had jumped to a conclusion.

"A day or two later," he said, "I recalled that on Guam there's an agricultural station where they were attempting to breed a kind of rabbit which can withstand tropical heat. I requested that they send me on the next flight two male rabbits—the *biggest* they had; I needed them for a demonstration. The rabbits arrived on the next plane, and they were gigantic angora types."

He arranged for two cages to be built: one down by the dock and another by the intermediate school. They labeled them in English and Japanese: RABBIT—USANGI. People came from all over Truk Lagoon to see these creatures, completely new to them. They looked very big, furry, and attractive.

"We made the point with the students," he said, "that they are even larger in Australia, and they aren't anything like rats. From then on the students began to eat the canned hare. It saved the day for me."

Deciding he needed to learn to speak Trukese in order to do his job more effectively, Herb began going for a week or ten days at a time to Fano Island in Truk Lagoon. At the same time he intended to work part of each day with the island's elementary teacher. He arranged ahead of time to live with the teacher and his family. "They had an extra house," he recalled later. "I hoped they'd give me that house to have alone with my dog, so I could get some rest at night. But they didn't.

"You know how they like to be with other people at night. Well, while they let me sleep in that house, the teacher and some of his friends immediately moved in with me. Because of their great fear of the dark and the unknown and ghosts, they kept a jar filled with kerosene, with a rag for a wick, burning all night. It gave off black, heavy smoke. And they kept all the wooden shutters closed, so there was absolutely no air in this stifling room. I would wait until I thought the others were asleep, then I'd creep to the windows and try very quietly to open some shutters, because it was so terribly hot and humid, and there was that strong smell of kerosene fumes. They usually woke up or weren't yet asleep, so it was a problem every night."

The teacher and his wife had two small boys. The older one was named Cigarette. the smaller one was called Papa. This intrigued Herb. He asked how they came up with those particular names. The teacher said they'd heard the words spoken by some Navy men and liked the sounds. Herb explained carefully the meaning of each word, but the parents never wavered; they stuck with the nice sounds. Other Trukese had heard similar words they thought had a nice ring, so we Americans smiled when we met or heard of youngsters named Piano, Ivorysoap, and Guitar.

Herb wasn't on Fano Island long before he concluded that one of its main problems was the large number of flies. He was certain the island's garbage was largely to blame, especially since this wasn't the breadfruit season. He resolved to give them a helping hand.

"When I thought I had set the stage over a period of weeks, through discussions of the island's sanitation problems with some of its movers and shakers, they called an island-wide meeting one evening. After wonderful singing, I steered them onto the big question. "What do you need to do to improve your island?"

"'Another store!' someone sang out, and they all agreed."

Retail stores throughout the islands were high risk enterprises. The store-keeper would get enough breadfruit wood and thatch or tin roofing together to make a little kiosk-like structure and stock its two or three shelves with trade goods bought at wholesale from TTC. The fatal weakness in the system was that tradition required him to share whatever he had with members of his extended family. They inevitably came shopping, and in a matter of a few weeks or a few months they usually cleaned the storekeeper out, with never a suggestion of paying.

"I thought the last thing they needed on Fano was a second store," Herb recalled. "But I said, 'I'll help you start a new store if you will help get rid of some of the flies.' They agreed. But the island cleanup venture never got very far. Their hearts weren't in it. Flies multiplied faster than anybody could control them."

In time, Lou Gardella and his Trukese sanitarian assistants, through a slow process of education, were able to get the people in some places to understand why flies were bad. On such islands they began to make progress. Herb came away from Fano all the more convinced that education had to meet daily village needs. I was sure he was on the right track.

Dinner parties were among our most popular social activities. After the dishes were cleared away, we'd sit in a circle in the living room, and make small talk, play parlor games, sing or have bull sessions, or all four. Often our bull sessions worked around to America's role in the islands. How well did the High Commission staff in Honolulu and we Americans on Truk—my own staff and the dozen or more headquarters people also stationed on Moen—understand and carry out our responsibilities? I recall one such dinner and "fireside" vividly. It was during our second year in the islands. Guests included both Americans and Trukese. Talk got around to island education.

"Education—*for what*?" a young American wife asked, a deadly earnest ring of challenge in her voice. Her animated gaze moved from Herb to Cy Pickerill, head of PICS, then to me. "What sense does it make to introduce United States educational patterns? You even have American textbooks and library books! What makes you think you're providing at PICS, where you have at least six different cultures, what each district's students really need? Or want? Do you really ever *ask* the Trukese people what they want their children to learn? Do you know what's truly *meaningful* to them?"

"But, but—" someone cut in, ready to protest this assault.

"From the little I see of it," she brushed aside the interruption, her voice tight with emotion, "it looks like we're giving the Trukese a pretty standard American education, and they're not getting much in either quantity or quality!"

A shower of reactions flew around the room like sparks from burning cedar kindling. Some were as emotional as the young wife's comments. Listening to the lively talk, my thoughts turned to Grimble. Young Arthur Grimble was appointed, at age twenty-six, as a cadet in the British Colonial Service back in 1913. He was assigned to the Gilbert and Ellice Islands Colony (now named Kiribati and Tuvalu). The northern part of the former lies just below the southeastern edge of the Marshall Islands. They are part of Micronesia, but were not part of the Trust Territory. He spent most of his working career there, rose to the rank of Resident Commissioner, roughly equivalent to our High Commissioner. At the end of his career he was knighted for his services.

A few months before this dinner party, my brother Ken sent me Arthur Grimble's delightful book, which had just been published. Called *We Chose the Islands,* it was about his first six years in the tropics. He told how he had sensed during his first years, and later came to know, as my staff and I did, the potential for danger in situations where well-meaning but fallible foreign administrators and their staffs started to "fiddle" with pieces of island culture. Such actions could upset clan life and other deep-rooted social institutions. From many of the old ways flowed strong benefits—too often unseen and unfelt by the outsider—in an environment where most parts of the culture were delicately balanced and all were closely linked.

Grimble's warnings made a strong and lasting impression on me. I worried more about the dangers inherent in fiddling with the Trukese culture than about any other part of my job—except fire danger around headquarters. I was concerned that my staff and I, well-intentioned but with limited understanding, might unwittingly upset and weaken fine old ways. Eventually I corresponded with one of Grimble's successors, Governor Michael Bernacchi of the Gilbert, Ellice and Line Islands, but only after we both had retired and left our respective former island homes.

As anthropologist John L. Fischer wrote in a monograph published in 1979, many of the CIMA reports were slow to appear in the islands. "When they did, the number of typewritten copies was limited, and the language was oriented toward the professional social scientist rather than the lay administrator..."

My counterparts in the other districts and I were grateful that the Navy had the wisdom and foresight to staff their Micronesian operations with a cultural anthropologist in each district. I considered our anthropologist one of the most valuable Americans at Truk.

In no area did I have greater concern about our fiddling than in the matter of the *eterenges* (extended family) relations. The extended family was, as an institution, still very much intact, as Frank often pointed out. How could we teach students new things without contributing to the weakening of some of the best of the old ways? Like respect of young people for the lineage, respect of children for their elders, and sharing?

Could and should we teach, in or out of classrooms, things that would in time weaken a particular custom we thought should go—like wife-beating, or women crawling in the presence of men? Both of those customs bothered us Americans greatly. We knew the missionaries were working to get them changed. Some of my staff and I spoke to island leaders against the customs, but we should have done more. They allegedly took place mainly in the western islands, but we heard about spanking wives in other parts of the district. Would such teachings trigger some unforeseen and unwanted cultural chain reaction? We knew decisions we Americans made could set in motion changes that would echo down through decades—even generations—ahead, and profoundly affect the lives of the Trukese. Hard as we tried, we walked headlong into a cultural problem now and then. One such experience was the canoe class.

Herb breezed into my office one morning brimming with good cheer and suppressed excitement. "I have a proposal," he announced, "for a much-needed innovation in our intermediate school program."

"You have my undivided attention," I responded. "Shoot!" I sat back expectantly.

"The ancient art of canoe building," he said a bit dramatically, "is dying out in the Mortlocks and here in Truk Lagoon. In another generation or two it could be gone. Only a few old master canoe builders remain. Before this precious knowledge disappears completely, I propose we initiate on an urgent basis a special class in canoe building. It will be part of our manual arts program."

"Who'll teach it?"

"We have a fine instructor lined up. His name is Kechuo, from Nama Island. He's regarded as one of the best of the remaining artisans in all the Mortlocks. He is prepared to come up here to Moen and teach canoe building for fifty dollars a month and a place to sleep. He has relatives at Mechetiu village who will feed him."

Herb described the plan in some detail, and I asked many questions. In the end it was agreed that he would check out some points I raised, and report back to me. A week later he returned to my office, accompanied by Principal "Rip" Ripsom. Herb said he and his staff had examined the proposal from all angles. The male students had been sounded out. Their response was enthusiastic.

A little-used quonset could be cleaned out and made ready for the canoe building class. Several big breadfruit trees, at the end of their bearing years, were located in a nearby village and could be bought at a fair price to provide wood for the canoes. Old Kechuo wanted to bring his own simple tools, along with several modern ones like a couple of chisels, a plane and a drill. The class would construct two outrigger paddling canoes during the semester. Finished canoes would be used by older students to catch fish in the lagoon for the school dining room.

"Go ahead," I said.

During one of my periodic walking inspections around the district center a few weeks later, I dropped by to look in on the new canoe building class. What I saw was heart-warming. Old Kechuo, barefooted, his stocky body and weathered face bent over the rough outline of a canoe hull, was using a traditional island-made adze, fashioned from a shell lashed to a smoothed branch from a tree. More than fifteen students, gathered around the hull, watched intently his every move. Making paper-thin shavings fly, he expertly shaped the hull to follow a penciled tracing. Then he asked several students, in turn, to try their hands at the exacting work. *Good instruction*, I thought. *Tell them what you're going to do. Do it. Ask them to try it. Check their work.*

One day after the class had been under way for about six weeks, I entered the quonset and found it empty. Assuming they must have changed the day's schedule, I thought no more about it until my next walking tour, when I found the building empty again. A canoe hull sat there in the same state of partial completion it was two weeks earlier. That afternoon I phoned Herb for an explanation.

"I'll be right over," he said. His face was clouded as he walked in and slumped into a chair. "We had to terminate the class," he said unhappily. This news jolted me. It was the most enthusiastic intermediate school class I had seen.

"It was going beautifully," Herb explained, "until they reached a certain critical step in the hull construction." He paused and sighed. "At that point the whole thing broke down. Kechuo told the students they'd have to leave the shop while he performed a certain step by himself. When the students protested, he told them it was secret, passed on to only a few members of his own clan. Apparently the students all knew this sort of thing was generally the case, but thought that here at school such things might be different."

"Why did Kechuo ever agree to teach the class if he was unwilling to show the secret part?"

"I asked him that," Herb said, still sounding distressed. "But he wouldn't budge. He's waiting to return to Nama on the next field trip ship."

"Did you talk with Frank before you started this project?" I asked.

"No. We never dreamed...." I suddenly realized I had contributed to the project's failure. This was one missing item on Herb's feasibility check list I had failed to catch.

That same afternoon I called Frank in. "Herb told me the canoe class had to be disbanded," I said. "How come you didn't know there's a secret step in canoe building?"

"I knew."

"Then why didn't you tell the Education office before they wasted all that effort?"

"Nobody asked me."

At that point I had a long talk with Frank about the role of a district anthropologist, as I saw it. There was a general understanding among head-quarters and all district administrators that anthropologists were not to be pleaders for either the administration or the islanders on any issue. For one of them to do so would, in the eyes of the islanders, damage his role as a neutral observer—a bridge between two cultures. With displays of such partiality, his sources for many kinds of cultural insights could be expected to dry up.

While I liked that policy, I also believed strongly that a staff anthropologist should help keep us out of trouble by pointing out cultural barriers before we crashed headlong into them. Often we Americans didn't know the questions to ask. Without our anthropologist, Herb, Clark, and the rest of us would be at times like a ship moving down a channel in a heavy fog without radar.

Bob Gibson

Bob, our Director of Education for the Trust Territory, was one of the clearest voices to come out of headquarters. Starting life as a Missouri farm boy, he earned his PhD at Stanford, became an educator, and moved up in the California school system.

When Americans of Japanese ethnic origin were ordered into detention camps early in WWII, Bob first strongly protested that action by our government as a very shameful miscarriage of justice. Then he became an education advisor for the program. After the war he spent three years as a civilian with the U.S. Army in South Korea, where he served as an advisor to the Ministry of Education. He was fifty-three when he came to the Trust Territory. He brought with him more experience in dealing with other cultures than most of us had.

On his first visits to Truk, he didn't start telling us what kind of programs the people needed. He looked, listened, asked questions. He didn't spend his time mainly around our offices and the hotel, like some visitors from headquarters did. He'd go out regularly with Herb and Napo DeFang, our Trukese Superintendent of elementary schools, to the villages—on islands in Truk Lagoon that seldom saw an official from Honolulu for more than a very short visit. Sometimes I'd go with them. After sitting in on classes, Bob liked to walk around the villages with the teacher. He wanted to know about island conditions. He talked with island chiefs and carpenters, farmers and parents. Was there enough food all year? What about the drinking water supply? Did they dry their copra on racks or throw it on the sand to dry? To him, these problems were all grist for the education mill. He began urging us to find ways—through adult education as well as in classrooms—to help the people meet those needs.

When he visited a school where the teacher failed to show up that day, as often happened, Bob didn't shrug or growl and walk away. Sometimes he asked his companions to take him to the teacher's village. They might meet the teacher along a pathway, dressed only in shorts, machete in hand, and bathed in sweat, returning with a shoulder load of taro from the family garden. Or they might learn he went fishing at the barrier reef, or was simply passing the time with friends. When he met an absent teacher, Bob would put out his hand and begin a conversation. He tried to size up the teacher: his degree of commitment to the job, his ability to speak English, and his ideas about how to improve elementary schools in general. He left it to people in the Education office to talk with the man about sticking closer to his teaching schedule.

During one of his first visits, Bob said to several of us "It concerns me that we Americans are giving them an educational system built around the classroom. But we do it because it's the way we know...."

On another of his visits about six months later, some of us sat with him during a day-long session in Herb's office. We were soon on the most familiar theme: *What kind of education makes the most sense in these islands?* Each of us present was painfully aware of the elementary schools' weaknesses: students were being taught the three Rs, a smattering of geography and history. Little more than half of those teachers had a ninth grade education—equivalent to no more than the sixth or seventh grade at home. There was a very small number of PICS graduates teaching. Less than a dozen elementary teachers were females. The other regular subject was music—time earmarked for one of the things students enjoyed most: singing. About the only music instruction involved there was to teach the words to a new song. Efforts were made in some schools to teach English, beginning in the fourth grades. Many teachers didn't even try to tackle this subject. They knew their own English was too poor.

After listening to the give-and-take for a while, Bob asked, "What do the Trukese people think? What do *they* want you to teach their children?" He turned to Napo.

"We tried to ask people on all islands this question," Napo responded.

"Some don't give us any answers. Sometimes carpentry and sewing are suggested. Mostly, they tell us they want their children to learn *those new things.*"

By asking questions throughout the district, we learned that many parents believed if their children could learn English and those other "*new things*" from American books, it would lead to jobs, and jobs meant dollars. This response was seldom heard in the western islands. Most people there seemed to place higher values on the old ways. Through contact with us foreigners, many Trukese were acquiring a desire for many of the material things we Americans, and the Japanese and Germans before us, enjoyed. Yet, with Truk's extreme shortage of natural resources, high hopes for substantial and wide-spread material gains seemed likely to lead to disappointments and frustrations—especially for the younger generation. We looked at Bob, waiting for his reaction to what Napo said. He swept us with his gaze.

"Napo... Herb... Will..." he spoke in that resonant Missouri drawl, "let me ask you three questions: Shouldn't the whole community be the subject for school teaching? Shouldn't the education we offer meet daily needs? How much of what the children are being taught now in the elementary schools can they put to work on their islands? Can you give me positive answers to those questions? If not, shouldn't we re-examine what we're doing? At this point in Micronesia's history not many children from each island are likely to go on to higher education." At that time, around 1,700 children were enrolled in Truk District's schools, grades one through six.

"We Americans aren't here to do things *for* the people," Bob said. "No, we're here to *help them help themselves*—point out to them choices that seem within the realm of possibility. Then let them choose." That was a part of Bob's philosophy we heard him repeat over and over in the years ahead.

Before he left to walk back up Telegraph Hill to the hotel and get ready for a dinner Herb was hosting that evening, we talked for a few minutes about "*those old things.*" The Trukese educators there with us agreed that this phrase, which they sometimes used in talking with us, meant the kinds of activities that had been taught from time out of mind on their islands: farming, food preservation, fishing, house-building, canoe building and sailing, midwifery, weaving, sewing. In that afternoon discussion, the Trukese didn't say anything about traditional medicine, forms of magic, and preparing young men for leadership roles in the clan, but they surely also were part of what they considered the "*old things*." Until about 1900, training for warfare between islands—even between villages on an island—was part of the education for young men.

Sometimes I tried to imagine what Trukese education was like more than a hundred years earlier—before the first foreigners regularly began to touch their lives. Because most Trukese children now attended elementary schools, did that mean their families no longer taught them the old things? We Americans knew it didn't. We were seeing daily evidence to the contrary.

Still, Herb and others of us who got around to other islands and villages throughout the district, were surprised and disappointed when we looked more closely to find how many boys and girls were not in school. At starting time if some were in the middle of a game, they finished it before going to classes. Or they started a whole new game. Some children didn't go to school at all. But wherever we looked we also saw that boys and girls were learning traditional island skills by watching and sometimes helping men, women, and older children in their extended families at work.

A favorite place for boys around eight or nine years old to play was in paddling canoes in shallow water. A few years later they could handle the canoes skillfully in those waters. About the same time, they learned to climb coconut trees and they became interested in spear fishing. Some wore home-made diving goggles with whittled wooden eyepieces. A few made their lenses from old TTC sunglasses or bits of plexiglass. The latter was ripped from wrecked WWII Japanese fighter planes, a small number of which still remained on some islands, half-sunk on a sandy beach or in the boondocks, with vines growing out of them.

We watched boys wade out, spear in hand, until they had to swim; then they duck-dived. They swam off of outrigger paddling canoes. Sometimes an older brother, father or uncle on shore watched a boy trying to spear a fish, then swam out and showed him how to do it right. Boys of fourteen or fifteen occasionally were invited to go along for a day's fishing in the more dangerous waters beyond the reef.

In the Mortlocks we saw older boys helping men build fish traps. Other boys often sat in the dappled shade of a tree, watching men shape and chisel out a canoe hull. On Punlap, Tamatam and other far western islands small boys stood or sat around watching while older boys helped men build a new grass hut. A few such houses were still on islands in the Mortlocks, and fewer still in Truk Lagoon. We saw girls learning in the same way to weave baskets and mats, work in gardens, and fish with butterfly nets. That was the pattern wherever we looked around the District: watch, help, do.

"Frank," I said one day after I'd been talking with Herb and several of his staff about such observations, "Trukese kids are on a two-track education system, aren't they?"

"Two-track?"

"Yes. They're learning '*those new things*' in school. Outside school, their families and friends are still teaching them things their parents and grandparents had to know—and most of these kids are going to need."

"You're surprised?" he said, grinning. "I keep telling you the people remain very Trukese. But there have been changes. They don't learn all the old things."

"Like warfare?"

"Warfare's gone. *Itang's* less important now. How many know how to build the big sailing canoes any more? Or to navigate the old way? And as the church's influence grows, magic has less importance. For some people, even their fear of island, reef, and sea spirits is fading a little."

Frank had told me during my first months at Truk that clan elders in earlier times handpicked a few young men around fourteen to sixteen to become men of *itang*. Those so honored always came from the clans that held the hereditary village chieftainships. But even in *itang* times, a potential leader had to be acceptable to his people. Sometimes a weak one came along. The people recognized it and bypassed him. In those times there were no island-wide chiefs. Those young men were chosen because clan elders had observed they were among the bravest and brightest, demonstrated good judgment, and probably were among the strongest and most athletic.

Over many years they were taught warrior leadership knowledge. While that was one important part of *itang*, its main emphasis was on overall leadership skills. They learned traditional lore, magic, the arts of oratory, and other ways of influencing the people. Beyond all that, they were instructed in the secret language known only to the men of *itang*. Their status and esteem were higher than that of a chief.

When the German administrators came to Truk at the turn of the century, they confiscated all the islanders' guns and stopped warfare between islands and between villages on an island. The men of *itang* got together and decided to de-emphasize their special leadership role. The times, they decided, had changed that much. Only a few men of *itang* were widely known to remain in Truk Lagoon while I was there. Chief Petrus—leader of leaders—was one of them. The Germans started the system of appointing top hereditary clan leaders as *island* chiefs. The Japanese continued it. This arrangement made it easier to administer by indirect rule.

One of the main outgrowths of Bob's visits and our talks together was agreement that higher priority must be put on adapting lesson materials to the Trukese culture. American textbooks with pictures of and references to trains, busses, escalators, a farmer's barn and machinery, simply weren't usable.

Developing such materials was a burdensome task. Much of the work fell to Herb, Napo, and a couple of Trukese and American teachers at headquarters who pitched in and helped. They began writing teaching materials with island settings. Children then began to read about familiar things: canoes, breadfruit and bananas, cooking fires, the lagoon. When they studied arithmetic, American examples of arithmetic in use gave way to problems like how to calculate the price a man should be paid for a bag of copra, how to calculate local distances, and the dimensions of a plot of land. In those years they had no computers to use as word processors, or copying machines. They had typewriters and slow, somewhat messy mimeograph machines.

Over at PICS, Cy Pickerill and her staff were faced with the same problems. For them the Navy had at least developed a couple of such story books, in English, illustrated with island settings and professionally printed. The PICS staff tackled their work in pretty much the same way as Herb and his crew, except PICS used only the English language.

Most new Truk District teaching materials were in the local language. Bob had become convinced by linguistic studies, followed by trial use, in other countries like the Philippines, that children learned better when they studied their own language in the first three grades. Herb, Napo and I listened to the pros and cons on this and agreed. There was, as Bob sometimes pointed out, no practical alternative. In Truk—and the situation was quite similar in other districts—many elementary teachers didn't know English well enough to teach it. I personally found on field trips that I had a hard time understanding a third or more of the elementary teachers trying to speak English.

These new elementary school reading and arithmetic materials were stapled together, sometimes with show card covers, and sent by the next field trip party to outer islands. This, too, was a never-ending process. Those modest publications proved perishable. Like translations of the legal code, which Chief Justice Furber had arranged for our field trip parties to deliver to island judges, the mimeographed Education materials quickly became sun-faded, dog-eared, dirt and salt water stained—even lost.

Sewing was introduced for upper elementary girls. Herb and Napo talked about the need to add instruction for boys in the simple use of hand tools: saws, hammers, chisels, drills. This was already being taught at intermediate school. We hoped that some of those intermediate students would learn to use such tools competently enough to pass that knowledge along to elementary boys back on their home islands. Most tools we saw around the islands—mainly in the Truk Lagoon—belonged to the small scattering of local carpenters trained in Japanese times. We also saw that small number of elite craftsmen, the canoe builders, using very simple adzes and chisels, made from local materials such as hard shells, and a few also used a modern tool or two such as a chisel, drill, or plane.

The main job of all Americans on our district staffs was to help prepare islanders to eventually replace us, and we could go home. An important job for several members of our Island Affairs staff and for my deputy and me—though all our staff contributed to it indirectly if not directly—was to try to help the people build up a productive economy. Regarding that first main task, we saw modest progress being made in specific education and training areas. Looking around our headquarters, we became increasingly aware that a substantial amount of good on-the-job training was being built into each of our Trukese employees by our own American craftsmen and professionals in many fields.

We began to pay more attention to adult education. Our agriculturists worked to get a simple but good extension program going on the outer islands as well as in Truk Lagoon. When we finally got funds we'd been requesting for several years to install rugged short-wave radios on a few outer-islands, our radio operators at headquarters taught Trukese on those selected islands how to operate them. We installed the sets in central outer island locations. That became a good additional form of medical extension. Our Trukese and American doctors could answer radio calls for help regarding patients with medical problems the outer island health aides and midwives lacked knowledge to cope with. Our doctors back at headquarters could talk them through some treatments—like a broken limb. And they could talk a midwife through a difficult delivery—like an air traffic controller might talk down a plane in distress.

Our doctors were helping to upgrade Trukese doctors, already impressively trained in their fields at the Fiji medical school. We had a number of capable, experienced Trukese nurses who had been trained years earlier under a Navy nurse training program on Guam. About two years into the civilian administration, a new Trust Territory-wide nurse training school was set up on Truk. Classes were conducted full-time under the American nurse trainer, who once had been a missionary nurse in China. The U.S. Weather Bureau office, under John Norris' skillful guidance, operated a school to train weather observers. Some young graduates were well on their way to standing independent watches. Staff sanitarian Lou Gardella was making noticeable progress upgrading his people.

Don McGrail and another American surveyor were teaching Trukese how to use their instruments to locate, map, and describe plots of land. At our Public Works shops each American foreman, whether in carpentry, plumbing, electrical, heavy equipment, refrigeration, boat pool, or garage crafts, also continually conducted on-the-job training. In most of this training we were building on the fine work the Navy had done in the half-dozen years before our civilian administration began.

Because of the primary teaching program weaknesses, it was an almost overwhelming task to prepare intermediate school students to become well-qualified teachers by the time they were graduated from the ninth grade. Furthermore, the four American teacher trainers at the intermediate school had double duty. They had to carry out the main job for which they were hired: conduct on-the-job training of the Trukese teachers. They also had to teach classes until the day when the islander teachers could take over.

Bob, Herb, Napo and I all knew we urgently needed four or five well-trained American teacher trainers to go on roving assignments to the different islands and spend a few months upgrading the local teachers' skills there. Then follow up periodically on the progress of each islander teacher with whom they had worked. Through Bob, who moved his headquarters to Truk after the first two years, we made strong requests to headquarters for roving teacher trainers. We kept receiving replies that they simply didn't have funds for any more staff. Sometimes they made us cut staff we already had and needed.

The Navy and, later, our civilian staff tried to get parents in each community involved with their elementary schools. All three high commissioners for whom I worked over the years, emphasized clearly to me and the other five district administrators one central aspect of Trust Territory policy: *All economic and social programs, including not only staff but also related buildings, utilities, roads, docks, and equipment, should be developed and conducted in such a way that the Micronesian people's own economy might some day be able to support them.*

One example of such islander involvement: the people were expected to construct most of their own elementary school buildings, using local materials. The Navy and, later, our civilian staff, helped when funds permitted. The typical school was about twenty feet wide and thirty feet long. Many school buildings had coral limestone walls several feet high, with supporting roof columns of the same materials. Roofs were of corrugated tin or thatch. The simplest schools had a framework of poles for uprights, crossbeams and trusses—all tied together with *senet*, and topped with a thatched or tin roof. Most schools had sand floors. We helped with the construction mainly by providing metal roofing and some cement to mix with coral limestone for foundations, partial walls, and roof support columns.

The schoolhouse was, with very few exceptions, a single room for the six grades. Open sides permitted refreshing trade winds to blow through. But a sudden wind-driven squall sent children scurrying, while papers went flying—often rained upon and stepped on by rushing bare feet. With few exceptions, the only furniture was a worn table which served as the teacher's desk, and a blackboard. Abandoned Japanese ammunition boxes sometimes were used by Trukese teachers to stow their reading materials and other papers. The blackboard was a sheet of plywood covered with green paint. On a few islands, part of a canoe house or the community building served double duty as a school. The Japanese had built on several of Truk Lagoon's biggest islands—especially Dublon, their headquarters island—excellent school buildings, each with a half-dozen rooms and wooden floors.

Periodic visiting United Nations inspection teams criticized this aspect of our operations throughout the Trust Territory. They said school buildings were too simple. Too many were inadequate. They were right. We didn't spend enough on materials to help islanders build them. Two factors kept us from doing more: tight budgets and the High Commissioners' policy regarding eventual islanders' self-support. The Territory needed more than the four-and-a-half to six million dollars a year it was receiving from Congress in the 1950's to help carry out all activities in the six districts, at headquarters, and to finance our shipping and airline contracts.

Another example was requiring each island to pay the teacher's salary, whether in cash or in kind or both. Encouraged by our Education and Island Affairs officers, island leaders in the districts created a new tax on cigarettes, and on other luxury items like perfume, to help pay elementary school teachers' salaries. After that, teachers were paid quite regularly.

The Pacific Islands Central School (PICS) covering grades ten and eleven, was the only high school in the Trust Territory. It served all six districts. Why not grade twelve? Our Education people at Truk and elsewhere in the field often asked that question. The buildings and staff available wouldn't accommodate more than 120 students. Headquarters swore funds were that tight. Sometimes the PICS staff squeezed in an extra half-dozen.

Under its very capable and dedicated lady principal, "Cy" Pickerill, PICS was staffed by a half-dozen American teacher trainers and two islander teacher trainees. The district agriculturist and his American assistant also were required to teach agriculture half-time to PICS students.

The school provided a program of general studies intended to help prepare students for higher education. There were classes in arithmetic, English, some general science, and several electives. One was sewing. Students who wanted to become teachers obtained some specialized training from PICS teacher trainers. Part of the teacher training also was offered at special summer school programs or "workshops" operated by each home district Education department.

PICS was located in two elephant quonsets, positioned in an L-shape. One building, partitioned, held the classrooms. The other was used as the school's auditorium and for student social affairs. Nearby stood several rows of smaller quonsets, painted snow white. Six of them were dormitories for male students; the other two were for girls.

Despite its humble physical plant, we Americans and, I believe, islanders who visited the school occasionally and had some contacts with teachers and students, saw that the place had a very strong spirit. The teachers were highly motivated. They seemed to relate very well with the students from all six districts.

Late in my first year at Truk, headquarters sent us a telegram saying they were going to close PICS due to lack of funds. I read the message a second time, stunned and dismayed. We all knew Bob wouldn't agree with the action. Without consulting headquarters, and after talking this bombshell news over with Cy Pickerill and Herb, I sent cables to my counterparts in the Ponape and Marshalls Districts regarding the matter. Then I took the next plane to those districts and met separately with District Administrators Kevin Carroll at Ponape and Don Gilfillan in the Marshalls. All three of us agreed to make painful cuts in other parts of our district budgets in order to keep PICS operating. We then cabled headquarters to that effect.

Shortly after returning to Truk, I received a cable from headquarters telling me to knock it off. On the next plane flight, I received a letter from the Deputy High Commissioner saying if they were going to have trouble with a district administrator, this is the kind of trouble they liked to have. Not long after that, all districts received a letter from headquarters saying a decision had been made to keep PICS open.

On my periodic visits to the high school, I saw clearly the good feelings which prevailed at gatherings of students from all parts of Micronesia: in classrooms, on the playfield, at performances students put on in the auditorium, and in friendships with each other. Cy and her staff knew they were helping to shape Micronesia's future leaders. And indeed they did. PICS graduates became, over the years ahead, leaders in their home district administrations, legislatures, court systems, and their Congress of Micronesia. Some became successful in business and in medicine. Some were prominent among leaders in the late 1960s, calling for negotiations with the U.S. government regarding their political future, and in the actual negotiations. Still later, some rose to top leadership roles in government in the three new nations and one new U.S. Commonwealth (Northern Mariana Islands) which evolved from the Trust Territory.

Besides those government schools, the missionaries—both Catholics and Protestants—operated a number of excellent schools within the Truk Lagoon. One was the very impressive Xavier High School for boys created and conducted by Jesuit fathers. The Catholics also operated a school for girls beyond elementary level. It was located at Tunnuk village on Moen Island, and taught by Catholic sisters. On Dublon Island stood a Protestant three-year boarding school for girls, ages 14-20, from all over the Truk District. It was created and conducted first by the German Liebenzell Mission and later by the Americans Commision for Foreign Missions.

The Germans and other protestant groups also had schools on Tol and other islands in Truk Lagoon, as did the Catholics. For the first two years after we arrived, Anna Dederer, trained in Germany as a nurse and missionary, was the beloved, very capable head mistress at the Dublon school. Reverend Kaercher and his wife and staff down on Tol, like Anna Dederer, also were highly dedicated, and were there long before and during WWII. They had harrowing stories to tell about their lives in those times.

Late in our fourth year of civilian administration, Bob finally talked headquarters into giving us one new roving teacher trainer position. He then came up with an idea which Dick King (who took Herb's place when he left to study for a PhD), Napo and I liked immediately. It was to get a replacement at PICS for Cy, a highly skilled, experienced teacher trainer; then have her demonstrate to headquarters what could be accomplished by such work in upgrading elementary teachers' job performance. Thus, we hoped, they would be moved to find us funds for three more roving teacher trainers.

Could we really get Cy? Would she, at age sixty-five, agree to that truly tough assignment?

Cy Pickerill Goes Circuit Riding

The proposed new assignment for Cy, after she had served superbly for four years as Principal at PICS, would be one of the toughest of all we had. She would be our only full-time trainer and up-grader of elementary teachers throughout the far-flung district. She would have to live for weeks at a time on a remote island, working with the teacher(s), then move on to the next island. With few exceptions, she would be the only Westerner wherever she went. The exceptions were those few islands where American missionaries were stationed far from headquarters. She also would see, from time to time, visiting field trip parties within Truk Lagoon for a few hours to a day at a time. In the outer islands, she'd see field trip parties once in two months, and then for one or two days.

When approached about this new assignment, Cy was not only willing to take the new job. She looked forward to it.

For the previous four years this feisty, wiry little lady with the bubbling spirit and gray-black curly hair had given more than generously to PICS of her professional time and talents, including much of what should have been her free time. She knew personally every one of her students from all over the Trust Territory.

Realizing they could become important among Micronesia's next generation of leaders, she was determined from the start that each graduating student would return home as well-prepared as possible.   Seeing Cy's commitment and devotion to the students probably accounted in part for the fact that all her staff seemed to share strongly that same attitude. Her work at PICS, where students represented nine different language groups and an even larger number of dialects, had left her little time to study the Trukese language. The first task she set for herself on her new job was to go down to Tol Island, fifteen miles away in the southwest part of Truk Lagoon, live with an island family, and learn to speak their language.

After three months of intensive study, Cy set out to ride circuit. In time, she visited every outer island. Later on, she settled down to work mainly on a half-dozen islands in Truk Lagoon. On far western islands like Puluwat and Pulusuk, where women crawled before men, Cy found that being a lady was no problem for her. Those chiefs and their people knew American women and men continued to act like Americans. And that's what they expected of us.

Now she began to see daily the painful shortcomings of the elementary system. Our Education people at headquarters had seen some of them on field trips and reported on such problems. But on those outer island visits we saw the teachers for a day or two; then we sailed to the next island. Someone like Cy was clearly a priority need: a person who would work intensively for several weeks or a month at a time with the teachers on one outer island.

Then return a few months later, check on the teacher's progress, and build in more training.

Any additional roving teacher trainers recruited would need to be people with very special attitudes. They would need to be either single or have a spouse with similar qualities of devotion to the work. They would need to live most of their working assignments in very simple houses with no electricity, stove or refrigerator, running water, indoor plumbing, and medical assistance limited to boy scout level first aid offered by the island corpsman.

Cy was not on the job long when I knew that high on the list of my mistakes as district administrator was that I hadn't fought harder and with more constancy for a roving elementary teacher trainer in the first years. Yet, we had to fight hard—sometimes unsuccessfully—to keep the positions we had. In my work diary entry for August 20, 1952, I wrote about a conversation with Mr. Delmas Nucker, then Executive Officer for the Office of Territories, stationed in Washington, DC. At the time he was visiting Truk on a swing through the whole Trust Territory. That was more than a year before he became our new High Commissioner and my immediate boss:

"He seems to feel Trust Territory must cut drastically size of organization. I told him we need a 10-year period to train Trukese teachers, doctors, agriculturists, government administrators etc. I believe we can cut our U.S. staff 2/3 to 3/4 in ten years..."

Cy would arrange with our boat pool to drop her off with her tent, duffle bag, and other camping gear on whichever island in the lagoon she planned to work next. Sometimes she caught rides on Trukese outboard motorboats or outrigger canoes headed for neighboring islands.

We'd see her down at the dock, ready to go, dressed in a simple tan skirt and lightweight jacket or blouse, scarf around her head and wearing tennis shoes or rubber *zoris*. Leather shoes just weren't the thing around salt water and sand. High humidity caused them to mold and salt water bleached them. Sometimes we bumped into her out on an island or arriving back at Moen after a trip. If the lagoon was a little choppy that day, her hair would be damp and salt-caked, and her clothes also damp and blotched with drying salt. She'd blink in the sunlight when removing her glasses to wipe them dry. We could see welts on her legs from coral cuts, mosquitos and "no-see-ums" (gnats). The sun reflecting off the water burned and dried her skin. About these things she offered no complaints.

I sometimes wondered if Cy shuddered inwardly a little at the sight of the dorsal fin of a big, blue-black or a gray shark following near her outboard motorboat. There were lots of sharks and barracuda around, and the sharks had a disconcerting habit of following a small craft about fifty feet away on a parallel course.

What she did mention to us in unadorned language, both in conversations and in her reports, was the quality of teaching she found in elementary schools. Discouragement often dripped between the lines. For this lady who had spent years at the University of Hawaii supervising education majors' internships, it must have been unsettling.

"Will, damn it all!" Cy fumed to me once in frustration and discouragement when I met her on an outer island several months into her new job, "these teachers are so pitifully prepared! Very few do any lesson planning. Most still teach by rote, you know. They don't even know how to organize their classes."

"But Cy," I said, reacting too defensively. "Herb and Napo and their people began three years ago to teach them in summer workshops how to organize classes. They touch on it during field trips."

"Then if they know, they don't care!"

"Do you think they believe some things we're teaching them don't make sense?" I asked. "Those workshops also teach lesson planning. And they're told not to teach by rote."

"I think many just don't give a damn!" she said.

I had to agree. But I also saw, as our Education office staff did, that in some schools the summer workshops were beginning slowly to make a difference.

Cy began to look more closely at what children were doing when they should have been in classes but weren't. As the months went by, it became increasingly clear to her that while they were absent from their classrooms, some were learning those old things—kinds of work and attitudes every adult had to know to survive on an island. Children learned not only what to do but also what not to do. Like the need to ban fishing from the island reef every so often so fish stocks would survive at levels to provide the island's needs indefinitely. And to let farm lands "rest" some years so they wouldn't wear out. Small children learned not to defecate on certain parts of the island, and they learned not to brag or boast or push themselves forward, because those weren't Trukese ways.

When she came to see these things, Cy was a little less upset about children not in school. Still, she believed strongly that she needed to help every teacher do a better job. She said she kept thinking of the need for every island teacher not only to help prepare students for a better life on their home islands, but also to feed better educated children into the intermediate school and PICS. Somehow, she said, it should be possible to better coordinate the timing of teaching of the old things with the newer things. She kept working at it.

Teachers tended to be among the smarter young Trukese. But after getting this extra training for a year or more, too many left teaching for the bright lights and better-paying jobs on Moen. Some of those who continued to teach backslid into old habits. But a few started to show the results of their extra training. She began to see a little payoff here and there for her tutoring. The young teachers couldn't help but sense and see how much she cared— how much she thought good teaching mattered. And some must have been moved when they understood that she respected them as potentially fine teachers.

There were other island education problems. "Where are the teaching materials?" she'd ask Dick King and Napo.

Herb and his staff had tried to replace damaged or lost teaching materials whenever they saw or heard of a need. They had a hard time trying to keep up. If some mimeographed reading lesson and other materials got damaged beyond use a week after the field trip ship called on an island outside Truk Lagoon, the teachers had to wait two months to get replacements. If the next ship missed calling at that island because we couldn't get ashore due to rough weather, it would be four months before replacement reading and arithmetic materials were delivered.

As she tutored young teachers, Cy was learning more and more island lessons. She learned to respect and admire the all-important place of the *eterenges*—extended family—in the life of every Trukese, and its very strong role in shaping one's personality and attitudes from earliest childhood. She learned that island chiefs were not always the most important leaders. Village council members often were the real movers and shakers. Even a very strong chief like Petrus on Moen, Ring at Lukunor or Aluis on Ulul in the western islands had to listen to the island council. A council was made up of the leading males of the longest existing *eterengeses*, which might own the most land. Those "district chiefs" often also knew the most about the history of land ownership on their part of the island.

She learned that Trukese medicine had some good qualities. Cy had heard something about these matters from Clark, Frank, Dr. Michi, and other members of our medical staff. And she had picked up bits from Trukese PICS students. But seeing such things at first hand out in the islands was something else. Like some of us, Cy occasionally walked innocently into confrontation with Trukese taboos and superstitions. She was a sensitive lady and coped with them with good judgment. Such encounters did not seem to diminish her effectiveness at all.

Cy stayed on at Truk for several years after I left. She continued to travel in her little boat around the islands, helping young teachers to do their jobs better. When she did finally return to the United States, she left behind legacies. Besides building a bit of herself into every teacher she worked with, her insistence on striving for excellence and her ability to bring those young people to believe teaching was a highly important work, endured. This showed up in some of her teachers who later became principals in the larger schools, leaders in their communities, and leaders of their own State governments.

Clearly, we needed more highly dedicated people like Cy Pickerill out there as roving teacher trainers.

Cy chose a young PICS graduate, Chutomu Nimwes, to be her assistant. She believed, after working with him for some time, that he had the ability to take her place some day. Years later Chutomu became Chuuk State's first Trukese Director of Education.

Sergeant Kumio
and "Those New Ways"

Frank Mahony's main aim as a member of our staff was to help the Trukese and Americans understand each other's ways as we came together from two very different cultures. A part of wisdom is the distillation of experience. Among the Americans on our Truk District staff that first year or two we had little experience, except for Frank's and Herb's, in working with other cultures.

Frank believed that one important step in helping us steer our way safely through the cultural hazards was to give us some understanding of village life, including how the individual Trukese fitted into his extended family—*eterenges*.

"Next to life itself," I once heard him tell an orientation class for new civilian employees, which also included wives and older children, "the most important thing for any Trukese is the *eterenges*. When a young man marries, it's the bride who takes the groom into her mother's home to live. The reason for this is that in Trukese society, inheritance of land and some other clan property flows matrilineally." He noted that an *eterenges* traditionally covers a wife's blood relatives from all living generations—usually three.

Different from most American families, we learned, the Trukese extended family functioned as a very tight-knit social and economic unit. When a new husband arrived to live in his bride's house, he might find himself living also with her mother and father, one or more of his wife's sisters and their husbands, and his wife's brothers below the age of puberty. When a boy reached that stage, he moved out and stayed with another family where he had no female blood relatives or only distant ones. This latter pattern related to the strong taboo on incest. There also could be other female blood relatives of his wife living in the same house, depending upon house space available. If space wasn't available, the new groom likely would also find himself and his wife living in a somewhat similar relationship pattern in another house nearby, sitting on her mother's *eterenges* land.

Land is a scarce item in the islands—a fact about which all grown Trukese seemed very conscious. The institution of the extended family was even shaped so that not only did land inheritance flow through the wife's extended family, but the oldest lady of the family, often in consultation with other lady members, controlled and assigned use of it to *eterenges* members. When the new husband joined his wife's extended family, he brought with him a gift of the right to his share of land in his mother's own extended family. Here what goes around comes around. The new husband's mother's *eterenges* would likewise receive land as young women in it got married.

Most extended families had thirty to forty members or more. A clan includes the *eterenges* members grouped together on their own part of the island, plus other members, usually only a few, who may be living on one or more other islands for various reasons. There also were situations where a young married couple, for special reasons—perhaps his not getting along well with his wife's family—were permitted by both the girl's and her husband's extended families to go and live with his mother's *eterenges*. A young man usually married into a nearby family for practical reasons. He had work and certain other responsibilities to both his wife's and his mother's extended families.

We Americans noticed, and sometimes were confused by the fact that all Trukese referred to cousins, brothers-in-law and sisters-in-law as "my brother" or "my sister." They also referred to aunts and uncles in both their mothers' and fathers' extended families as "my mother" and "my father."

"When we look at the *eterenges* today," Frank liked to say, "we're getting a fairly clear picture of family life as it existed a hundred years ago and earlier. German and Japanese civilian administrations and the Japanese military government came and went," he'd tell the classes, "but the people have remained very Trukese." A young lady's suitor seeking her hand in marriage, had to get permission from the her parents and other adults in her extended family. They needed to be satisfied that he would fit in well.

Frank told one group he was briefing that American mother-in-law jokes wouldn't work in the islands. "When a young man joins his bride's family," he said, "it isn't mainly the mother-in-law he has to cope with; it's his wife's oldest brother—usually living in another house fairly nearby. The oldest brother has certain traditional authority over his sisters' husbands, and he usually doesn't hesitate to use it."

"What does he make them do? What does he want from them?" a listener once asked.

He makes them work!" Frank said, grinning. "And he wants money—and *pisek:* any material goods the sisters' husbands might have, like a radio, a knife—almost anything, to borrow—and sometimes keep."

He would go on and explain that the oldest brother, for the good of the lineage, ordered and supervised the men's work in his mother's *eterenges*. They might be asked to cut and haul breadfruit and taro, repair a house, catch fish, help cook certain kinds of food. Similarly, the oldest sister in her mother's *eterenges* supervised women's joint tasks, like gardening, some kinds of fishing and cooking. Failure to comply almost certainly would mean a terrible clash—possibly expulsion from the lineage. "No worse fate can befall a Trukese than to become estranged from his or her extended family," Frank would emphasize in his lectures.

As we Americans first learned from Frank, and many of us later saw, there were corresponding benefits. Here the new husband would find secure economic and social relationships. Sharing was the rule in preparing and eating food and in most other aspects of extended family life. In clashes with people outside the *eterenges,* the husband was expected to stand rock firm with the family and vice versa—unless the trouble happened to be between his wife's and his own mother's family; then he was in a really tough spot.

Younger girls in an *eterenges* had to obey and respect their older sisters. This was strictly observed in practice. Any girl who failed to do so was reprimanded. Younger sisters were also expected to do the same for brothers beyond the age of puberty. If a girl failed to do so, she could not expect to receive support of any kind from her brothers.

Tied in with all this, the young anthropologist would explain in his *eterenges* lectures, is the need to conform. This whole set of extended family relationships is a powerful force in shaping the Trukese personality. A person, ideally, is expected to be quiet in manner, calm of temperament, modest, generous and courteous. He smiles readily and seldom raises his voice. A younger person is polite and deferential to all older family members. It's instilled in Trukese from earliest childhood to avoid conflict as much as reasonably possible. Thus it is also built into the Trukese child not to compete, not to try to rise above others.

Frank noted that exceptions to this were in sports competitions like canoe racing and baseball—the latter introduced by the Japanese and made popular by them. He would tell how today the Trukese had competitive feasts: inviting another *eterenges* or village members as guests. The aim was to provide more fine food than the guests could in a later reciprocal feast. If the latter didn't outdo the former in the quantity and quality of their feast, they were the losers.

Even with Frank's illuminating insights, and with the best of intentions, we new American civilians sometimes blundered into cultural mistakes

One afternoon Sergeant Kumio (not his real name), who held an important position in our Constabulary, came into my office in his khaki uniform. "*Kepina*," he said, standing in the erect way Marine officer Harry Reed had taught them, "I have a request for you. I want to ask you that you will help me with one thing. It is a private problem."

I looked across the desk curiously. This fine, big man, in his early thirties, with a heavy black forelock and a normally easy, relaxed manner, lowered his eyes and squirmed uncomfortably.

"I'll help you if I can, Sergeant Kumio," I said, and invited him to sit down.

"*Kepina*," he said, looking up, "I want to ask that you will order my family not to come on the base."

My surprise at this request must have shown. "You know the district center's open to everyone," I said. There was a steady stream of people who came walking up the road from the dock area and all other parts of Moen Island. Those people were on their way to the hospital for sick call or to visit friends there, see relatives or friends at one of the schools, sell fruit at the dining room or to American families, and for a dozen other reasons.

"Why would you want me to do that?" I asked curiously.

"Every time I get my *peioff,*" (pay) he explained, still looking thoroughly uncomfortable, "some of my family comes to the brig, and they ask me for that money." He paused, frowning deeply. I waited for him to go on.

"Mr. Muller, you said to me—some of those other American people told me and other Trukese workers we should try to save some of our *peioff.* But I cannot save anything." His eyes met mine imploringly.

Sergeant Kumio's extended family lived on one of the high islands in the Truk Lagoon. They had enough land, with a good number of coconut and breadfruit trees, papaya, mango trees, and good yielding taro patches, so they could eat well and cut copra to sell.

Kumio seemed to be having doubts about the rewards of hard work and living away from his home island—not very often seeing his wife and children or joining male friends on fishing expeditions, not often visiting around the villages or enjoying dances and special feasts and songfests. What he did see and could count on was the appearance of members of his extended family each payday at the Constabulary headquarters, or waiting for him near the pay line in front of the Finance and Supply quonset. After obtaining from him a good part of his pay, they headed for Truk Trading Company.

I had encouraged him to save a little money each payday. That conversation took place during a field trip we made together to an island in Truk Lagoon. While we walked down a path toward the village we planned to visit, we came to a house built during Japanese times. Much nicer than most other houses, it sat back from the beach in an expanse of grass. Built mostly of wood, with a tin roof, it was a two-story affair, with a long, screened porch on the first floor in front and a big balcony on the second floor.

Kumio had made an admiring remark about the house, and I told him, "You could have a nice house like it some day..." The sergeant stopped walking, turned and looked at me surprised, questioningly.

"...If you want it badly enough to save a few dollars each payday," I added.

Now Sergeant Kumio sat gloomily in front of my desk, and after a little more conversation he stood and I walked with him to the door.

Here I had been guilty of causing another headlong encounter between traditional ways and Western concepts we foreigners were bringing into the islands—sometimes unconsciously. How could we get a sure feel for modern ways that would blend well with the old? One evening shortly after Kumio made his request, I invited Frank up to our house for a cup of coffee, and told him about my conversation with the sergeant. His voice shifted to a slightly higher pitch and intensity. "What did you tell him?"

When I answered, he relaxed and a smile crept over his face. "Kumio's engaging in a little wishful thinking. When he became a constabulary man he knew he would have to start being assertive in certain relations with other Trukese. When he became a sergeant, he knew he'd have to give orders to the men. He was willing to change some. Still, he's very Trukese. He knows the extended family ground rules. They'll keep coming," Frank said, still grinning, "and he'll keep handing over his money to them. He hasn't changed that much."

Nearly a year after that conversation with Kumio, I happened to be visiting his island when he was home for a few days' leave. I walked over to his village to visit with him. We sat and talked in the shade of a big mango tree. "Kumio," I asked, "are your brothers and sisters still looking you up on payday?" It was the first time we had talked about the matter since his request to bar his family from the headquarters area.

He turned toward me, his face showing a slight frown. "Yes, Mr. Muller," he said slowly. "But it is all right now. That one time I came to see you about my family, I wanted to save some of my *peioff* then to make a bigger house for my family and me." His resigned voice implied that he had given up that dream.

"You decided not to do it?" I pressed ungraciously.

"Maybe one—two months after I come to *kepina's ofis,* I talked with my family one night. I tell them maybe I will build a house like that Japanese one you saw, but not so big. I must keep one part of my *peioff* each time and buy TTC stocks so I can save for that house."

In those years, Truk Trading Company sold a share of stock to Trukese for twenty-five dollars and paid a yearly dividend of about twenty percent. I made a few rapid calculations. Even using some of the family's old breadfruit trees, purchasing other old ones for lumber, and with several male members of the *eterenges* pitching in to help the local carpenter he'd need to hire, a two-story house more modest than the one we saw that day would cost around a thousand dollars. Kumio would be lucky to be able to set aside eight dollars each month out of his salary of forty dollars. At that rate, even with TTC's annual dividend of five dollars a share, and selling all his stock at the time of construction, it would take him about seven years to accumulate enough to build.

"Did your *eterenges* agree?"

"Yes, they said it will be all right."

"Did you purchase some TTC stock?"

"I kept some money at the brig each month until I will have enough for two shares. Then some of my family come to the base to see me. They tell me they need some things and I gave them most of that money for the stocks..." His hands moved in a gesture of futility.

"I'm sorry it turned out that way, Kumio," I said.

"After that one time," he continued, "when I talked with my family again, I tell them I will like to buy a Johnson 10-horse." At least, I thought, he's improved his odds greatly on his new dream. Such an outboard motor then cost more than $300.00 at TTC.

"Did they agree?"

"Yes," he said and smiled without humor. "But, Mr. Muller, it was the same way. That time I can save for only one share and fifteen dollars to the next one share. Then my family come to the brig and need things."

"Did you keep trying to get the outboard?"

"No, *kepina.*" He was quiet for a while, then looked over at me again, this time his face brightened and his voice sounded cheerful. "But I saved some money. Then I bought something at TTC."

"Oh, great!" I said, surprised and pleased that he finally got some cooperation from his *eterenges.* "Your family let you save this time?"

"No, I didn't talk to them that time. That first month they didn't come to Moen, and I saved some of my *peioff.* Next time I got paid the water is too rough for them to come, so..." he grinned triumphantly, "I saved more and took the rest home. Next time I went on a field trip to Mortlock Islands and save some more, because when the ship came back to the dock, I got my *peioff* and I just went down to TTC and bought that Coleman lantern and that aloha shirt."

I laughed at Kumio's delight in having managed even this much, and I felt good with him.

That evening I had dinner with him and some other men of his *eterenges*. They lived in houses near where he and his wife lived with some relatives. The women and girls, who traditionally ate separately from and later than the men, served us a fine meal of breadfruit, fish, chicken, and fruit. The food was set on a long line of banana leaves spread out in a grassy area beside the house. We sat, legs tucked beneath us, on either side of those very practical, deep green tablecloths.

For the occasion, Kumio wore a checkered short-sleeved blouse shirt, faded from many launderings at the creek. Sitting several places to my right was his oldest brother-in-law, a very jovial man, who seemed popular among the others and had a fine reputation as a spear fisherman. He wore the same new looking, bright blue and white aloha shirt I recently had seen Kumio wearing once or twice after working hours around the district center.

I felt a surge of resentment toward the brother-in-law and felt sorry for Kumio. Having given up his dream of a new house for part of his family and, later, an outboard motor, he couldn't even keep the dress sport shirt he'd managed to acquire despite the clan's unrelenting demands upon his earnings. I wondered if the lantern hung over in the brother-in-law's house.

After dinner we sat out on the grass, visiting with several of his relatives and friends. I commented to Kumio on the extensive repairs that had been made recently to several houses near each other, including his own mother-in-law's, judging by the newness of the reddish-light brown breadfruit wood. On two of them, half the siding on the wall facing the lagoon had been replaced, along with a number of hand-sawed boards of the big, combined living room-sleeping room floor. On one, new screen wire gleamed in the setting sun. Kumio nodded toward the jolly nimrod brother-in-law and three other male relatives. "My 'brothers.' just did that work," he explained.

Later, a young girl handed around drinking coconuts. It reminded me of the dinner we had enjoyed. Once more I praised the meal and, in the conversation that followed, learned that several of the men had gone fishing that day down south by the barrier reef. One of the young boys in the big family doubtless had climbed a coconut tree to pick our liquid refreshment. Other family members—men and women—had contributed to preparing and cooking the breadfruit chunks with coconut cream from the soft, gelatinous inner part of the not yet fully ripe nuts. This was placed as a garnish over the breadfruit chunks.

The next day when I was ready to leave, Kumio walked with one of the Trukese boat crewmen and me down to the little dirt and coral pier where the picket boat was moored. Nearby, a small group of men got ready to go fishing. I saw among them Kumio's oldest brother-in-law, now shirtless and in shorts. They laughed and called with high spirits to each other as they removed palm fronds, for protection against the sun, from two outrigger paddling canoes high on the beach and hauled them to the water's edge over more palm fronds used as a skidway.

"Nice canoes," I said admiringly to Kumio. "Are they your family's?"

"Yes, they are ours," he said. "My 'brother' made them."

While the picket boat headed back toward Moen Island, its bow rising and falling in the chop from the northeast, and we took spray over the wheelhouse, I kept thinking about Kumio and his *eterenges*. I pictured his wife and children living in that house as part of a larger family. The children were surrounded by doting aunts and uncles, and there was always someone to watch after them while Kumio's wife worked away from the house—if the youngsters didn't tag along. She might have to help tend the family's taro patch and join other women in fishing with butterfly nets, and do some cooking, washing, cleaning, and help with sewing. But there were many kinds of work only men did, like fishing beyond the barrier reef, keeping the canoes repaired, and harvesting, hauling and cooking some kinds of food.

I saw vividly again the men sitting at the outdoor feast, and Kumio's relaxed enjoyment among his family, and the brother-in-law in Kumio's sport shirt. My resentment of the evening before drained away. Like Frank sometimes said, there was no need on Truk for the government to create a social security system. And no one knew it better than Kumio.

Ghosts, Sorcerers and Hexes

We saw that most Trukese were still living in an environment populated with ghosts, spirits and sorcerers. Some spirits dwelled on their village lands and others lived in the sea or sat on island reefs. Every misfortune was attributed to the violation of a taboo. For every broken taboo, the hapless man or woman involved knew, an unhappy consequence would flow from it as surely as the ebb tide followed the high tide. Much of that was built on fear.

There were those "good" magic men. One such kind of persons knew breadfruit magic. They were called upon to insure a good crop. Love magic, too, was secret knowledge—a clan treasure, to be passed on very selectively to lineage worthies. There were said to be rain magic specialists, but the only successful one, a wise and widely-informed Trukese leader told me, was a man from Nauru who once lived at Truk in Japanese times.

Then there was the "bad magic" that hovered over the people: the ever possible but apparently seldom invoked threat of evil from a sorcerer (*chon pout*). Sorcerers practicing black magic (*rongengau*) are not to be confused with the entirely different, benign, often helpful, and always compassionate medicine men (*sounnsafei*) described in an earlier chapter. The Trukese were, understandably, most reluctant to talk with foreigners about evil spirits, sorcerers and hexes.

Since the first American missionaries arrived in the Mortlocks in 1872 and in Truk Lagoon in 1879, they had made many thousands of converts to Christianity. Large numbers of islanders—Catholics and Protestants—became regular churchgoers. Their new faith helped alleviate for them, increasingly day-by-day, their past constant fear of ghosts and other capricious spirits. Yet the missionaries saw, as we sometimes did, that some Trukese were still hedging their bets. It was somewhat like their approach to modern medicine, though usually in a reverse sequence. If their own medicine men didn't bring quick, visible results, many were willing to give hospital medicine a try. When a Trukese was faced with having displeased a reef or island spirit, he might call first upon his Christian religion, but at some point turn to ancient ways for reinforcement. And when a catastrophe or death touched them, the people were certain that unfriendly gods and ghosts were abroad in the village, waiting for incantations or other offerings that might appease them.

Often precautionary measures were taken before trouble struck. Some people still constructed their houses with small windows. Those with more modern houses kept their doors locked at night. Some families kept a candle or lantern burning at night to ward off bad spirits who might be abroad. Grass huts existed mostly in the western islands, but there were still a few in some of the other outer islands. They had small entrances and no windows. One explanation for this part of their design, we learned, went back to the era of inter-island warfare. If a warrior, or some other unfriendly person tried to enter a hut, he would necessarily be on hands and knees.

Missionaries like Father Rively and especially Father Fahey, who spent much time on Puluwat and near neighboring islands, witnessed western islands sailors coming safely through a *noto* (typhoon) at sea. The first thing their navigator did when he reached shore was to stalk and kill a bird, which he tied in a tree or laid on the sand near the canoe as a thanks offering to *Mwaresi*, the sea god.

Once when I sat with old Anton, a Mortlocks chief, he told me how he tried to help protect his people from what sounded like, from his description, a *tsunami:* high waves rolling across the low island at about half-hour intervals. He had ordered all the people into the community building and a church—the two buildings sitting on the highest ground on the island: perhaps thirty feet above sea level. The people had been in the buildings for many hours and done much praying.

After the third wave, he said, he went outside with some other men to inspect the damage. Hundreds of breadfruit trees were knocked down. Some had washed into the sea. Their chickens went with the big waves; only a few were saved, because they roosted up in the coconut trees. All the pigs were gone. The big waves carried them into the sea. The island path was now covered with many down breadfruit trees and broken houses. In the afternoon the chief went out again from the church, this time alone.

"I took out my *toropwe* (a worn, water-stained notebook with hand-written notes in black ink) "and went to the beach to find out what is going to happen to us."

"What did you do then?" I asked.

"I just made the magic then."

"What did you want the magic to do?"

"Make the waves stay back."

"Did you tell the people about that?"

"I walked back to the *imwen mwich.* (meeting house). I told the people not to worry any more about those big waves. It is going to be all right now. Maybe it is because God heard our prayers..."

Cy Pickerill, while serving as the district's circuit-riding teacher trainer, sometimes was amazed by experiences involving the supernatural. "Once while traveling from one island in the Mortlocks to another in my fiberglass boat with outboard motor, she recalled later, "my young Trukese traveling assistant that day became very upset when he saw a rainbow. He wanted to turn back." Ancher (not his real name) was at that time one of Truk's few PICS graduates who had gone on to attend and graduate from a four-year high school outside the Trust Territory.

"In the end, when I persisted, with my reasons for continuing the trip, he made incantations to *Mwaresi,* the sea god, whose sign is the rainbow. I'll be damned if that rainbow didn't disappear shortly after that!"

In our years in the islands, one of the most common family household signs for appeasement of and protection from spirits which might do harm involved weaving thin leaves of a coconut frond into intricate patterns. These sometimes were hung on coconut or breadfruit trees in plain sight of the passerby. We saw them around in the villages, dried out, frayed with time, sun and wind. Some of them simply protected a farmer's patch from being pilfered, or they honored a recently deceased relative who had worked that ground. Occasionally we saw such woven tokens in a house, hung from a beam or attached to a wall to protect its family from a particular unfriendly spirit.

Through the years some missionaries took a harsh stand with the Trukese in dealing with such matters. The result was, not surprisingly, that they built a wall between themselves and the scolded islanders—cutting off opportunities to learn from them their true feelings about the ways and extent to which ghosts and spirits—friendly and unfriendly—and witch doctors affected their daily lives.

"The Catholic missionaries in these islands have been more sensitive and have responded more wisely to Trukese customs and beliefs than we Protestants," Dr. Hanlin, who took Anna Dederer's place on Dublon, once told me. My observations supported that view—the Hanlins being exceptions. One day a new, young German Protestant missionary visited a Trukese home in the south of Truk Lagoon and saw a sorcerer's sign dangling from a beam inside. His eyes flashed revulsion, like Moses eyeing the golden calf. He turned to the man and wife and the wife's sister who lived with them, his face reddening.

"So! What do I see here? What is this evil thing? Why is it in this Christian home?" He strode across the little room to the woven charm, ripped it down and threw it upon the breadfruit wood floor.

"Look!" he spoke with emotion. "I cast it upon the floor! I stomp on it—break it all apart! It can do no harm—none at all! Because it is nothing!" He paused, made an effort to compose himself, then resumed speaking in a more modulated tone. "These things must go," he admonished the shaken family. "They have no place in a Christian home."

Although he was an earnest, dedicated, intelligent, if not always wise, young missionary, in that encounter he had caused three more Trukese to become increasingly defensive and secretive. He probably cut off permanently any possibility of learning their honest feelings about their beliefs in and fears of gods, evil spirits or ghosts they had somehow crossed. He would never know how they were groping for ways to cope with such scary matters, invoking for the time being, anyway, both their Christian beliefs and other kinds of protective measures reaching back into time beyond memory.

I wondered whether the same young man was aware that his older fellow missionary's wife, when outside at night under a tropical full moon, wore a big, old-fashioned bonnet to keep from getting moon-struck. Did he know that at least a few of his American acquaintances on Moen seriously studied newspaper columnists' predictions of their fortunes according to their particular signs of the zodiac and the current juxtaposition of sun, moon and stars? It might have surprised him had he known that a few Americans on Moen carried good luck charms, had "lucky" numbers, and wouldn't undertake certain tasks or book a flight on Friday the thirteenth. A few of them appeared to believe the portents for their future revealed to them by another American wife who claimed special gifts in palm reading and divining tea leaves.

What would the same young Protestant missionary have thought had he known about the treatment, involving use of an old Trukese method, Reverend Hanlin was willing to receive for his earache? Early in his assignment to Truk, and before Mrs. Hanlin and their daughter arrived, Reverend Hanlin developed a painful, continuing earache. One young Trukese lady on the girls' school staff heard him refer to his discomfort. The second time he mentioned his earache some days later, she shyly asked if he would want her to try to help it with a Trukese remedy. He smiled at the thought.

"Well, yes," he said, "I'd be grateful if you will treat my earache."

She made a little fire and asked him to sit near it. Then she found a piece of old newspaper—substitute for a big leaf. She shaped it into a long funnel with one end very small. Positioning the large end so that it collected the rising smoke, she placed the small end barely into the opening of his ear.

"You know," he told me, grinning, "in just one treatment my earache was gone. That smoke felt warm and soothing and had a curing effect."

Even some Trukese ministers had not completely shed their beliefs in the existence of evil spirits and curses. The impressive looking new church on Udot had just been dedicated. A great feast helped mark the occasion. Breadfruit and taro in coconut milk, baked fish, chicken and pork, rice and a fine array of fruits were spread invitingly on many long rows of banana leaves on the grass. After the speeches, congregation members and a large group of guests moved to the feast area. The ordained Protestant minister, in snowy white duck trousers and white shirt, obtained silence and commenced the blessing. He droned on for several minutes, while some eyed the food with growing hunger pangs. Finally he concluded:

"...and, oh Lord Jesus, please take away from this food any curse that may have been placed upon it."

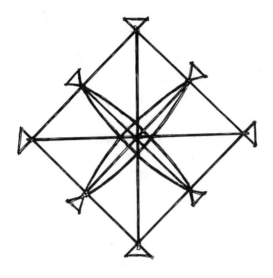

Line Squall

Most American wives on Moen Island probably were more conscious than their husbands of fast-approaching rain squalls that pound down upon tropical islands. The men and women least affected by them were those employees who spent their working hours in offices, shops, the radio shack, schools and the hospital. Wives normally didn't have a jeep to use, so they walked to visit a neighbor, the commissary, post office, or the community club's snack bar at the hotel for a mid-morning cup of coffee or tea.

The only privately owned vehicles on any island in the district were those on Moen. They were owned by Truk Trading Company and by the Catholic mission. Nearly all TTC trucks and jeeps had been acquired from the Navy, which helped establish it. There wasn't even one sedan on the island. To ship a personal vehicle from the mainland would have been very costly and, understandably, our government wouldn't pay for it. Anyway, there were only a few roads on Moen, and there were no private repair and maintenance services. Government policy did permit us to use some jeeps after hours for such recreational activities as visiting each other's homes, the hotel, or going to the swimming beach, dock, or airfield.

One morning deckhands on our tugboat *Bailhache* cast off lines soon after the field trip party was aboard. The *Bailhache* was a beautiful seventy-one foot vessel that our headquarters Supply office had obtained for us from government surplus. Shortly after it arrived and we all stood admiring it, I asked Chief Petrus to recommend the best man in the district to be its new skipper. He suggested Konrad, a gentle fellow from Uman Island who was highly respected by the Trukese for his seafaring skills. On this particular morning Captain Konrad stood barefooted in the wheelhouse and steered a course for Udot Island, about ten miles to the southwest. The tropical morning still held some of its coolness.

This was a one-day trip in Truk Lagoon, with Trukese and Americans from Medical, and Island Affairs, including an agriculturist, along. Kenchi Uehara, the tug's mate, and a deckhand stood in the bow watching for coral heads. After little more than an hour, Konrad steered past the southeast tip of the island's sandy beach, spoke into the brass tube, near the spoked wheel, to the engine room below. He ordered dead slow speed and at the same time sharply altered his heading to westward. He ran a short distance on that course; then, after a hand signal from Kenchi, he again spun the wheel hard right. The tugboat's high bow swung rapidly until it pointed shoreward. Now Konrad guided the tug skillfully through the narrow, dog-leg channel between big, submerged coral heads close by on either side. Less than a hundred feet from the sandy beach, the skipper signaled the engineer for slow astern and, almost simultaneously, stop engine. A second later he motioned to the deckhands to drop the anchor. The tug drifted back slowly until the anchor line took a strain and held. Several outrigger canoes came alongside, and all of us except the crew went ashore.

At the end of our work schedule with island counterparts, Chief Kanis told us that the people of his village had prepared some food and invited us to share it with them. The feast, in typical island style, was laid out in a cool, grassy area in a line, twenty feet long, of broad banana leaves, which served as a fine table cloth. We sat on the ground, legs tucked beneath us, and faced each other.

Before us were set wooden ceremonial food bowls, shaped like double-ended boat hulls, and tin pans of baked chicken, several kinds of fish, breadfruit, taro in coconut milk, and a fine variety of fruits. Of all the tropical fruits, the favorites seemed to be mango, in season for only about a month, in

July, and sweet, juicy slices of pineapple. While we ate and visited, teen-aged island girls stood behind the three or four highest ranking Udot officials and our field trip party. They languidly waved woven fans to cool us and keep away flies. It was a special islander gesture of hospitality.

After lunch the chief, other island officials, and several of us in the field trip party walked down the path toward a nearby village. Chief Kanis wanted to show us some new copra dryers the people recently had constructed, using designs suggested by our agriculturists. When we neared the beach, I glanced toward Moen Island, to the northeast. I stopped and for a few seconds studied the horizon with growing concern. The sky was still clear and blue two-thirds of the way to Moen; yet the island was invisible. A heavy line squall, miles wide, like a huge, gray-black curtain, had blanked it out and was moving fast, directly toward us.

I excused myself, saying I wanted to return to the tug for a few minutes, and hurried off down the sandy beach. I had no reason whatever to doubt Konrad's ability to cope with the oncoming line squall, even with the tug in that tight situation, hemmed in by the island reef and scattered coral heads. But we'd had the *Bailhache* only six weeks, and I was being overly protective.

Once out of sight of the chief and the others, I broke into a fast lope along the curving beach, then stopped, breathless and sweating, just before rounding the point. I wiped my forehead and walked ahead at what I tried to make seem a casual, leisurely pace. A few dozen more steps, rounding a point of land, the tug came into view. It lay quietly at anchor. By now, though, I felt the first stiff breezes, and they grew steadily colder. Konrad, Kenchi, and the deckhand stood with the engineer on the forward part of the bow, peering over the rail at the anchor in shallow water. On the beach two barefoot men carried on an intermittent, shouted conversation with the crewmen. I asked one of them to take me out to the tug. He agreed and they pushed a small paddling canoe down the sandy beach and into the water.

Aboard, I joined the men in the bow, still trying to act casual and unworried. Together, we studied the squall bearing down upon us. If the crew had any concern, they masked it well. Did they think a single anchor on a sandy bottom would hold the tug? I didn't. I wanted to ask them about that, but remained silent. If the *Bailhache* drifted backward only 150 yards or so and a few yards to either side of the narrow, crooked channel, it would get hung up on the coral reef. It might not rip out the tug's sturdy steel bottom, but could hold it in such a grip we might never be able to pull her free.

"Maybe we put down other anchor," Konrad spoke to Kenchi in Trukese. I breathed a hidden sigh of relief. Kenchi turned to the second deckhand. They moved rapidly to rig it, this time from the starboard side. When it was ready, Konrad, now in the wheelhouse, called to the engine room for dead slow speed ahead for only a few seconds, then signaled full stop. The tug glided silently toward the beach on its momentum. When its bow was along-side where the first anchor lay, the deckhands quickly tumbled the second one over the side. Kenchi made a hand motion to Konrad. The tug backed at dead slow speed very briefly; then the engine became quiet again. The anchor line took a strain and held.

I continued to stand with the deckhands in the bow, watching the thick, black rain curtain, driven by wind gusts of thirty to forty knots, racing straight at us. We felt the first cold drops of rain, followed in seconds by a deluge. I hurried along the deck, pushed by the wind, climbed the ladder to the elevated wheelhouse and tugged hard at the door.

Now the full force of the wind struck us. Sheets of rain beat and tore against the wheelhouse and streamed down the windows. Konrad looked at me sideways from where he stood at the wheel. He still seemed calm and re-laxed. The beach was invisible. I turned and looked astern from the fogged-over side windows. I could see nothing. The only possible way to locate coral heads—sometimes fifteen feet or more wide, hard, razor-sharp, and often barely submerged, was to sight each one visually. In this weather that would be utterly impossible.

The tug lurched backward. The two anchors had dragged. In a few sec-onds the motion stopped. The anchor flukes dug back into the sand. My palms were sweaty. Konrad still looked almost casual. I had to control myself strongly to keep from ordering: "Start the engine! Run ahead just hard enough to stay in place!"

A minute later the anchors slipped badly a second time. Before I could turn to Konrad and open my mouth, he leaned over the speaking tube and gave an order to the engineer down below. The big diesel roared to life. Its pow-erful, steady, pulsing sounds gave me great comfort. It sounded positively beau-tiful. Konrad and I stood silently, peering through the streaming wheelhouse windows.

Up forward, Kenchi's tall, dripping figure pivoted around occasionally, and he made hand signals to Konrad. Once when he did this, Konrad spoke into the tube to the engineer. The engine's revolutions increased slightly. I saw that part of the anchor line nearest the bow slacken. Konrad spoke again to the engineer. The revolutions decreased, and the anchor line took up new tension. But Konrad had the engineer keep enough revolutions on to prevent the tug from drifting backwards.

After five more minutes, the wind's force slackened a little and visibility improved enough so that we could see the far end of the anchor line. Thirty seconds later we barely made out the beach through the rain. Konrad looked over at me and smiled. In another two minutes the squall had passed. Soon the air became clear and warm again and the sky blue.

One more line squall had swept the lagoon and was heading for Tol Island and the open sea. One more lesson learned: Never worry about Konrad's and his crew's handling of the *Bailhache.*

Love Magic

I first heard the phrase from "Shelley," a Public Works shop foreman, during small talk at the hotel one evening. He voiced the words in a manner which left the clear impression that here was tantalizing, esoteric knowledge held by a most select and enviable few. Two weeks later Herb Wilson spoke these same words: "love magic," and they drifted around me like a tropical fragrance. When, during the same month, I heard Frank use the phrase, I decided the time had come to add a new dimension to my knowledge of island ways.

Several of us, Trukese and Americans, were aboard the picket boat for a one-day field trip to Tol Island in Truk Lagoon. The morning air was still cool and the rain-washed sky was bright blue. The twin diesels hummed steadily, contentedly. Frank and I sat on top of the low cabin aft of the wheelhouse. Russ Curtis, Island Affairs department head, and Herb walked up and joined us. We listened as Frank talked about the islanders' strong belief in some things supernatural. When he mentioned love magic parenthetically, I stopped him abruptly.

"You're the third American I've heard mention love magic. Tell me about it."

He dramatized a surprised look, grinning impishly, and said, "What—*you*, 'father' to these island people, and with a wife and two little daughters of your own, *you* are interested in *love magic?*"

Russ and Herb laughed. "Purely professional," I said, feigning injury. "Didn't you suggest I dig deeply into island lore?"

"We-e-ll..." he began, and his voice and expression warned me I was in for more of his Hibernian humor, "it's a powerful magic!" Here comes some artful evading and dissembling, I guessed.

"Love magic isn't useful," he proceeded after a well-calculated pause, "to anyone except a young, unmarried man with very serious intent or a man or wife who believes the mate's ardor is cooling."

I waited again. After fifteen seconds I said, "Well? Continue."

"You want to know *more?*" he asked, again with theatrics.

"Of course," I responded in kind. "Please get on with my education."

"The best place to learn about love magic is on Satawan," he went on in the same mood. "They have the strongest love magic. That's where it all began in these islands."

"Is that where you carried out your studies on the subject?"

"I should be so fortunate?" he said, his voice turning suddenly mournful and his eyes rolling upward. Here his manner changed in a way that was one of Frank's hallmarks when discussing a subject that strongly interested him: his voice became softer and slightly intense. "I learned about love magic from several different informants, including one in the Mortlocks and some from this lagoon. They assumed I would maintain a kind of secrecy..."

Before I could ask what he meant by "a kind of secrecy," he continued on a related tack. "Have you heard how a young man of courting age first goes about trying to create a girl's interest in him?"

"No. How?" Herb asked.

"He might sit down and begins writing love letters..." At that point there was a shout by the lookout in the bow. The man on the wheel slammed both engines into reverse. Those standing on deck were thrown forward. I hurried forward to see what was happening. The boat now sat dead in the water, except for rolling gently. Ten feet forward of the bow and three or four feet under the surface was a huge coral head. Its razor sharp edges were capable of ripping a big hole in the picket boat's laminated plywood hull. I didn't get back during that trip to my conversation with Frank. I learned nothing from him that day about love magic.

While we were in the islands, the oldest Trukese could still remember when a young man seeking a lover's tryst used a love stick. People, young and old, delighted in telling us how they were used in their fathers' and grandfathers' times. Taking a straight piece of breadfruit wood eighteen to twenty-four inches long, a young suitor shaped it to have a short handle and a long, graceful "blade," tapering to a spear-like point. Along the length of the blade he carved his own unique signature of intricate designs: serrated edgings of diamonds, triangles, half-triangles, small curving wings. The flat part of the blade was decorated with more carvings. Some love sticks were stained with island dyes.

A young man with courtship on his mind carried his love stick around the island. He made certain the girl whose heart he sought to win had full opportunity to study and memorize his special carvings. In this way, he unmistakably signaled his interest in her, and that she should expect him as a caller.

Then he went to her grass hut at night after the village was asleep. He pushed his love stick through the wall and into that part of the room where, he had learned surreptitiously, she slept. If she was asleep when he arrived, he either prodded her gently with the love stick or entangled it in her hair and tugged softly until she awakened. Then her fingers traced and read his design. If the girl still was not certain she recognized the pattern, she would whisper, "Who is it?"

The traditional reply was simply, "I."

If she was still not certain, she'd repeat the question and he'd whisper his name. If she rejected him, she pushed the love stick forcefully back to him. If she liked the suitor, the young lady then pulled the love stick into the hut. This was a sign that she was ready to consider him seriously as a suitor and would try to leave the house quietly and see him outside. Both the young lady and the suitor feared his nocturnal call on her might awaken other members of the household. Part of an extended family's ways was that the girl's parents and other older relatives might already have their own ideas as to whom she should marry. With the coming of houses with wooden walls, the usefulness of love sticks began to die out. We saw them on sale at TTC along with other handicraft.

It was several months after that day on the picket boat trip to Tol, when I first heard Frank mention love magic, that he and I began having some follow-on conversations on the subject. He gradually educated me. Much of it was in bits and pieces. One of his early narrations on Trukese courting ways returned to the subject of how a young man might begin trying to win the love of a young lady by writing love letters. He emphasized that he had learned much about this and other aspects of Trukese culture from Tom Gladwin, who had done research on the subject related to his CIMA work at Truk, and written about it as part of his dissertation for a PhD from Yale University.

Frank told me how the boy would describe in his letters to the girl his ecstasies of pain as he dreams of her and longs to be with her. While attempting to fill his letters with flowery phrases, he offers profuse apologies for his lack of skill in expressing his deepest feelings for her. He begs her to discount this inadequacy by realizing his total sincerity and devotion. The letter would be delivered by a trusted go-between. Trukese tradition dictated that the girl ignore the first letter or two. The young swain persevered with further expressions, heavily sprinkled with more poetic adornments, of his love for her, describing more fervently in each new epistle his sweet agony in waiting to be with her. If he receives no answer after sending several more letters, he might simply give up. Or he might turn to love magic.

I was surprised to learn that there isn't just a single, ancient, unvarying prescription for the love magic potions, or for the way the man or woman mesmerizes the targeted person with it.

"Love magic," Frank told me, "is very soundly based psychologically. For it to be effective, both the man and the girl whose love he wants to win must believe strongly in it. When they do, it should work fine."

I had been in the islands nearly three years before I first raised the subject with a Trukese man. Like trying to learn more about witch doctors, I felt that my Trukese acquaintances wouldn't expect the *kepina* to question them on such matters. He seemed willing enough to talk, but he gave me little more than enough information to confirm broadly what Frank had told me. Still later I also talked about love magic with Trillie, a lady from the Northern Mariana Islands, who came to Truk and taught at the Catholic girls' school on Tol. Not being Trukese, she had a more detached view of the subject, although love magic was not limited to the Truk District.

Trillie once saw love magic indirectly affect her work situation. A Trukese young lady, whom I'll call Niwisa, was her teaching assistant at the school on Tol Island and was from a prominent family there. Niwisa had separated from her husband. He was an older man, and their marriage had been arranged by the two families. Now she lived in a little house near the school. She left him, she told Trillie, because he beat her regularly. She vowed often to Trillie that under no circumstances would she ever take him back.

"One afternoon when school was out," Trillie told me, "I walked down the path with some other girls, including Niwisa. We were going to the church for mass. Niwisa walked somewhere behind me. Then I saw a man coming along another path, so he would meet us just where the two paths crossed. It was Niwisa's former husband. He wore a *mwarmwar* (head-band of flowers). We could smell the strong, special perfume on him. It was from those buds of the plant the Trukese call *pwallan*. I think it is the same as that plant they call *lior*."

In Truk Lagoon it was an unwritten law that when a man and woman met alone on a path and one or both were married, they did not speak to each other. To do so might have suggested the man had illicit intentions. When Niwisa's husband went past Trillie and the girl she was walking with, he did not speak.

"We were near the church, so we stopped at a little pool to wash our feet," Trillie told me. "When we finished and were ready to go on, we didn't see Niwisa. Some small boys were playing nearby, so we asked them, 'Did you see where Niwisa went?'"

"'She just went to her family's house with her husband,' they said. That evening she left the village where the school was located and didn't return to her school job."

Some days later Father Hoek (an American Jesuit priest) learned about this. He went to Niwisa's village to talk with her. "She was smiling and told him she was very happy," Trillie told me. "Father Hoek asked her if she wanted to come back to work at the school. She said, yes, but she wanted to live here with her husband. So she came back and they lived together in that little house by the school where she had been staying."

"Did you learn what happened that day on the path?" I asked.

"Yes, I asked her about it. She said, 'My husband used love magic on me.'

She said it had made her so she had no power to resist. She suddenly wanted to be with him again, and the love magic made her feel very happy."

I wish I could say the story ended there, but, alas, real life is not always so kind.

"Did it last? Did they stay together?"

"For a few weeks," Trillie answered. "Then he had to go away to take care of some animals. He returned and they stayed together a little longer; then he started to beat her again and she asked him to leave and not come back to her." He knew he had to leave because if he didn't, her older brother would have ordered him to leave—this time permanently. She kept working at school but started living again in her mother's village.

When I fitted together the various pieces of information I had been gathering, a picture emerged. The following story represents my understanding of the essence of love magic, how young Trukese men learned it, and how they went about putting it to use.

Ichiro's Story

It is no secret throughout his part of the lagoon that Ichiro knows love magic. While not as highly treasured as canoe building secrets, it is, like some other forms of magic, valuable clan property. That is why a person who knows it normally will teach it only to a few younger clan members. To give it out too widely would dissipate its value. Once in a while a man or woman may teach it to someone outside the lineage for valuable consideration, providing the giver's grown children agree. They have a voice in the matter because a few of them will inherit the knowledge.

The year Ichiro turned seventeen, his sister's husband, a carpenter on Fefan Island, agreed to teach him the trade. Today, at thirty-five, Ichiro is looked up to on Fefan for his carpentry skills and for his quiet, forceful voice at island meetings. He is also respected and liked for his ready smile, for having the best bass voice in the group that sings in his village at one house or another before breakfast several mornings a week, and for his talent as a softball player.

His wife's *eterenges* owns enough good farm land on this high island so they can live well. Although his carpentry skills are in demand, he still finds time to work some mornings in the family garden at the edge of the village.

He finds much pleasure in joining male members of his extended family on trips to their part of the barrier reef for spear fishing. Steeped in tradition, he believes many of the old ways should be kept—that they give strength and unity to the extended family.

One evening Ted Hall was in Ichiro's village near the end of a three-day field trip in Truk Lagoon. Ted, a junior professional level technician for the district administration on Moen, was nearly one year into his second overseas tour. He was twenty-eight, still a bachelor, disliked report writing and other paper work, and was happiest when he was out in the villages working with the people. Over the past two years a close friendship had formed between him and Ichiro, bonded in part by the fact that Ted's father was a carpenter and cabinet maker, with a small shop in the Midwest, where Ted had helped him during summer vacations.

Several times in recent months Ted had tried, when he and Ichiro sat alone visiting in the evening, to probe gently, tactfully on the subject of love magic. He appreciated that this kind of knowledge was not freely given. Believing that he and Ichiro were close enough friends by now, he had tried to leave a veiled hint that the imparting of such knowledge would be treated as a *niffang*—a gift gratefully received and anticipated to be reciprocated with some future gift or favor. While his Trukese friend didn't seem at all uncomfortable on those occasions, Ted had learned from him little beyond common knowledge. Yet Ichiro had ended the last talk with an unspoken suggestion that more might follow.

Not long after dusk on the first evening of this visit, the other men drifted away, and Ted and Ichiro walked down by the beach near the pier and seated themselves in a sandy area. Ted welcomed the opportunity to be alone with Ichiro, but he was fearful that his friend might want to leave soon because the night was sultry, the breeze had died down, and the mosquitoes and no-see-ums were bothersome. Ichiro got up after a few minutes and dragged dead palm fronds and dry leaves over to make a smudge fire. He turned and called to several boys playing on the pier. One of them raced off in the opposite direction. He reappeared a few minutes later carrying between two pieces of palm frond, held like tongs, glowing embers of a chunk of mangrove wood to start the fire.

The two chatted light-heartedly for more than a half hour. Ted, seeing that

131

the carpenter was in fine spirits, decided to try again to get him to share some of his secret knowledge.

"Ichiro," he began, making a pattern in the sand with his shoe, "you have told me a little about love magic. I would like to learn it." He wanted to add: How did you find a teacher? How long did it take you to learn it? How do you prepare the magic? How do you use it? Fearing to push too hard or fast, he said only, "Will you tell me more?"

Ichiro didn't look back at the young American through the wisps of smoke. Instead, he sat gazing into the fire. Ted became worried that he had offended his friend. But Ichiro finally turned to him, seeming both serious and agreeable.

"Well, I will just tell you something. I was nineteen years that time when I liked those girls," he began. "I liked that one girl very much and I wanted her to like me. So I wrote letters to her, but she did not give her answer. Then I decided I will just try to learn love magic. Before I asked my uncle to teach me, I brought him a small gift—a little wooden box with a top, which I made from scraps of nice lumber. In a few days I just asked him to teach me, but he did not answer that time. The next week I helped him to make a fish trap. He told me, 'I will teach you the love magic because I watched you, and I see you are the kind of young man who will not follow the first rain.'"

"What did he mean by that?" Ted asked. Ichiro looked at him, appearing slightly irritated, and Ted resolved not to interrupt again. But Ichiro addressed the question.

"My uncle took many talks to explain this part to me," Ichiro said, his voice still equable, "until he knew I understood it, because that part is very important. He told me that to use the love magic in the right way I must not do things too fast. He made me understand I must wait for the right time to do things. The love magic must not be used in the rain because it will become weak. But that is not what he wanted to tell me. He wanted to say I must not use the magic on the first girl I see. I must use it on a girl I love and respect. *I must not follow the first rain.* When he saw I understood about that, he taught me more. But he always went slowly, slowly, slowly. I was impatient because I was young. I wanted to learn faster."

Ichiro smiled and paused, perhaps reliving moments of those long ago lessons.

"Our *eterenges*," he went on, "knows love magic *nom, nom, nom* (since old times). My uncle said it is very important for this magic to be in the lineage a long time because it gets stronger that way. He told me love magic can be used in different ways but the biggest reason for it is to make a woman feel love for a man. If the man learns it well and can make a strong magic, he will make the girl want to love him. Sometimes a woman learns the magic and uses it on her husband to make him love her more." He stopped, stood and laid another palm frond on the fire.

"My uncle said there are taboos I must follow when I use love magic." He half-turned his head, and Ted saw his serious expression through the smoke. "I must not eat some of that food—*opwot* (preserved breadfruit) or some kind of fish. I must not eat the eel or the octopus. The big eel found by the reef is strong taboo.

"He told me it is taboo to eat any food the day before I make the love magic. I must be alone when I prepare it." Ichiro walked away from the fire, came back with some more wood which he placed on it, and again sat by Ted.

"I must never tell anyone who I will use it on. That is very important. Bad things will happen if I break the taboos. The magic can hurt me. Maybe I will get sickness." He gazed steadily at Ted for some seconds to emphasize the point.

Ted returned his companion's level gaze. Ichiro's expression and whole manner told him that the carpenter believed every word implicitly.

"Can you believe love magic?" he asked Ted. "Can you believe it strong? If you cannot do that, you cannot make the love magic."

Ted was about to assure Ichiro that he thought he could believe in it, when his teacher spoke again. "The girl you use it on must believe in love magic, too. My uncle told me another very important part. I must make the magic only on a girl who is *tipemecheres* (good-natured). It takes very strong medicine to work on a girl who is *tipekoum* (angry at heart). After he taught me all these things, he made me tell them back to him many times. When he knew I understood them well, he started to teach me how to prepare the magic. Here are things my uncle and I gathered from our island and the reef:

6 buds from the tree called *lior*.
1 female white sand crab.
3 petals from the ginger flower.

Make oil from coconut.
A little sea water.

"When we finished gathering all these things, my uncle kept the lior buds and the flowers in a square tin box that once held tobacco. He put the sea water and the coconut oil we made in two small bottles. The next morning he brought out the tin box and the bottles. We took these things and went to a quiet part of the village. No one tried to follow us.

"First my uncle showed me how to pound the buds from *lior* and the ginger petals. He put them in the bottom of the tobacco tin. They smelled good. After that we just pounded the crab until it was like flour, and we pounded pieces of copra to make coconut oil. Then he mixed sea water with coconut oil and poured it into the box. He stirred everything slowly, slowly, slowly with the middle rib of a coconut leaf while we chanted these words he taught me:

Lior small flowers, o...*lior* strong
Lior small flowers, o...*lior* strong
Use your powers to make that girl
(her name) want to love me...

"He made me say these words over and over while he stirred. This was to make certain each part would give me strong help. My uncle said it was ready now.

"I told him I wanted to go then—that afternoon—to the girl's village. But he told me 'You forget one important thing.' He meant about first rain. Then he said, 'This magic will not work for you. You must make some by yourself.'

"I felt angry with my uncle because I could not use the perfume we took a long time to make together. There was nothing I could do. That same day I went to get those things I needed. My uncle let me use his little tin box and the two bottles. I just gathered all those things and mixed them the way my uncle taught me. Then I was ready. So that night I did not eat. I could not sleep well because I think, will the magic work? I did not eat the next day.

"I waited until the sun was almost on the sea before I started to the girl's village. When I got near it, I stepped off the path into the bushes and put perfume on different parts of my body." Ichiro tapped his right and left upper arms on the outside, and his forehead and chest.

"I went down the path until I can see her house, but I did not see her. So I just walked past her house and down by the beach. But I still did not see her. I was very unhappy.

"But the next evening I went back to her village. This time I saw her by a grassy place with those girls. I waited a long time. Then she left them and walked along the path toward her house. I walked fast so I will meet her on the path. I walked on the left side of her. I wanted the wind to blow the magic smell to her. At first I am afraid she will not like me. Then I thought about how my uncle said this is strong magic, so I felt better. When we went past, I walked very close to her and let my arm rub some good love magic smell to her arm. Then we both kept walking. I looked back and she looked back and smiled. But we did not say anything then, and she went to her house, and I just went to my village."

At that point, Ted interrupted Ichiro again. "Did the magic work? Did you win the girl?"

"Oh, yes," Ichiro said and smiled happily.

"How did you arrange to meet her?"

"I went to her village the next day," he said. "I did not see her, but I can talk to one of her 'sisters.' I said I want to come to see this girl tomorrow night after dark and meet her just outside her house. I waited by the edge of the village and then the 'sister' came back and said it will be all right.

"The next night I waited until her village sleeps. Then she came out. I was wearing more of the love magic my uncle showed me to make. We sat and talked by the edge of the village for a long time.

Ichiro stopped again, as if that ended the story. The second time I am with her, she told me it makes her feel very happy. She feels like she is having nice dreams even in the day. Then I told her I love her and she said she loves me. After that we meet many more times secretly at night."

"Did you and the girl get married then?" Ted asked hesitantly.

"No," Ichiro said, "I wanted to marry her. But then there was this problem." Ted looked at his teacher expectantly.

Ichiro paused for a long time, as if deep in thought. Finally he turned back to Ted and continued. "Her mother told her the family wants her to marry an older man. But she said to her family, 'please do not make me marry with him, because I love Ichiro and he said he wants me for his wife.' When I learned this from one of her sisters, I went to her family and said I want her for my wife. Her family talked together for some days. After a while her family said it will be all right. So she became my wife and we are still very happy."

By now the smudge fire was nearly out. They walked back from the beach and along the village path toward the community house where Ted was staying. After standing and talking for a few minutes more, they said goodnight and Ichiro went on down the path in the dark. Ted heard him stop about a dozen steps away. He could not see him but heard the carpenter's low voice clearly in the village quietness.

"What I told you about—it will not work for you."

"Oh... Why not?"

"There is some part I cannot tell to someone not of our clan."

Western Field Trip

The departure of each field trip ship from Moen Island was a social occasion, with a holiday mood, especially for the Trukese. Friends and relatives of the passengers, and others looking for something to do, found entertaining diversion in a sailing—much in the same way small-town Americans several generations earlier dropped by the depot for the arrival of the daily milk-run train. Trukese and Americans—wives, children, friends—gathered on the pier alongside the ship to chat with those who were boarding.

A day before the departure, the Truk Trading Company loaded trade goods into the freighter's holds to sell at each island we'd visit. Similarly, Island Trading Company workers loaded weighing scales and bundles of jute bags islanders would need to load with copra for sale to ITC during later field trip visits. ITC was headed at Truk by John Spivey, a former Navy pilot, who reported directly to his ITC boss in Honolulu. It was a Territory-wide organization created by the Navy years earlier for the purpose of buying and marketing for the islanders their copra, trochus shells, and some handicraft for export. TTC and ITC each sent two Trukese employees on outer island field trips.

Hours before sailing time the deck forward of the wheelhouse was jammed with Trukese passengers, live chickens, a few pigs, fat packages of taro, and cooked or preserved breadfruit—both kinds wrapped in big green leaves and tied with vines or *senet* (coconut husk cord), stalks of bananas, and baskets of papayas and limes. On deck near clusters of passengers were bunches of drinking coconuts. Some people placed rolled up mats, bedding, and other belongings under great canvas awnings the crew rigged, draped over a cargo hatch boom like a big tent, to protect deck passengers from rain squalls and the sun's heat. There always were guitars, and singing began long before sailing time.

We field trip party members, especially Americans, tended to linger on the pier with families and friends until the ship's whistle sounded and the order was given to haul in the gangway. The Trukese must have been as impressed with the American custom of publicly kissing our wives and children goodbye, as we were with the shrieking wails of Trukese women. The latter began when the ship's lines were cast off, thus sealing the departure of some passenger they might not see again for months. The wails kept up, with much soulful calling and waving of colorful scarves until the ship was a few hundred yards out; then the women, whose hearts I would have sworn were breaking from their sadness, stopped crying instantly. They turned around and, chatting cheerfully and laughing, strolled off the pier and back toward their villages.

The Trust Territory had acquired from the Navy several 175-foot steel-hulled freighters. They were in those years, except for a few small sailboats such as Truk Trading had for picking up copra from certain closer-in islands, the districts' only sea transportation link with their outer islands. Those freighters were rotated and used, in turn, by the other districts. In our case, a freighter carried us to the twenty-three populated islands far beyond Truk lagoon. Pacific Micronesian Lines, the contractor for the Trust Territory, operated the ships with American captains, Filipino mates and islander sailors. We usually shared a ship with the Ponape District, east of us. We kept it four or five weeks, then rotated it over to them. The Trust Territory's shipping liaison man, stationed on Guam, often pressed us to keep the ships moving.

We made trips once every two months to the Mortlocks. After a day or two back in port, we put a fresh field trip party aboard and they went out to the Hall Islands, north of Truk Lagoon, then to the western islands. The

Mortlocks run took eight to ten days. The western trip was something else. The sea was always rougher out there and, except for Puluwat, none of the islands had good anchorages. When the weather was favorable and we didn't have a larger than normal amount of copra to pick up, we made it in eleven to fourteen days. Much more often than in the Mortlocks, we had to skip an island or two because of rough weather.

The first person on an island to sight our approaching ship would sing out, "*Sippo! Sippo!*" (ship). In a few minutes word spread from one end of the island to the other. To the people on these islands, which they called *fanoen fan*—islands below the horizon—the first sight of a ship in two months signaled a day or two of excitement. It meant a chance to renew contacts with the world beyond the few islands nearest them. The number of greeters and the exuberance of their greetings were usually more restrained in the western islands than in other parts of the district. They welcomed back their own people returning from the hospital or boarding schools on Moen, and perhaps two or three who went in on an earlier ship to visit friends and see the bright lights of Moen. The ship's call meant a chance to sell copra, buy trade goods, receive mail, hear news and gossip, get some medical and dental help if they felt so inclined, and meet and visit with the rest of the field trip party.

Puluwat

The Puluwat Island outrigger canoe, manned by two husky young paddlers, each wearing only a loin cloth, surged toward our freighter in rolling, pitching motions in the wind-driven sea. Through the haze of spindrift enveloping the canoe, we watched them maneuver cautiously to within ten feet of the ship's lee side. Quickly the ship's islander crewmen finished rigging a wooden plank "springboard" over the side—like a house painter's rope-suspended platform—and the Puluwat men eased their canoe to within three feet of it. The canoe might rise and fall three to five feet with each breaking wave.

Normally, the first canoe out to the ship carried a few bags of copra, which one of the paddlers would heave up onto the springboard, then hop up quickly onto it and boost the sacks to the main deck before salt spray could soak them. If copra gets wet it can't be stored because it becomes a fire hazard in a cargo hold, like wet hay in a barn. This first canoe had brought out no copra because, though the wind was gradually decreasing and the sea getting smoother, it was still too rough.

Captain Rathbun, on the wing of the bridge, called down. "How much copra?"

The Truk Trading Company man, a Trukese, standing nearest to the springboard, conferred briefly with the Puluwat men, then shouted up to the Captain, "Maybe 300 sacks." This was twice the amount we normally picked up from Puluwat every two months.

"Holy Jesus!—" the captain began—first words of his familiar outbursts, more out of habit and impatience than ill temper—and cut it short when he saw Father Fahey on deck directly below. Grinning, the captain lowered his voice slightly and added "—Son of sweet Mary...!" Father Fahey, the only missionary aboard this trip, winked at several of us standing nearby and crossed himself.

"Can you get it all aboard today?" the captain shouted down to me. Like merchant officers everywhere, he was conditioned to think of ship operations in terms of fastest possible cargo handling at each port, then sailing.

"If they already have most of it bagged," I yelled back above the wind. "If the sea gets smoother..." I had little hope that the first factor would work in our favor today.

"How much copra bagged?" one Island Trading Company trader asked the Puluwat man.

"Little bit," the canoeman replied cheerfully. "Need *tuk*" (jute sacks). This announcement brought derisive remarks from several Trukese and Americans in the field trip party and another salty outburst from the bridge.

"Always same on western islands," the ITC man said philosophically. He called for his partner to hand up several bundles of empty sacks from deep in the open cargo hold, made a charge note on the Puluwat tally sheet, and tossed the bundles down to a canoeman, now on the springboard.

Part of my job was to visit the islands lying far beyond the large Truk Lagoon. Sitting in an office back on Moen Island, I simply couldn't get a good feel for the district, and was certain my staff couldn't either. I tried to get out to these thirteen "northwest field trip" islands and the eleven in the Mortlocks, south and southeast of Truk Lagoon, on at least every other field trip. That way I hoped to absorb something of each island—get to know the chiefs, people, and village life a little better, even if visits were only for a day or two at a time. We Americans and our islander staff members needed this to make more confident and sensible judgments as to whether the kinds of help we were bringing to the Trukese were what they really wanted and needed. Were we doing all we could, within limits of our outer-island field trip time and resources we had available, to support the island chiefs, teachers, health aides, and the rest of the people, with their subsistence farming and fishing? Furthermore, I greatly enjoyed the trips. Except when the sea got really rough. Then one of those little freighters could roll, pitch and yaw with the best Navy destroyers. Trying to get off the ship into a canoe, or back onto the ship later, in such seas could be dangerous.

Dr. Michi and I would go ashore first this morning; others would come in on later canoe trips. He first handed down to one canoeman a cardboard box of medical supplies and a small handbag containing his instruments. Then he climbed down onto the springboard and was drenched immediately by waves breaking up from under it and against the ship's side. For several seconds he studied the canoe's movements, then stepped easily into it the split second before it reached the top of its upward surge.

My turn next. Before my feet touched the springboard, a cascade of cold salt spray thoroughly soaked my khaki blouse and shorts and dripped off my face and baseball cap. As I stepped into the canoe just forward of the rear paddler, my whole upper body was instantly propelled outward by the canoe's roll, far past the center of gravity. The long, slim outrigger on the outboard side began to sink. The rear paddler's muscular arm shot forward. His powerful grip encircled my right upper arm and pulled me back and onto my seat. The outrigger stabilized immediately.

Dr. Michi, who had whirled around toward me only an instant later than the Puluwat man, laughed and settled back onto his seat. "I have done that many times," he said with his typical kindness. The canoe swung around and quartered the waves as we rolled and pitched toward the thick green line of coconut palms a few hundred yards away.

The only conversation was an occasional brief exchange between the two Puluwat men, who had to shout above the wind and breaking waves. Today I wanted to get onto the island early and be satisfied that Chief Romelo was doing all he could to expedite getting the copra bagged and hauled. While Puluwat men had a well-deserved reputation as some of the world's best blue water sailors, their past record in moving copra out to the ship in reasonable time was dismal at best.

Fifteen minutes later the Puluwat men maneuvered the canoe through the reef pass into calm water. It was a much easier pass than most others for canoes to enter in rough weather. They drove the bow into shallow water, and we stepped ashore. Dr. Michi handed his supplies and kit to two young boys who had been among those watching us land. They followed us along the shaded path toward the village. We went only a short distance when Chief Romelo came walking toward us. Dressed in a red loin cloth and a faded, unbuttoned GI shirt, he greeted us with a warm smile and handshake. We walked back along the path with him to his village.

Dr. Michi went on to the dispensary while the chief led me over to the yard of his modest wooden house and invited me to take a seat on a log under a bower of breadfruit and coconut trees. He sat beside me and called toward the house. His wife came out the door and walked over toward us. I had met her on one of my early trips to Puluwat. She was buxom, cheerful looking, and wore a traditional western islands wraparound skirt woven from hibiscus fibers. I stood to greet her, while she made a half crouch-half bow, exchanged a few words with the chief and went back into the house. A few minutes later I saw her and another lady begin fixing an outdoor cooking fire. Soon she served us coffee in big tin cups.

Chief Romelo, whom I guessed to be in his middle forties when I first met him, was square-faced, with prominent cheekbones and black curly hair that was graying. Like many other men on the island, including all the older ones, he had large ear loops and blue tattoo designs on his thighs and arms. The chief was still full of life's juices. His thick-set build gave him a ruggedly powerful look, even among the men of Puluwat—once the most feared warriors in the middle Carolines. With all these physical attributes, he had warmth, gentleness, and a caring attitude toward his people. He favorably impressed us Americans who came to his island. As the years went by, our friendship grew to be one of the closest I enjoyed among out-island Trukese.

If any American who made field trips was asked what were the three most interesting islands in the district, he'd almost certainly list Puluwat as one of them, or Pulusuk, forty miles to the south. Maybe even smaller Punlap or Tamatam, twenty miles north of Puluwat. These were, much more so than most of the other islands, the old South Seas. Here the people's ways, at least in terms of their material surroundings, were much like they must have been hundreds of years earlier.

The first time I came to Puluwat, several years earlier, I saw, as I walked around the villages, that most families lived in grass huts with sand floors and no windows. They were colorful, but the thatched walls and roofs were hosts to insects. During the rainy season they often were damp inside. The only sunlight came through the low doorway. Our doctors believed their darkness and dampness contributed more than anything else to the high incidence of tuberculosis in the outer islands. Towering above these modest huts, a small scattering of wooden houses and some big canoe houses, were the Catholic and Protestant churches, with their coral limestone and cement sides, thatched (Protestant) and corrugated tin (Catholic) roofs.

Every family cooked over an open fire, using big stones to support iron pots. Around some cookhouses I saw a few tin cups and plates, a tin kettle or two and carved wooden bowls. Other material signs of civilization were scant. Most men had a machete for making copra and as a general purpose cutting tool. A scattering of lanterns glowed at night while the fuel lasted. The few medical supplies were kept in an old Japanese ammunition box in one corner of the health aide's station. In each school building was a blackboard made of painted plywood. That was about it.

Puluwat men, typical of those in other far western islands, wore a loin cloth of woven pandanus fibre or red cloth, sometimes with an economy of material. A few men had shirts, usually khaki, and wore them to keep off the sun, and during the typhoon season, when the combination of cold wind and driving rain could feel downright uncomfortable, especially at night.

The women's pandanus wraparound *lavalava* (skirt) extended from hips to ankles. Many skirts had alternate colored stripes and others displayed intricate designs, some like those of Navajo Indians. Handlooms on which they wove them were of the simplest kind: tree limbs trimmed and lashed together with small *senet*. Some women wore, mainly for church-going, bulky, hot "Mother Hubbard" dresses, made of cloth bought from TTC. Young boys went around naked until ages seven to nine; then they began wearing loin cloths. Younger girls wore breadfruit leaves with a *senet* twine belt.

Just as American men coming ashore in the far western islands could not help noticing the bare-breasted women, I observed that American women who occasionally made field trips when space was available, seemed equally aware of the superb male bodies, mostly uncovered. More than once I saw an American woman on a visit to one of these islands, who normally could walk with no difficulty down island paths in other parts of the district with just as many uncovered tree roots across them, suddenly begin to stumble when Puluwat men came walking in their direction. Since most American wives had a limited knowledge of spoken Trukese, and our field trip party was too busy much of the working day to interpret for them, they missed fine opportunities to get acquainted and exchange ladies' talk with the island women.

By the time Chief Romelo and I finished our coffee, a half-dozen older men and some young boys had drifted up, gathered around us in a semicircle, sat in a typical squatting position, and listened. There were so few visitors to outer islands that, as an American missionary once observed, any visitor is everyone's visitor. While such listeners hung onto every word of news from other islands—especially those fairly nearby—they rarely asked about the world beyond Truk Lagoon.

A muscular fellow with thick black hair, spokesman for a group of Puluwat men who had copra to take out to the ship, walked up to where we sat. He and those for whom he spoke already had heard from the canoemen who brought us ashore that we planned to stay only one day.

"*Sippo* wait for tomorrow," he said, making the request in English. Facing me, he looked deadly serious. I had observed on Puluwat and other far western islands that most men seldom smiled around an American. They didn't act unfriendly. They just didn't smile. Men smiled readily in the Truk Lagoon, in the Mortlocks, and in the Hall Islands. In those islands they also often took the initiative to greet Americans. Not here.

"We put *taka* (copra) in *tuk* (sack) today. Take *sippo* tomorrow." Not only was most of the copra on the island not bagged, his further conversation revealed; some of it was still on the uninhabited neighboring Alet Island, separated from Puluwat by a narrow channel and used mainly for growing coconuts and raising pigs.

"Every time the ship comes to Puluwat we ask your people to buy enough sacks to have copra ready to load for the next trip," I reminded Chief Romelo and the assembled listeners, trying to sound matter-of-fact and friendly, yet firm. "They never buy more than a few sacks. We have forty passengers on deck waiting to get home. Every day the ship is at sea costs..."

I stopped in mid-sentence. Here I was on Puluwat acting like an American ship captain: trying to highball the operation. On this lovely, remote island, much more so than on most others in the district, our Western concept of time was as foreign to them as strawberry shortcake. I was not prepared to believe they should become like us in that respect.

"Okay," I said. "We stay one more day." Then I turned to the chief, who had listened expressionless to all this, but began smiling when I announced my decision. "Please, Chief Romelo," I appealed to him, "try to get the men to buy enough sacks while the ship is here so they can have all the copra in sacks—ready—next trip."

"*Ewer!*" (yes) he agreed readily. But the sack problem didn't really change.

Spokesman and his two fellow copra makers walked away a few steps, squatted and conferred together. Then they got up, came back to us, and he spoke again to me.

"We use *sippo pot?*" (ship's motor whaleboat) he asked with good expectations in his voice. Our field trip officers had been telling the Puluwat men, as had Bob Law, Tom Gladwin and other Navy Field Trip officers before us, that they had plenty of canoes on Puluwat. We expected them to haul their own copra.

"No ship boat," I said. "You have two days—plenty time—to take copra in your canoes." I realized I might have to backtrack on this if the wind didn't die down a little more. With this sea, their copra would get too wet in the canoes. Spokesman and his companions received my response with no apparent disappointment. They left for the beach. Past experience certainly warned them I'd be most unlikely to say yes to this latter proposal.

Inter-island warfare was common prior to the arrival of the German rulers at the turn of the century. The sight of a Puluwat flotilla approaching other islands was a terrifying prospect. Puluwat men had dominated that part of the Carolines. We sometimes heard young men in Truk Lagoon joking about their country cousins to the west, but never in their presence. Now they sailed their big canoes around the western islands and occasionally journeyed 160 miles to Moen for the high adventure and camaraderie of sea voyaging—and for a look at the big city and to buy a few packs of cigarettes at TTC.

On each visit to Puluwat my feeling grew that here were a people with a strong sense of identity and self-sufficiency. They gave us Americans—and probably our Trukese field trip companions even more—the impression that they believed they were as good as anyone anywhere, and better than most. Father Fahey expressed his opinion to me on several different occasions that western islanders, more so than most people in other parts of the district, had a deeply rooted feeling of security.

Times were changing much faster in the Halls, Mortlocks and Truk Lagoon. There, people were adopting more and more foreign ways. On Puluwat they liked the old ways and took pride in them. They transmitted to us, unspoken, their belief that they could take care of themselves with their own resources and skills at hand. They had a strong sense of who they were: builders, sailors, navigators of great seagoing canoes. The central fact of Puluwat life was that it was a canoe culture. Building and sailing their big canoes was at the heart of the way of life here. Because it was, it did much to shape the spirit and attitudes of the men who sailed them and of everyone else on the island. The canoe builders were greatly respected. A *pono* (navigator) was held in higher social esteem than a chief. The Puluwat people were keeping their customs and traditions pretty intact.

After leaving Chief Romelo, I walked around the island, watching other field trip members at work with their Puluwat counterparts. We had a typical field trip party along this time. They were from Education, Medical (a doctor and two sanitarians), and Island Affairs. The latter checked on island government, including any court cases. Sometimes Island Affairs brought along an agriculturist, but not this trip. There were only two Americans agriculturists to cover the entire district. They even had to teach part-time at PICS and the intermediate school. Shortly after John Smith, our senior agriculturist, arrived, he began to pick up on and carry forward the Navy's earlier work to train Trukese to become extension agents. In the first few years, those islander employees weren't yet quite prepared to travel out on their own.

By early afternoon the wind had moderated. Going over to the beach to see how copra loading was moving, I found Chief Romelo there, talking with other Puluwat men. Three paddling canoes of different sizes were being loaded, each with six to ten sacks. The chief told me they ran out of sacks, so he sent a canoe to the ship to bring more ashore. In mid-afternoon all copra work was halted by a heavy shower which lasted nearly an hour.

I invited the chief to come aboard for dinner that evening. He readily accepted. We went out together in an outrigger at six o'clock. In the modern setting of the ship's dining hall, the chief, dressed as he had been ashore, sat among ship's officers and our field trip party with poise, dignity and all the relaxed self-confidence of a Puluwat man. Captain Rathbun was host in the dining hall. I had not asked him for permission to bring the chief aboard. Early in the meal I tossed out a little fact about Romelo and his people that broke the ice.

"Captain," I said, " I think you know these Puluwat men are some of the world's best blue water sailors. They navigate only by wind, waves and stars, and watching sea birds. They can hit tiny islands I've seen some freighter captains, with all their navigation gear, miss." I could say this to him because he was an unusually good navigator, and he'd know I wasn't including him in that group.

"By God, you're right!" he said, and began to talk with Chief Romelo about canoe sailing, with the interpreting help of several field trip members.

This was before I made it a policy that all field trip parties would spend evenings ashore any time we remained at an island for more than one day, whether because of the amount of field trip work ashore, weather, or an extra large amount of copra to be hauled. Usually it was a combination. When we began spending more time on the island, we started getting better acquainted with the people. Except in the rainy season, the days were hot, but in the evening the air became cooler and the whole island seemed more relaxed; cooking fires glowed in the dusk and, especially in the breadfruit season when food was plentiful, during and after mealtime the whole island seemed more sociable. More often than not the island people shared their food with us, and we left our "C" rations and other food with them. Community meetings were held after dark. This, too, helped create a more relaxed, unhurried atmosphere for visiting and talking about island matters.

One of the many dividends growing out of our evening visiting was that the people sang for us, though they did so the least in the western islands. In those evening gatherings under the stars or in the community building or a big canoe house, hundreds of voices blended beautifully, in several parts and with harmony in some of the finest folk singing I have listened to anywhere around the world. They composed songs themselves, about experiences, hopes or problems in their daily lives; others were hymns, as well as songs with their own words set to hymn music. Almost every island had its singing stars. They were men with wonderful, deep bass voices, and they enjoyed using them. They knew they stood out—were especially appreciated by their own people and by us. After entertaining us, the islanders sometimes asked us to sing for them or tell a story.

We usually chose to tell stories, although occasionally we were able to produce a soloist or duet. I often wished we could bring along a piano accordion player, or at least a harmonica virtuoso, but among all of us Americans on Moen there wasn't one.

The chief engineer of the field trip freighter, who was part Hawaiian, sang beautifully. We often asked him to come ashore at night to sing his best number, *Beyond the Reef*, and other songs.

Sometimes the islanders composed songs on the spot about their American and Trukese visitors. They occasionally divided into groups and had singing contests. It was their custom that the winners be sprinkled with inexpensive perfume, which islanders liked and women purchased in quantity from TTC. One time Ray McKay, our freckled-face young industrial arts teacher at the intermediate school on Moen, and George Davis, one of our agriculturists, were doing several weeks work on an outer island. The evening came when it was their turn to pick the winners, but they had no perfume of any sort to award. Ray resourcefully produced a spray can of pungent insect repellent, which seemed well-accepted and brought a laugh.

Walking around Puluwat, I was again impressed by the fact that the men didn't smile much around Americans. Why was this? Was it a throwback to the times before the turn of the century, when Puluwat warriors and those from other far western islands occasionally sailed their flotillas of canoes into Truk Lagoon, shouting challenges to the local people? Did they still have a wariness of all people foreign to their little cluster of neighboring islands? Was it because Puluwat, Pulusuk and Tamatam men were sensitive about the sharp differences between their own culture and those in some other parts of the middle Carolines? If it were, I believe their reaction would have been disdain rather than the least flicker of inferiority. On Puluwat, different from many other parts of the district, there apparently was little inter-marriage with the

Japanese in those pre-war and war years.

What we Americans didn't like about Puluwat and some of the other western islands was that they were too much of a man's world. Father Rively, the handsome young Jesuit Father down on Lukunor in the Morltocks, had spent some months here on Puluwat a few years earlier. He told about once seeing a man spank his wife because he wanted to be hospitable to a visitor and she had almost no food on hand to serve him. And here in the western islands, much more than on other islands, women had to walk with their heads lower than men's when they passed them. If a lady had to pass a group of seated men, custom decreed that she must crouch or crawl, so that her head would be lower than theirs.

Puluwat women quite often smiled at Americans in our field trip party. They seemed to know we didn't want them to genuflect for us, and I don't recall that they ever did, except when we were with Puluwat men. On another trip to this island, I was walking along a village path one morning and stopped to watch women cooking food. One of the younger women, who might have been in her early twenties, left the group and walked just behind me when I moved on. As she approached her home, one of the few small wooden houses, she caught up and spoke to me.

"Good morning, *kepina*. Come to my house. Come meet my father."

I was amazed. In the middle Carolines women simply didn't speak to men like that. My thoughts whirred. The last thing I needed was to get my head knocked off by a Puluwat superman for breaking some of their most sensitive traditions related to women. Yet she looked like an intelligent young lady, and the way she spoke made me think she would feel rebuffed if I said no. I wanted to have the experience. Maybe her father told her he wanted to talk with me.

"Thank you," I said.

She opened the door and waited for me to go in. I was again startled, as I studied her father's face closely, that it didn't register any surprise when I entered his home. The house was a simple one. Among the furnishings were an old table and three metal folding chairs. After I introduced myself to her father, who appeared to be in his late forties, and asked the young lady her name, I sat back and waited for him to question me. He sat looking friendly and solemn and said nothing.

I had found that talking with people in the western islands always was more difficult, because their dialect is quite different from that in Truk Lagoon, or in the Mortlocks, which had still another dialect. We managed to talk, and the girl, who knew some English, helped me with my language struggle. She went outside and returned a little later with a kettle of coffee which she served to her father and me in tin cups. I learned that her father, like everyone else, farmed and fished and the daughter had attended the Protestant school.

It was the only time I was ever invited into a Puluwat house. Even Chief Romelo always sat with me in their yard. Still amazed at the invitation by a Puluwat woman, I thanked them and stepped back out onto the path, half-expecting to be met by a couple of husky men. If people noticed my visit, and they must have, they gave no indication that they did.

Walking around the island some more that second day, I visited students and teachers at the government school, and watched Dr. Michi. He was busy with his outdoor sick call in front of the dispensary, where a rickety wooden table had been set to hold his bag and medicines. Men of all ages stood talking, and women sat, waiting their turns. Dr. Michi told me he talked with the family of one young man who had died since the last field trip. Based on the family's and the island's health aide's description of symptoms, Dr. Michi decided it probably was appendicitis. This re-enforced my belief that we had to install in a central part of outer island clusters, simple, short-wave, voice radios, powered by gas generators. We were able to install a couple during my fourth island year, when funds finally became available and Trukese on selected islands were trained to operate them.

After a while, I walked along the beach past the front of the canoe houses. I stopped twice to exchange greetings with old men sitting and standing inside them. Nearly all young men, except those working with our field trip party, were occupied with copra bagging and hauling.

The canoe houses were located along a graceful curve of the sandy beach in a sheltered cove. They were, except for the churches, the tallest buildings on Puluwat. They had a massive look, with thick corner posts, high ridgepoles, thatched sides, long pitched roofs and eaves which came to within a few feet of the ground. Inside the canoe houses, if not moored or beached in front of them, were the superbly crafted, graceful and sturdy sailing canoes. That afternoon I saw two canoes, pulled up on the beach in front of the canoe house. They were covered with mats woven from coconut fronds to protect the hulls from the sun.

Their sailing canoes were typically about twenty-five feet long and over four feet high from keel to gunwale. They almost always were made entirely from island materials. The biggest breadfruit tree was not large enough to make such a hull, so they built up its sides from bow to stern by cutting and shaping large pieces of breadfruit wood, using island-made tools much like their ancestors had. The canoe builders made minor concessions to modernity by using a chisel or two, plane and a little hand drill. Years after leaving Truk, anthropologist Tom Gladwin wrote a book about Puluwat's superb builders, navigators, and sailors of those great canoes. He titled it *East is a Big Bird*. I have been assisted in several of my construction descriptions by Tom's careful study of canoe building on Puluwat.

Untold centuries of experience had taught them the best hull and outrigger designs, every part of which curved gracefully. The mast would be set at a rakish angle to best help the sail catch the wind. Each plank of the hull was precisely shaped to fit perfectly with the one it adjoined. The hull parts were secured together, first by sealing them with gooey breadfruit sap "glue" which hardens somewhat, but is not nearly strong enough by itself to hold the parts of the hull together.

After the joints were caulked with coconut fiber rope, the built-up sides were further secured very tightly with *senet* criss-crossed through tiny drilled holes. On Puluwat, and on islands all over the district we field trippers would see men sitting around in canoe houses, sometimes in community buildings, visiting and passing the time, while at the same time making such rope. They would take coconut husk fibers, after they were soaked in water and carded, and roll them between the palm of their hands and one knee. The rolled strands were then rolled into other strands to make rope of different sizes. It is very strong and much more resistant to rot than manila rope.

Tom emphasized, after his detailed study of canoe building by those masters, the subtlety required in shaping the hull. "Every aspect of a canoe's performance," he wrote, "is determined in the last analysis by the contours of the hull. Yet the distinctions are too fine and the various contours too complexly interrelated for them to be taught in any other way than by example, or learned except by skilled observation and experience. Not everyone is equal to this challenge."

Some men started taking their own sons on voyages at the age of four or five, to create in them a love for the sea and the big canoes. Lives were at risk on such voyages. Should they have the bad fortune to encounter a *noto* (typhoon) at sea, their chances of survival were very poor. Sheets of rain, driven sideways by howling winds, and the fury of mountainous seas, with blinding spindrift, tossing those canoes of breadfruit wood and coconut fiber rope, around with little or no control, could throw the most skilled navigator badly off course. Puluwat sailors always were mindful of the sea god *Mwaresi,* and other sea spirits. Navigators were known to take a sea detour at a particular point on a voyage to avoid certain spirits which, they believed, ate canoes.

Going on past the canoe houses, I walked toward the copra loading area farther up the lagoon. It was now late afternoon, near our planned sailing time. I became aware of many young men and women standing quietly for several hundred yards along the beach. Down the middle of the narrow channel between Puluwat and the Alet islet, a paddling canoe moved silently, except for the dip of paddles. Two paddlers were near the bow and two more toward the stern. In the middle, the lone passenger, a man of about thirty, sat, head bowed, with a sad expression. Dr. Michi, standing near the copra loaders, told me he was sending the canoe passenger to the hospital at Moen because he had been losing weight steadily for no apparent reason and was becoming weak.

The young men and women along the beach called their goodbyes to him in subdued voices. Some women were crying. I watched this little drama, fascinated. Except for the physical setting, it might have been happening in any American small town. I made a point to follow the young man's case. He was cured and returned home two months later.

The captain, anxious to get moving, sent in the motor whaleboat to pick up our field trip party. The wind had come up again and was now blowing shoreward at fifteen to twenty knots and the sea was very choppy. After brief farewells to our island hosts, we climbed aboard and headed for the freighter. A few hundred yards out from the island reef a large wave suddenly hit our whaleboat. While the boat shuddered, its stern lifted sharply, then dropped. The jarring wave action caused the two copper pintle bolts which held the heavy wooden steering rudder in place, to jump out. It was a freak accident. The strong current, wind and waves combined to suddenly shift the course of our now unsteerable motor whaleboat away from a heading toward the ship. In seconds, it started drifting us rapidly toward the surf-pounded reef.

Sitting in the stern near the cox'n, I told him to shut off the engine since we couldn't steer. Other field trip party members looked anxiously toward the cox'n, who seemed baffled by this crisis. When I swung around to study the problem with the rudder, Tosiwo Nakayama, our young Trukese Island Affairs representative this trip, who had been sitting near the bow with several others, hurried back, knelt near me and peered over the stern. There was only one way to get out of this mess. The rudder pintles had to be slipped back into the empty, tube-like copper sleeves attached to the stern. Someone had to go over the side, into the rough, shark-infested sea. He'd need to descend until his face was below the surface, then horse the thick wooden tiller around until the pins were properly positioned and pushed into place. Meantime, the sound of waves pounding against the reef, and of surf breaking over it, grew louder.

While I hesitated, thinking of the sharks—some a dozen or more feet long, and the odds that one might attack a person dangling behind and under the stern, Tosiwo acted. He quickly removed his shoes, slid over the stern, sank below the surface and began to maneuver the pintles into place. In less than two minutes, after bobbing up breathlessly for air several times, and calling clipped instructions on how to position the upper part of the heavy wooden rudder, he had the job done.

I felt like a miserable coward for hesitating while this young islander took the risk. The cox'n started the engine, swung the bow until we quartered the waves and headed again for the freighter. It was nearly a year later before another small craft crisis—this time when our tug, *Bailhache,* ran onto a big coral head in Truk Lagoon, also with many sharks around, gave me the opportunity to partially redeem myself.

At sailing time the half-dozen Puluwat men still on the ship, some trying to make last minute purchases, were warned to get into their canoes. Several moved toward the rail, then drifted back to the traders. When they saw the dripping anchor chain coming up out of the water, they reluctantly slid into their bobbing outriggers piled with trade goods, and paddled clear of the ship.

Watching their canoes moving toward the island, after one more visit when their copra wasn't ready for loading, I smiled as I recalled the words of a Navy field trip officer's official report, written several years earlier, following a visit to Puluwat:

"The stubborn lack of cooperation of these people in trading, both with TTC and CIVAD (Naval Administration) personnel and among themselves has always led to confusion, waste of time and effort... The proper way to handle it," the writer concluded despairingly, "was explained to them several times."

Pulusuk

I was up shortly after sunrise and went out on deck. The sea was blue and much calmer than the day before. Captain Rathbun had made the short run during the night and brought the ship, bless him, to within less than a quarter-mile of the Pulusuk island reef. Some of our more cautious captains would have stood off much farther, even in fine weather like this. Two paddling canoes already were tied up alongside, and the dozen bags of copra they had hauled lay on the deck.

After breakfast, Eskiel Malon, a Trukese from the Mortlocks, who was our Education representative on this trip, and I got a ride in one of the canoes. It headed for the reef pass—barely wide enough to let us through. For us field trippers, to enter some of the most difficult passes here in the western islands or in the Mortlocks was a real hair raiser when the sea was kicking up. Trukese paddlers would position their canoe some yards outside the usually very narrow, sometimes crooked, pass into the lagoon. When a big wave came from behind, it suddenly started carrying them rapidly forward. As the canoe neared the reef, the swell would crash against it, sending spray all around, sometimes dampening down all aboard. The canoemen then had to use their highest skills, paddling and steering, to guide it through the reef opening without crashing against either side. Once inside, in bad weather, they had to work fast to keep the back surge from pulling the canoe backward onto the reef or open sea.

Today's weather made it a relatively easy passage from sea to atoll. As Eskiel and I stepped out of the canoe onto the sandy beach, a boy of about ten, wearing only a faded T-shirt, ran toward us, shouting urgently, *'Misineri uon sippo? Misineri uon sippo?"*

Father Fahey had stayed back on Puluwat. *"Ap!"* I answered, and Eskiel laughed.

The boy raced back up the beach, shouting this intelligence to the ladies who had despatched him. If my answer had been yes, the bare-breasted women would have slipped quickly into their ankle-length, baggy, shapeless "Mother Hubbards." These "costumes" were introduced first to Hawaii and later into these islands by New England missionaries. The Pulusuk women's concern about whether a missionary was aboard related only to the Protestants—excluding Pastor Hanlin, a sometimes field tripper, who took a tolerant view of traditional dress. None of the Jesuit Fathers spent any time worrying about or lecturing the people on female attire in these hot, humid islands.

A rain-soaked dress might take days to dry during a spell of stormy weather. Mother Hubbards had to be uncomfortable in the normal 85-degree daytime temperatures. They were easily dirtied if women wore them, which they rarely did, while performing such work as bathing their children, gardening, net fishing, cooking (except large starchy foods and a few others such as turtles) and cleaning the grounds around their homes. Most of the time they wore their *lavalavas.*

Walking up the sloping beach toward the village, I saw Chief Fatan standing in front of a canoe house, talking with two other men. I joined them, shaking hands. The chief was an old man—old by island standards, though he couldn't have been much past sixty. Taller than many Trukese, lean and angular, with blue tattoos, he didn't have then, if ever, that ruggedly powerful look of so many Pulusuk and Puluwat men. It was his face that drew attention. He had gray, thinning hair combed straight back, long ear loops, a patrician nose and chin, and calm watery dark eyes which fitted his weathered skin and seemed to reflect amused tolerance of all he saw around him. Even the most casual visitor could observe that his people liked and respected him. He impressed me as one of the oldest and most relaxed chiefs out in those western islands.

We sat in front of the canoe house and made small talk, pausing once to watch two older boys trying to maneuver a paddling canoe, overloaded with sacks of copra, out through the reef pass. Then I began asking him about the island. Our conversation followed a pattern now familiar to both of us. He spoke no English, but was thoughtful enough to speak slowly for me, so I thought I understood at least part of what he said. I wasn't sure he understood my spoken Trukese. I tried to speak in short, simple sentences. Sometimes I'd stop and ask if he understood. He always said yes. It was a form of politeness.

"Anybody with big sick?"

"Nobody sick."

"Maybe some little girl—little boy—sick?" I persisted.

"Nobody," he reconfirmed, looking at me steadily. I gradually concluded that persisting in questioning those western island chiefs, and some in other parts of the district, regarding illness wasn't useful, and stopped asking them. After the initial statement, they never changed their answers—never suddenly remembered that there was indeed a very sick woman or child. Why did they do this? Frank thought they still had great faith in their traditional medicine men. More often than not, it seemed, if there was a sick person and he or she didn't show up for sick call, the island health aide didn't mention it either, unless the family had come to him for help.

Far too many times after such a conversation with a chief, I'd walk around the island and learn from talking with small children that, yes, a little girl is sick in that house, or a man over there. My informant would point to the hut or house, and I'd go over and ask the mother if I may see the sick child. Quite often, in these western islands, he or she would be lying on a mat on the sand floor. (In Truk Lagoon and the Mortlocks, it would most likely be on a blanket on top of a mat covering a wooden floor.) I'd bring Clark or Michi over. Too often he would look at the child and say, especially in the case of tuberculosis, "If they'd just let us know last trip!"

"Any canoes out now?" I referred to canoes that might be out voyaging.

"One canoe to Namonuito."

"When did it leave Pulusuk?"

He paused. "Three nights."

Out here, they often used nights rather than days as a time reference. Father Rively said it was because they navigated by stars. So it wouldn't be overdue. I told Chief Fatan we'd look for it when we got there tomorrow. He didn't seem concerned. After all, Namonuito atoll was only eighty miles away. Occasionally people out here would tell us about an overdue canoe, and ask us to look for it on the way to and at the canoe's destination island. About once a year they sent word to us at Moen of an overdue sailing canoe. Would we please look for it? Depending upon weather, availability of our field trip ship, and other factors, we either searched or radioed the U.S. Search and Rescue people on Guam, to send an Air Force plane or a ship based there. Sometimes we'd ask pilots on the regular weekly flight through the district headquarters islands to circle over an island where the canoe would most likely be if not lost. They would drop a message in a cannister, asking if the canoe was there. If the answer was yes, the people were to form a big circle on the beach or make some other reply visible from the circling plane. Quite often the searchers found them at sea.

"Is there enough food now?" I asked.

"Food all right." The question was more in the nature of small talk.

This was the breadfruit season; with the tasty big green breadfruit balls hanging from almost every branch, it was their best eating time of the year.

"Any new court problem?" There was no Trukese word for case that I knew of. There was a word for trial or judgment—*apung.* The chief reached to scratch one greatly extended ear lobe, from within which, by tonight, he'd probably be carrying a package of Japanese brand cigarettes that TTC sold.

They hadn't come ashore yet. "No. No problem."

His answer did not surprise me. Court records were sketchy to non-existent out here. Island leaders had dealt in their own ways for centuries with offenses against all their unwritten laws and customs. I was convinced, and Frank agreed, they were continuing to handle many of them in the old ways, with very little thought for or mention of the "American" laws on the island, and thus with little or no need for records. Why should I be surprised? Even American department heads and the Constabulary would agree to handle certain problems outside the modern legal system if they thought by doing so justice would be better served. This type of arrangement seldom happened.

An example of where it did happen, at headquarters, was the Constabulary's dealing with Clark and Dr. Michi in the case of the hospital patient with hysterical blindness who had "kited" the check (raised the amount).

I wanted to ask Chief Fatan, Chief Romelo, or Chief Aluis on Ulul, if there were any sorcerers (*chon pout*) on his island, and where he stood regarding the matter. I hesitated to do it, partly because of my limited language knowledge—especially with the western islands' dialects. Moreover, I was concerned that any one of them might be offended that the *kepina* would raise such a delicate subject like this. Even so, I went so far as to try to put together words and phrases I'd need for my part in such a questioning.

I imagined I'd start by telling a chief how, in ancient times in the Hawaiian Islands, there were the *kahuna 'ana'anas:* sorcerers capable of placing a hex on an enemy or, for a fee, on someone else's enemy. The victim would fall ill, and he simply began to wilt away. Unless someone intervened on his behalf, he would likely die. Mostly, though, people did indeed intervene, and the man with the hex on him was saved.

I first heard about the *'ana'ana* type of *kahuna* from a friend who had grown up in Hawaii and later became a business executive with one of Hawaii's Big Five companies. Bob, who was my WWII cabin-mate on a destroyer in the Pacific, told me one of his great grandmothers had been adopted, as a child, into the Hawaiian royal family. He said modern doctors had examined hexed patients and found nothing physically wrong with them to account for the fast wasting illness of the victim. As soon as someone intervened and arranged to have the hex lifted, the victim rapidly recovered. When I saw Bob again in Hawaii in the early 1950s, he told me this situation still existed to a very limited degree in modern Hawaii. He had seen, over the years, several members of his own staff—those with some Hawaiian blood—who had been hexed. "I knew what was the matter the minute one of them walked into my office."

Years later, at the University of Hawaii Library, I read with fascination Thomas T. S. Leong's thesis for his Master's degree (1962) from the University of Southern Californa. It was titled, The Kahuna Institution of Hawaii. He indicated that in old Hawaii there had been at least seventeen different kinds of *Kahunas.* They ranged from community high priests, prophets and seers, to skilled navigators, canoe builders, herb doctors, and several kinds of traditional medicine men. All but the *kahuna 'ana'anas* were benign, respected, and they tried to make life better for the people.

But the sorcerer—*kahuna 'ana'ana*—was despised and regarded as virtually an evil spirit rather than a human. He worked mainly at home and at night, with his hexes, potions and other evil actions to help kill his targeted person. In modern Hawaii, I learned, most people have never heard of the *kahunas*. Of those who have, many of them seemed to very wrongly assume that, because of the *kahuna 'ana'ana's* reputation, most, if not all the other kinds of *kahunas* were evil.

In the end, I never raised the question with any of those three chiefs. I talked with Frank regarding my idea of asking them about sorcerers. His response was predictable. It is, he warned, a very delicate subject. He had talked about it with several of his closest Trukese informants. They indicated that a few *chon pouts* did exist in islands of the Truk District. More than a year after talking with Frank, I had separate conversations on the subject with two different Trukese friends whom I knew quite well. Each listened to my story about the *kahunas 'ana'ana* in ancient Hawaii. "We have that, too," one said solemnly. He didn't offer to elaborate. The other man told me they are known to be on the different islands. People know who they are, fear them, but didn't talk about them. I did not pursue the matter further.

People of the middle Carolines lived under three foreign governments before the Americans came. The Spanish made few changes beyond religious training. German rulers at the turn of the century confiscated guns and stopped warfare among the islanders. German missionaries organized and taught in some schools. Germans also helped plant coconut trees and build up copra trading. The Japanese brought many changes. Some lasting ones, besides the descendants of inter-marriages, were elementary education built into children of the era, and vocational training. Some Japanese-islander trading patterns continue.

Here, as in the rest of Micronesia, the church continued to grow as a powerful force for cultural change, and some of its beneficial effects were being felt. Some old ways were fading. Leaving Chief Fatan with his companions, I walked around and came upon Lou Gardella, our district Sanitarian. The Trukese affectionately called him "Mr. Lou." He stood surrounded by a circle of women, children and men too old to take part in the copra loading. His Trukese assistant, Nachsa Siren, translated for him. "It's no good to build nice *penchos* (privies), then walk past them and make poop-poop all along the beach," he told them, bubbling with vigor and goodwill. Mr. Lou had a way of impressing his listeners that, despite his light-hearted manner, his messages were serious and important. But with the combination of long, sandy beaches and high tides, mother nature provided one big flush toilet.

The Pulusuk people weren't convinced.

After one of the first visits to this island under Interior, our field trip officer presented in his written report a brief summary of island conditions, and concluded: "We held what we afterwards felt was a very unsatisfactory village meeting. We explained our hoped for program of agricultural development, the role of the UN in our Trusteeship and the change in administration from the Navy to Interior. There were no comments or questions." Chief Fatan would have smiled at that. I did and Frank doubtless did, too.

I believe most Americans on my staff who made field trips to the outer islands were convinced that the people here on Pulusuk and Puluwat were just as intelligent as any of us Americans, or any Trukese in other parts of the district. At least a few Americans thought it was fortunate in some respects that they had been much less exposed to foreign ways. Yet, we believed we had something worthwhile to offer them—even keeping in mind the plea of American Admiral Carleton Wright, who once was the Navy's Inspector General, and later its Deputy High Commissioner for the Trust Territory. Amazingly, the Admiral had visited every inhabited island in all six districts. He pleaded, in an article he wrote for the *Saturday Evening Post*:

> "...Let them alone in their happiness!...What a temptation they offer to the brisk missionaries of modernism, the bureaucrats, the sentimentalists and the busybody do-gooders."

We Americans believed we could help provide enough education and training so they could have better medical care, learn to grow better crops, raise better pigs and chickens, market their own copra, improve their fisheries, and learn a little about the world beyond Pulusuk and neighboring islands. Some day Trukese leaders would gather at the district government seat at Moen and beyond to make decisions affecting them. They might want an informed voice. Frank thought we could do these things with acceptable kinds of cultural change. Acceptable to whom? Frank believed that as the Trukese lived with changes we were helping to bring about, they would, in time see and believe the new gains were worth some cultural changes.

On this visit to Pulusuk, we bumped into one visible clash between old and new ways. Three teen-age boys had been judged by their teachers and our Education staff, over several recent field trips, to show exceptional promise as students. They were selected to attend the intermediate boarding school on Moen. All three accepted the offer.

The future of these young men took a sudden sharp turn when it came to the attention of their mothers that they had gathered their few simple personal effects and some food and were about to embark on the freighter to Moen. Either the mothers hadn't noticed their offsprings' preparations earlier or were slow to react. Now, near embarkation time, they announced firmly in concert, and in language no one could misunderstand, that no sons of theirs were going to leave Pulusuk to live for years on some strange, faraway island just to sit in a school. We sailed without them. That kind of experience seldom happened in the western islands. It surprised me.

A western islands man might spank his wife because she didn't have food ready in the evening. And she might have to crawl and crouch in the presence of men. But here was a matter about which some women obviously felt strongly, and had the courage to speak out. They prevailed. We admired them for that. Now, our Education people and Frank and I agreed, we'd better try to regroup: develop ways to convince mothers and other family members in the western islands of the reasons why at least a few of their children should be encouraged and permitted to get an education beyond elementary school. Then they could, like Dr. Michi, Tosiwo Nakayama, and other relatively well-educated Trukese, help them have a better life right there on their own islands. It would be a long, slow process.

I kept wishing we could talk with Arthur Grimble, that long ago Governor of the Gilbert & Ellice Islands, and other South Seas administrators like him, with decades of experience behind them. Especially I'd have liked to think with them about the part where government projects on any island inevitably tend to bring cultural change. The British island administrators in the Pacific, at least in Grimble's time, however, didn't try to make as many social and economic changes as we did. They were administering British colonies and not, like us, trying to help prepare their people for independence. Still, Grimble—like Michael Bernacchi, a later Governor of those same islands and the Line Islands—was very concerned about fiddling with the culture.

Namonuito Atoll: Four Tiny Islands

We sailed from Pulusuk during the night. Our ship had called at the four Hall islands early on the trip, before going on to these western islands. The people in the Hall Islands, being only about fifty miles north of Truk Lagoon, had closer ties with the people there and thus their ways were more alike.

Little Punlap and Tamatam, northeast of Puluwat, were in many ways an extension of the island life we were about to visit next: Namonuito Atoll—biggest in the western part of the district. It is triangular in shape, more than thirty miles wide at its base, and dotted with five populated reef islands, four of which are among the smallest in the district. Its reef passages are too small and shallow for a freighter to enter.

Long before daylight the next morning I was awakened by the sudden change in the pulsing rhythm of the ship's big diesel engine. It paused, then quickened and the whole ship vibrated as it went into reverse. I heard faintly an order called down from the bridge, an echoing acknowledgment from a sailor in the bow, followed by anchor chains rattling through the hawse pipe. Then silence.

We stayed less than a day at each of the first four tiny reef islands, where there is quite a similarity both in appearance and their struggle for existence. Each is less than a half-mile long and a few hundred yards wide. Each had a population of sixty or fewer. Seen from their curving white beaches, here was all the natural beauty of the tropics, surrounded by some of the world's prettiest shades of sea color, coconut and pandanus trees, bright blue skies, fat, fleecy convection clouds. Walk across each island, though, and it presents a different aspect.

Except for Ulul, which we visited last, those other four islands, sitting astride the atoll's barrier reef, are so narrow that plants are poorly shielded from salt spray Thus some could not produce bananas. On none of the four did plant life thrive. Coconut, breadfruit and pandanus trees were exceptions. After the breadfruit season ended, people often were forced to eat coconut meat (copra)—a sure sign that food was really scarce.

While visiting on those islands, where each person knew all the others and what they were doing almost every waking moment, I wondered how they kept from getting cabin fever. I tried to imagine the strong restraints in personality and temperament they had to practice—probably much more than on larger islands—so all could live together in reasonable harmony. They gave the outward appearance of being about as happy as people on bigger islands. Maybe an important part of their coping with smallness was that they looked out upon the atoll barrier reef, with its perimeter of about 100 miles, as a living community of plant and sea life and as part of their own home grounds. The men, especially, spent much time out on it. And their frequent visits to neighboring islands provided at least some diversion.

Ulul

Our last stop on the trip. Ulul is much larger than any of the other four islands. It was the home island of Tosiwo Nakayama, our Island Affairs department representative on this trip—who swam among the sharks at Puluwat a few days earlier when we lost our whaleboat rudder. Tosiwo was born on little, nearby Piserach, in this atoll. His mother was Trukese. His father, who was Japanese, had worked for a large homeland trading company until he was repatriated to Japan at war's end. Tosiwo was warmly greeted here on Ulul by people of all ages, including Chief Aluis Opich, his uncle. Tosiwo was our only western islands employee at headquarters.

Taller than most Trukese, with a big shock of black wavy hair, a quiet manner and almost shy smile, Tosiwo was looked upon by other Trukese and the Americans on our staff as one of our ablest young employees. Later, when the Congress of Micronesia was created, Tosiwo became its first President. Still later, when the Truk District joined together with three other districts to become a new independent nation—the Federated States of Micronesia—Tosiwo became their first President. This young man was born in a part of the district where Truk Lagoon people had tended to look upon western islanders as coarser, tougher types. Many years after my family and I left the islands, Tosiwo told me in a letter more about his educational background. Parts in parenthesis are my additions.

"Napo DeFang's mother and my mother were promised sisters. (Tosiwo explained the term: They were not blood relatives but became such close friends that they agreed to be sisters for life.) "I grew up on Lukunoch (Lukunor in the Mortlocks, to which area his father was transferred by his Japanese company, and worked for some years) knowing that Napo was related to me. When I went to intermediate school on Moen, (after the U.S. Navy military government took over) Napo was Superintendent of Schools in Truk District. He took care of me then. One day he and Thomas Gladwin came to my class... They asked me to quit school and work for Thomas Gladwin in the 'office' and that my salary would be $15.00 a month. I was not impressed by that $15.00.

"Thomas Gladwin then told me, 'You will have to learn how to type.' I used to admire those working in the office and pounding away on the typewriter. So I asked them, 'Did you get permission of my chief for me to work, because I am here studying how to teach so that when I finish I would go back to Onoun (Ulul) to teach? This I promised the people of Onoun and Chief Raatior.' They replied by saying that they did get Raatior's permission for me to work so I said, 'Yes, I will quit school and work for you.'

"My first assignment was just to type. I worked for Tom Gladwin for several years until 1951, when I told him I wanted to resign to go back to Onoun to learn the arts of navigation from my uncle Raatior. (Raatior Opich was his older uncle on his mother's side.) But when I went home to Onoun, he had already passed away. I stayed until six months later when PICS was opening up and accepting students from all over Trust Territory.

"Napo sent a member of his staff to tell me to come to Moen to attend PICS... So I stayed in PICS until I graduated. And I went back to work in the 'office'. When I applied for a scholarship to go to school in Hawaii, it was only for one person. Napo won the scholarship but he decided that I should share with him using half of the scholarship to study in Hawaii and he will use half to study in Guam. This was in 1955."

That ended Tosiwo's written description of the formal educational part of the making of a future president of a new island nation. His listing in the publication *Micronesian Biographies* indicates that he studied at the University of Hawaii (1955-58). He then returned to work for the Truk District government. In 1964 he became Assistant District Administrator. In the years ahead he moved progressively upward to finally occupy the highest public office in the new Federated States of Micronesia.

After meeting with Chief Aluis, who had been Chief Raatior's younger brother, I walked around the island. It is one of the prettiest of the western islands, and it gave a feeling of spaciousness and lushness. About 180 people lived here. Beneath the canopy of breadfruit, coconut trees, and banana plants, there was a profusion of color: tall green grass, hibiscus—some flaming red, others bright yellow—oleander, frangipani and ginger flowers. It also had the biggest coconut plantation in all the district, developed after the turn of the century by a German trader from over on Ponape.

I had not walked far when I saw Mr. Lou and Nachsa Siren, near a wooden house with a tin roof, talking with some people. They were gathered around a thick, square cement water catchment tank, built in Japanese times and used for collecting rain water. Coming nearer, I stood at the edge of the half-circle and listened.

"Look, see!" Nachsa carefully probed with a small stick at something floating on top of the water. "Baby mosquitos! Soon they will be big mosquitos! If they bite you, you can become sick, maybe with 'big leg.' Why don't you keep the tank covered?" he implored the gathering.

The little audience of several women and older men, looked at him undisturbed. One elderly man with ear loops and few teeth, said the children like to play around the catchment, and they forget to replace the lids. Nachsa spoke to me in English in a low aside, "They don't understand about larvae. They don't believe a mosquito bite will make them sick."

Lou turned suddenly and pointed in the direction of some tall grass and bushes beyond the edge of the village. "There's one of those damned ugly monitor lizards! I hate 'em!"

His exclamation evoked memories of our first trip together to Ulul, when, while visiting with Chief Aluis and some other islanders, Lou and I first saw a monitor lizard.

"What in hell is that?" Lou had asked in a voice filled with revulsion.

Chief Aluis smiled as Nachsa translated Lou's question.

"Lizard," he replied.

"Where did they come from?" Lou practically demanded. "I haven't seen them on any other island!"

I could appreciate his feeling, since I had reacted similarly to the big, ugly green creatures with reptile-like heads, flashing red eyes, moveable eyelids, and long, thin tongues which darted out and in almost faster than the eye could see to snare insects. The one we saw that day must have stood eighteen inches high and close to four feet long from the tip of its nose to the end of its long tail. It looked prehistoric, with feet shaped like an alligator's, a rough, scaly skin and serrated back.

The chief, obviously enjoying our reaction to the lizard, continued to smile. "Japanese bring them," he answered.

"For God's sake, *why?*" Lou asked.

"Rats," the chief replied. "Rats," he repeated. "When Japanese first come to live on Ulul, we have many rats. Rats everywhere. They go in our houses," he nodded toward a grass hut. "They eat our copra. Eat too much copra."

"Why didn't the Japanese just bring in cats?" Lou asked.

"Don't know," Chief Aluis grinned. "Maybe Japanese don't like *kattu.*"

"It sure as hell must have worked!" our usually equable sanitarian said grudgingly. "I haven't seen a rat on Ulul."

"Chief Aluis says it worked too much," Nachsa interpreted. The chief's tone became more serious. Nachsa listened, then turned again to Lou. "He says the Japanese brought in four, maybe five lizards. Pretty soon, maybe four months, maybe six, there were no more rats on Ulul. Then trouble started."

"Trouble? What kind of trouble?" Lou's tone was now moderated and curious. The other islanders, following every spoken word, were smiling. The Trukese greatly enjoy a good story. Although they doubtless had heard versions of this one before, they settled back and were savoring it again.

"They eat our chickens," the chief said, smiling. "Soon we had no one chicken on Ulul. Today no chicken lives on Ulul."

"How many lizards are there now?" Lou asked.

"Don't know," the chief replied. "Maybe twenty. Maybe more."

"Why don't you get rid of the bastards?"

The young translator smiled and turned to the chief. "Mr. Lou asks why don't you kill them?"

"Rats come back," Chief Aluis said. "We don't want one rat to come back."

By the time my family and I left the islands, Ulul still had its green lizards, no rats and no chickens, except for a few scrubby ones kept in pens.

I left Lou and his friends and walked back down the village path. Seeing a heavy rain squall approaching in the distance, I hurried toward a big canoe house. One end was piled with sacks of copra waiting to be loaded. At the other end, almost a fixture in canoe houses, several old men sat talking and smoking. I went over and joined them. The cloying aroma of the bagged copra filled the air. After exchanging greetings and a few other simply-worded pleasantries with them, addressing no one in particular, I asked, "Could Ulul people cut 700 sacks of copra each time the ship comes?" That would be twice as much as they made for this trip.

A man with blue tattoos of the rising sun of the Japanese empire on his chest, faced me. "*Ewer* (yes), he replied without hesitation. The others nodded in solemn agreement.

"Why don't they?"

"*Pweta?*" (Why?) he asked me. The impassive expression on the faces of the other old men told me they regarded his answer as serious and reasonable.

Trukese, like people in most of the Pacific Island world, place a high premium on leisure time, just as they do on hospitality. The income from the 350 sacks—more than seventeen tons—being loaded this trip would be enough to purchase all they desired or considered real needs at the time: rice, flour, sugar, cloth, cigarettes, perhaps a few tins of corned beef and, a Trukese favorite: oval tins of fish from Japan, packed in a rich, tangy tomato sauce. They might also buy new machetes, pomade, bottles of cheap perfume, and a few might purchase lanterns. After all purchases from the ship's hold were made, there would still be several hundred dollars in cash coming ashore at Ulul. Probably centuries ago these islanders had learned that one road to happiness is to minimize wants.

The clan-sharing tradition surely also affected copra output here. A man had limited incentive to cut more than a few bags between ship calls. Most of the extra earnings, if he did cut more, would end up being shared, like in Sergeant Kumio's experience, with others in the lineage, some of whom didn't bother to cut much copra at all.

The rain squall hit hard. In minutes, more than a dozen copra loaders came in, rain dripping off their skins, making them glisten. They talked and kidded with each other in loud, animated voices. Since wet copra would not be accepted, this seemed like a good time for the community meeting. Chief Aluis, who had joined the gathering, agreed.

A large conch shell was sent for and blown. This brought men, women and children, including members of our field trip party, who had sought shelter in the nearest place when the squall hit. Except for the chief and field trip party, which he invited to the front, everyone sat on the sand floor, women on one side and men on the other. The chief opened the meeting with traditional words for such gatherings.

"*Iwe, masanasana!*" (All right, let's have your attention!) Turning first to us,

167

then to his people, he spoke. "Ulul people welcome the ship and those people from the *Ofis*. They come to teach us how to live better. We must listen to them. We must remember words they speak."

We field trippers tended to follow a pattern in community meetings: the field trip officer spoke first, then called on department heads or their representatives. Too many Americans still had to speak with an interpreter, though some continued to study Trukese. Each speaker, depending upon the activity he represented, reported his findings on island conditions. He praised accomplishments, offered suggestions for improvements in health, sanitation, the school, or food production. We told of changes in copra grading standards—a sore subject, certain to bring a rumble of comment from males present, and reported any expected changes in copra prices. The latter was based on world market prices, the wild fluctuations of which were cushioned for the islanders by a copra stabilization fund operated out of Island Trading Company headquarters in Hawaii. Islanders usually were paid about $5.00 for a 100-pound sack.

Sometimes we told them about an upcoming special meeting of chiefs, a planned visit to Truk Lagoon by the High Commissioner or a congressional party. We were wasting our time with these last two items. Their little world was tightly circumscribed.

At this meeting, when Eskiel Malon spoke he reminded them that no child under ten was going to school at Ulul, though they were supposed to start at seven. Too many children, he admonished parents, never attend. He urged them to send their children to school and instruct them to obey the teachers. Maintaining class discipline was not, as Cy Pickerill later painfully noted, a strong point with most young teachers.

Herb Wilson had made a swing through these islands a year earlier. At the end of that trip he wrote in his report about his findings:

"In general, educational conditions in the western islands are poor. The teachers are ineffectual, mostly because of their own uncertainty and insecurity, and the program presented is sterile." He noted several exceptions—where teachers had introduced practical arithmetic lessons like how to figure the amount Island Trading owed the copra seller, and how much he owed Truk Trading Company for his purchases. The women throughout the islands doubtless would have loved to go aboard to look at all the trade goods, and purchase some. Selling copra and buying trade goods was, unfortunately for them, one more part of a man's world out here.

The rain stopped as suddenly as it began. The late afternoon sky turned blue again. Ulul men jumped up, brushed sand off their bodies, and began to move more copra to canoes at the beach. Chief Aluis offered no apologies for their abrupt departure. This was the way things worked during ship visits. Our field trip speakers completed their remarks to the remaining people: women, older men and a few children. Then Chief Aluis made a closing comment and adjourned the meeting.

We sailed after dark for Truk Lagoon's North Pass, where the captain estimated we'd arrive at noon the next day. We had more copra than usual in the holds, and fewer passengers—different from the Mortlocks, where we often had to turn away people who wanted to visit Truk Lagoon. Weather this trip had been better than we expected. For that reason and because the chief engineer experienced no troubles this time with his sometimes balky piston sleeve liners, we hadn't found it necessary to bypass any island. It was a good field trip.

Searching For Sea Dollars

Often on Saturday or Sunday mornings a half-dozen or more enthusiastic American weekend fishermen headed for the barrier reef with their fishing gear, lunches and soft drinks. They returned near sundown, sunburned and almost always loaded with big yellow-fin tuna, red snapper, grouper and other fine eating fish. They had enough to give to neighbors, and they spoke extravagantly of all the fish out there.

Several economic development consultants with whom our headquarters contracted over the years and sent through Micronesia, would fly in, look around each district for a few days to a week, and ask lots of questions. Each time they offered about the same conclusions: the three most promising sectors for expanding the cash economy are fisheries, tourism and agriculture. They qualified the tourism proposal by noting that this would have to wait until some future time when the Navy relaxed its tight security control over the area. And they qualified agricultural development prospects by noting the very limited amount of land in Micronesia.

Russ Curtis, his small industry development specialist Barney Chung and I were convinced that here was a substantial dollar-earning opportunity for the Trukese. Big Japanese fishing boats, some of them outfitted for purse seine or pole fishing, and others with forty to sixty or more miles of long-line with hooks, flags, and glass float balls strung out behind them, operated near Truk District and other territorial waters. Day after day they harvested tons of big yellow-fin and other tuna. U.S. Navy patrol ships out of Guam, enforcing the three-mile limit—changed years later to twelve miles, and still later, to 200 miles for fishing—reported their presence to us. Mother ships took their catches, so they could remain at sea for long stretches.

We saw that the Trukese fished with spears, hooks and lines, wooden fish traps, hand-held nets, and throw nets. A few owned big nets, requiring several men to handle them. While Truk Lagoon men fished both in waters around their own islands and out on the great barrier reef and beyond, women fished only in shallow waters off the island beaches and by island reefs.

By Moen's shores we'd often see a half-dozen or more women, fully dressed except for shoes, wading waist deep, proceed to surround small schools of fish by forming an ever-tightening circle with their fan or butter-fly-shaped nets. They fished mostly in daytime. Sometimes, though, they went out at night. When we drove along the beach road after dark, we saw them with their coconut frond torches glowing. The torches helped them see better, helped attract fish to their nets, and gave them a greater sense of protection against lurking, unknown spirits. Men often went fishing with their wives at night.

Barracuda, with rows of razor-sharp teeth, occasionally attacked the rough-woven pouches the women tied in front of them or draped on their hips to hold their catches. Too often, the hospital treated a patient who had been fishing when a barracuda lunged for the fish in her basket and nearly disemboweled her or tore flesh out of her hip or thigh. In deeper waters, sharks sometimes attacked men the same way.

Gil Korenaga, one of our two agriculturists, and Sam Mukaida, a teacher trainer at the intermediate school, sometimes went fishing with Trukese friends around Moen Island. Both of them, having grown up in Hawaii, were interested to observe that when the women fished with their nets at night, they chewed coconut meat and spat it out onto the water to make it calm and clear, just as the Hawaiians do.

One night Sam and Gil were invited by Trukese friends to go with them to catch octopus—considered a delicacy in those islands. That view was not shared by many Americans in the islands. The Trukese would spot one and call urgently to Sam and Gil, "Catch it! Catch it!"

"We couldn't even see it!" Gil told some of us later. He and Sam were fascinated and repelled to watch the men kill an octopus by biting off its head and squashing its brains while it coiled its tentacles around its human adversary.

When the Trukese talked with us about ways they might earn more dollars, one of our responses was to point to the rich sea harvest waiting in the ocean all around them. About a year after we took over from the Navy, Chief Ennis Nedelek from Fefan Island, who had shown interest in such discussions about commercial fishing possibilities, made an appointment for himself and two other men from Fefan to see Russ Curtis, Barney Chung, and me regarding that subject. Ennis was skipper of one of TTC's forty-foot schooners that traded around the outer islands.

"If the *ofis* can help men from Fefan get a boat about thirty or forty feet long, with a good storage hold and a little Japanese engine," Ennis said, enthusiasm showing in his eyes and expression, "we can go in deep water and bring back enough fish to help feed several islands."

Then he asked whether the Fefan fishermen might sell fish to our PICS and intermediate school central dining room on Moen and to the American Jesuit missionaries for use in boarding schools they operated on Moen. If this worked well, he added, they could think about acquiring more boats and catch fish for sale on Guam. Maybe they could even revive the dried bonito industry, which thrived under the Japanese administration. After all, for many pre-war years the Japanese had operated a big fish-drying factory at Truk and exported dried fish to Japan.

"How do you propose to finance this project?" we asked Ennis. This was all in English, which he spoke well.

"We Fefan people will save some money," he said. "Can the *ofis* lend us some of the money we will need?"

"How much can you raise on Fefan?" we asked. With Sergeant Kumio's experience still fresh in mind, I was skeptical.

"Maybe one-fourth. Maybe one-third.... We think we can earn enough in four or five years to pay back the *ofis*."

We had several follow-up talks with Chief Ennis and the two other men who came with him from Fefan. Once they brought in a roughly penciled sketch of a little fishing boat much like Ennis had described. We helped them draw up specifications. Then we located addresses and wrote to several Japanese builders of such small boats. A reply came back promptly from one builder, along with designs and specifications for a fine looking twenty-eight foot fishing boat with a wooden hull. It had a good-sized hold and a simple pompom engine that took up little space.

Wellington Ott, our Public Works officer, who was, along with his other skills, a diesel expert, studied the drawing spread out on his desk. When he came to the description of the little two-cylinder engine, his head came up and he whacked the desk-top in appreciation.

"My gawd! Like the man says, you could repair one of those little things with a chunk of coral, a piece of wire and a pair of pliers. We could teach a Trukese in two weeks to be a boat mechanic."

We worked with them on some estimates of a year's income and expenses after they could start fishing with such a boat. Then we wrote to headquarters, proposing to help the Fefan people get the boat. Following Chief Ennis's suggestion, we recommended that the Fefan fishermen should raise one-third of the total cost of around $3,500, and that HICOM make a loan for the rest to the Fefan Fishermen's Cooperative, which they'd organize. We thought if HICOM didn't have such a fund—and we hadn't heard of one at that point— it should be established to encourage islander initiatives by providing modest amounts of "seed money." Several weeks passed; then came a reply from Honolulu. The proposal looks economically and technically feasible. HICOM, regretfully, has no funds to make such a loan.

About the time headquarters said they couldn't help with the proposed fishing venture, I flew to Guam for a few days, where I bumped into Henry M."Hank" Hedges, District Administrator for the Northern Marianas. He was down on business from his headquarters on Saipan, about 120 miles to the north.

Before I first met Hank, a Trust Territory employee from another district who had become acquainted with him back in Honolulu, told me about him. "He's a wealthy retired businessman and yachtsman who always smokes big cigars, is chuckly and looks like a South Seas planter." The description wasn't bad, as far as it went.

He was tall, erect, florid, with a thick black mustache and thinning iron gray hair, and he always wore a woven, flat-topped planter's hat and a ready smile. About fifty years old when I first met him, he had owned a successful engineering firm in Chicago, which he sold and "retired" at age thirty-nine to go sailing with his wife, Connie, in their own big schooner in the South Pacific around Tahiti. The *Askoy* had, among other things, a steel hull, two Tahitian crewmen, thick carpeting and a piano. During WWII the Navy recruited him as an engineer to help build airfields on several Pacific islands. While spending some time after WWII in Honolulu, Hank sang in a barber shop quartet with an admiral and a couple of businessmen with whom he had become friendly. Those barbershop buddies urged the High Commissioner to persuade Hank to come out of retirement and join his staff.

Hank and I had dinner together the following evening at a little downtown restaurant. I'd spent enough time around him to know that his spirits were usually strongly upbeat. But this evening something was wrong. He was the most subdued I had seen him. When the meal was finished, Hank carefully removed and cleaned his glasses; then he told me his sad story.

Somewhere along the line Saipanese men had lost their deep-sea fishing skills. That did not seem important to them because there were plenty of fish around the island reefs. Meantime, the Japanese were off Northern Marianas shores a few miles, like at Truk, harvesting yellow-fin tuna with their longlines. Hank had decided, he told me, to do something about it. He identified a small group of Saipanese men who sounded seriously interested in getting into a commercial fishing operation.

"I talked it up with them for two or three months," he said. "When the Navy was still running Saipan, there was a young officer who also had seen the fishing possibilities. He got the people stirred up, but he was transferred before he could get something going.

"I got a few of the most interested ones together—maybe a dozen—and told them I'd be willing to find an old reefer and get it in working shape. I showed them how we could fly frozen fish down here to Guam and sell in this wide-open market. The military would be a big market. We get a lot of flights into Saipan, and most of them return with empty cargo space."

He stopped, got the waiter's eye, and called for more coffee. Then he turned back to me. "Things started out fine. I got the freezer going nicely. We began sending small shipments of frozen tuna down here by air..." He stopped again. Leaning back in his chair, he half-closed his eyes and puffed slowly on his cigar a few times.

"By God, Will!" he said, sitting forward, "those Japanese fishermen must have known we were opening a market here! They sent word in to some Guamanians that they'd sell unlimited quantities of tuna for twelve cents a pound. We just couldn't compete with that..." I saw the pain in his eyes. The infant Saipan commercial fishing operation was dead.

Back on Moen, I told Russ and Barney about Hank's experience with the Marianas fishermen. They also found his story pretty discouraging. It seemed clear that we'd better not build up any hopes on the part of the Trukese about exporting fish to Guam or Japan.

Still, we continued to see Trukese, and our own enthusiastic American fishermen, returning from the barrier reef with their impressive reminders of the wealth out there. How to capture some of it on a larger scale? We kept seeing the Japanese fishing boats beyond the three-mile limit. Occasionally one of them had a crewman with a medical emergency, and the Navy gave permission for them to enter our harbor. Alongside our dock, they would open a hold, give away a few beautiful big frozen tuna, then offer to sell unlimited amounts at ten cents a pound.

We became encouraged again. This time we took a different tack. We talked with Chief Petrus, Chief Ennis and others about trying to interest a major American seafood corporation in coming to Truk. It should be a joint venture, we suggested, with the corporation putting up the money and technical know-how and the Trukese providing shore sites and most of the work force. The corporation surely would need a processing or freezing plant ashore and they'd need sailors to help man the fishing boats and do the fishing. The Trukese were all for it.

We sent a letter to HICOM, outlining such an approach, and asked them to contact several of the largest West Coast seafood firms. After many weeks replies arrived, forwarded by our Honolulu office. Each answer was brief, similar and disappointing. They had no plans at this time to expand operations into our part of the Pacific.

By now, we began to wish we could ask the Japanese to come in as fishing partners, and I'm certain the Trukese did, too. But we knew the Navy's security policy. Besides, we thought, the Japanese commercial fishermen seemed to be doing fine without shore bases in the islands.

Years later, long after I'd left the Pacific, Van Camp Seafoods finally checked out the Trust Territory as a new source of tuna supply. They conducted surveys in all six districts, then built a freezing plant in the Palau Islands of the western Carolines, about 1,000 miles west of Truk. Palauan and some Asian fishermen caught the tuna and Van Camp hauled them back to their processing plant in American Samoa or San Diego.

One day many years after I had left the islands, out of curiousity I phoned Van Camp in California. Soon I was talking with Bernard Fink, then a Vice-President of the company. He had been involved in the 1964 survey and follow-on operations in the Palau Islands. "Why," I asked, "did you pick Palau over Truk or Ponape or the Marshalls, which are 1,000 to more than 2,000 miles closer to the West Coast?"

"Well," he answered, "the thing hinged mainly on *bait*. We found the best bait supply in Palau. We used a little anchovy-like fish called *nehu*—maybe a Hawaiian word. They are about an inch-and-a-half long. The waters off Palau are a meeting place for the north equatorial current, which runs westward, and the north equatorial counter-current, which runs eastward. Where these two meet, the water is roiled. This causes the fish food supply to become enriched.

"Another important consideration," he added, "was that the Palau area had been heavily and rather successfully fished by the Japanese, so we knew the fish were there."

"How's the project working out?" I asked.

"We're just closing down out there after about twenty years," he said. "Each year over that whole period we either operated slightly in the red or just broke even."

Pearly Shells Below the Water

The pre-war Japanese civil administration introduced the shells into Truk Lagoon. A cash-earning, self-regenerating marine harvest, the trochus shell is conical shaped, gray-green on the outside, pearly on the inside, and when fully mature has a base of four to five inches in diameter. Living inside its shell house is a member of the snail family. It exists only on underwater plant life and needs oxygen, so it thrives in the warm, shallow water that covers a barrier reef. After the war, the Trukese continued to harvest the shells. They sold them to firms in Japan, where their pretty interiors were used to manufacture mother-of-pearl type buttons, ornaments and jewelry.

When the U.S. Navy moved into Truk after the war, they wisely brought in marine biologists who surveyed the trochus beds and recommended limiting the harvest season to two weeks a year. One of my first official acts as the new civilian district administrator had been to continue that Navy district order, which controlled shell harvest, and had the force of law.

Trochus season was an exciting time for the Trukese. Paddling canoes from every island in the lagoon congregated at the barrier reef. Each extended family had its own section of the reef for taking trochus. The place swarmed with young and middle-aged men in shorts, equipped with spears, prying picks and home-made diving goggles. After a few days of harvesting, drying and removing the snails, the first canoe and power boat cargos began to arrive at landings near Baker dock. Workers unloaded wet gunnysacks filled with shells—exceedingly foul-smelling because of the dead snails recently removed from them.

They sold their shells to Island Trading Company, which exported them. The Trukese people earned about $40,000 a year from the total harvest, which was a good return for the short season. We helped them expand trochus planting to atolls in the Mortlocks. This, in time, aided in modestly boosting their dollar earnings.

George Davis, who replaced Gil Korenaga at the end of his tour, as assistant agriculturists, might have argued with anyone suggesting it was easy money. George, who was assigned additional duties as the district administration's monitor of trochus activities, believed in understanding problems at first hand. One day he joined some islander harvesters down at the southeast part of the reef beyond Uman Island. Unlike Trukese divers, the young Vermonter decided he wasn't an agile enough swimmer to carry a spear gun to guard against sharks and at the same time carry a pick to pry shells loose from the reef.

"I had just loosened a shell maybe six or eight feet under water," he recalled. "when I noticed some movement off to my left. A shark ten or twelve feet long swam past maybe twenty feet from me and kept hanging around. I was plenty scared. Then I saw one of the Palauan scrap metal project workers who had come along with us that day, swimming slowly toward me with his spear gun. He motioned me to follow him slowly. The boat was about forty feet away. When we finally got to it and our heads were out of water, he told me to take it real easy getting into the boat. It was awfully hard to keep from hurrying up over the side, but I followed instructions and the shark swam away."

I learned some years after leaving Truk that Japanese shirt and other clothing makers eventually found themselves priced out of the market for this button material, due to the continued scarcity of trochus shells in relation to a soaring demand and thus rising prices for them. The clothing industry shifted to buttons made of cheaper materials. That was a hard blow for Truk's trochus harvesting.

"This Is My Food"

John Smith was in his middle twenties when he came with his wife, Lola, to Truk two months after I did. A farm boy with all the freshness of a spring morning, and a degree in agriculture from Iowa State, he soon realized he had his work cut out for him.

How can a cheerful, energetic young man from the Iowa heartland help South Sea islanders become better farmers, when they have been growing food by their tried and proven ways for many hundreds of years? And when this American, until coming to the Pacific, had never seen a breadfruit tree or a taro patch? That was the problem our new district agriculturist faced.

Russ Curtis was, as Island Affairs officer, John's immediate supervisor. He told me he liked the way John was tackling his new job. John began by traveling around the islands to study the farming situation at first hand. Considering that most farms in the community where he grew up were 160 to 600 acres or more, what he saw those first few months must have shaken him. If it did, he never let on.

He began to see that the Truk District's greatest shortage is arable land. The entire district has about fifty square miles, scattered over an ocean area of 180,000 square miles. At least fifteen to twenty percent of the land was used for houses, other buildings, pathways, roads—the latter on Moen and Dublon Islands only. On the dozen high islands in Truk Lagoon, parts of the mountainous areas were too steep for agricultural uses.

This was extremely serious for two reasons: Truk's economy was historically based on subsistence farming and fishing. The population was increasing at the rate of approximately three percent a year—one of the fastest growing in the world. Anything that grows at three percent, whether it is interest earned on money, increase in forest tree volume, or population, will double in twenty-four years. And the Trust Territory had no family planning program.

Every part of Truk—like the rest of Micronesia—is a fragile environment, but the low coral outer islands are fragile in the extreme. Rainfall is about 125 inches a year, with much of it falling at night. Weed and insect control in the tropics is a harsh, running battle.

Frank Mahony, who became one of John's close friends, was fascinated by the Trukese people's preoccupation with food—especially breadfruit.

"Despite all the rain," I heard him tell John and several other newcomers in an orientation session, "Truk still has three—sometimes four—very dry months. This can be disastrous for an island's food supply, even when much of it comes from trees. When a typhoon hits an island even a glancing blow, much of the food-producing capability is wiped out for months—even years. Thus," he would emphasize, "we see food as an extraordinary concern to all Trukese. But on low islands, where population pressures are greatest, their preoccupation with food is greatest."

When Trukese men showed us Americans their crop lands they never said, "This is my land." They always said, "This is my *food*."

John began to see how the Trukese had developed over many centuries practical ways of growing food. He also saw that the mainstays of the food supply in this part of the middle Carolines, besides fishing, were breadfruit and taro. Breadfruit is a tree crop. Taro, a plant with beautiful big green leaves shaped like arrowheads, has thick, fleshy, edible roots. Hawaiians make their *poi* from taro. Crops of less importance were sweet potatoes and yams, squash and manioc (tapioca). On the high islands there was a thin scattering of sugarcane and vegetables such as Chinese cabbage. Then there were those wonderfully tasty fruits: pineapples, mangos, papayas, bananas, and limes.

He decided to start out by working on something an Iowa farmer would know a lot about: pigs and chickens. Later, when he became better educated about island agriculture, he would take the next steps.

When he told me he wanted to revamp and expand the pig and chicken projects, which the Navy had started, I asked, "Why?"

"The Trukese diet's mostly starch," he said. "Fish, pork and chickens are about their only other sources of protein. People have very few pigs or chickens. You've seen the pigs. They look awful—scrawny, inbred. Trukese students at PICS tell me that in the dry season when there's no breadfruit, the people, especially on low islands, eat coconut meat. They consider that rock bottom. But it's the only bulky food left, besides taro."

"What'll they feed the pigs?"

"Coconuts. Breadfruit that falls and busts up. Fallen papaya.... Things like that...."

"But wouldn't it be better to use the nuts to make more copra to export?"

"How's that better? They use a lot of their copra sales money now to import rice, sugar, flour—even canned fish in tomato sauce. Why not produce more food here so they won't need to import so much?"

"Sounds sensible," I agreed. "How fast will they improve what they have now by crossing them with those new purebred pigs and chickens you want to import?"

"Fast! Take one of their worst looking sows, cross it once with one of those purebred Poland China boars the Navy project left us, and the new litter will be half purebred. Cross them a second time and you've got a three-quarter bred." There'll be a good increase in weight, too."

"I understand they really like pork and chicken, so what'll keep them from eating the new purebreds you send them for breeding stock?"

"Oh," John said, arching his heavy black eyebrows, "we won't let them do that. They have to promise to keep them for breeding stock."

"I hear that's what the Navy told them," I said. "But you've reported, yourself, that they've eaten a lot of the breeding pigs the Navy brought in."

He agreed it was a risk. "Before we put a purebred hog or chicken on an island," he said, we'll have to educate the people not to eat the goose."

After getting more information, Russ and I approved the expanded pig and chicken projects and so did headquarters. Things went quite well. I was surprised, though, as were John and other field trippers, to learn how prone those purebred boars were to falling into holes on those outer islands, breaking legs—and ending up on a roasting spit.

One of the best and most lasting things John did quite early on was to recruit and start training Nori, a young Trukese who showed a strong interest in learning better farming methods. He became the first of many Trukese agricultural extension agents.

Absolutely Marvelous Tree!

The first territory-wide Director of Agriculture under Interior was from Wisconsin's rolling dairyland country. Milton Button had been head of the state government's Agriculture department. In his new job, he came to Truk only twice. Both times he was a walking case of severe culture shock.

"There—there just isn't much out here," he said to me in his deep, gravelly voice during his first visit. He sounded and looked truly shaken by what he had seen on his swing through Micronesia. "So little land," he said mournfully. Such poor soil...."

Maybe he never overcame his initial shock. Or perhaps it was the tropical heat, or both. He returned to Wisconsin at the end of his first tour. One of many fine services he performed, though, was to send Dick Pieris to us as a consultant.

Dr. Richard V. D. Pieris, a native of what was then Ceylon, earned his degrees from several of England's best universities, and he spoke softly, with a British accent. By the time he was forty, he had earned a world-wide reputation as a geneticist—a plant breeder with special knowledge of coconut palms. Dick was on the staff of the South Pacific Commission, with headquarters in Noumea, New Caledonia, when he was "seconded," as the British say, to the Trust Territory.

When John told the Trukese that Dr. Pieris was coming to show them how to grow more and better coconuts, they were skeptical. They regarded growing coconuts as one of those *old things*—something they didn't need to be taught.

He came in on the weekly flight from Guam one Monday afternoon. We Americans and the Trukese were attracted at once by the informal, bright-eyed manner of this man with dark brown skin and an erudite manner. We also liked the feeling he gave us that he was absolutely delighted to be here and could hardly wait to share with the Trukese his knowledge of coconut trees.

John and Nori, his new extension agent, took Dr. Pieris around to villages on Moen and other islands in Truk Lagoon. When they arrived on an island, a large group of Trukese of all ages would surround this man who looked a little like them and apparently had some special magic with coconuts. They walked together through the villages, showed him their coconut trees, then studied his facial expressions intently for clues as to what he thought of them. Before leaving each island, he would tell the people their trees looked fairly good.

There are, however, he always added, a few things they could do to grow even more and better nuts.

Before Dick came to us, we knew the coconut is an amazing tree. We had seen islanders weave its spear-shaped leaves into baskets, mats, hats, and use them to make dancing skirts and for roof thatch. The meat is crushed for edible oils and to make soap, while leftover pulp makes good animal feed. Tree trunks were used for rough construction like bridging over swampy parts of trails and for corner posts of building when breadfruit wood couldn't be spared. Its husk's fuzzy covering is used to make cord, rope (*senet*), and parts of the tree, as fuel for cooking fires. The tree has at least a dozen other uses.

He was the most enthusiastic man I ever heard talking about coconut trees. He never lost an opportunity to let us know that it was one of the best things that ever happened to the Pacific islands world.

"Without it," he said, "people on many low islands couldn't survive." Dick delighted in dropping on us and the Trukese at dinner parties, staff meetings, and village meetings, little facts we should have known but didn't.

"Did you know," he asked some of us at the hotel bar one evening, "that the coconut is the world's largest seed? That its origin is unknown? That the coconut tree is one of nature's finest factories? It starts bearing at about six years and produces steadily until it wears out in its old age of fifty to sixty years." This was the kind of attention-getting knowledge he liked to dip out in little spoonfuls.

One day I was with him, John and Nori on a trip in the lagoon. Pausing while talking to his usual following of Trukese, he turned and spoke to me in an aside. We had just been gazing with him at a cluster of nuts in the top of a tree.

"Will, if you climbed up there you would see not only nuts but the flowers on some. You would find every gradation in size all the way back to soft green balls no bigger than a walnut. In one year those walnuts will be ripe nuts."

Dick also pointed out to me what the Trukese, and probably John, already knew: how well nature adapted this tree to its tropical home. "Its roots are so shallow, you know, it can absorb much rainfall, so it's highly drought-resistant. Yet its root system is widespread; it's anchored well enough to withstand some typhoons."

Most Trukese simply let nature take care of the reseeding. Dick came across a farmer now and then who said he took the two bottom nuts from his best bearing trees and replanted them. Hearing this, the coconut expert beamed.

"But how did you know to do that?" he would ask. Always they gave him the same answer: they didn't know why. It was the way their fathers and grandfathers had done it.

Dick suggested refinements on the ancient patterns. Most important of them was how to identify the best seed nuts. He also told the people how far apart to space trees, how deep to plant seedlings and better ways to mulch trees and to dry copra.

After he left, John had Nori and a helper collect the best nuts and start seed beds around their own houses in the villages. This attracted attention. The seed coconuts, lined up in rows by the hundreds, each had a bright green flag of a sprout sticking up. Nori and his helper gave them to anyone interested who promised to plant by the "Pieris method." John suggested that the Trukese set a goal of doubling coconut production in ten years.

HICOM's staffing chart for our district listed two full-time agriculturists. We kept asking headquarters to send us the second man. I reminded them that they required John to teach at PICS half-time. Subsistence agriculture was the main way of life out here, and we had only one-half a man-year for field work. Eighteen months after Interior took over, Gil Korenaga flew in one day to become John's assistant.

Gil, who had earned his degree in agriculture from the University of Hawaii, didn't take long to get his feet on the ground. He pitched in and helped

John and Nori with the pig and chicken projects and the coconut improvement work. He also started looking around early on for ways to help the people earn more cash.

One day Gil met a young farmer who lived in a distant village on Moen Island. As they talked, Gil saw that the young fellow showed unusually strong interest in learning to produce better garden crops. He confided to Gil after several visits that he had a dream of growing enough so he could market some of it.

Gil offered to send to the University of Hawaii for better watermelon and cucumbers seeds. When they arrived, he drove a government jeep over the rough road to the farmer's village. The young man planted the seeds and nurtured his new crops carefully. Soon he had the best watermelons and cucumbers to be seen in all Truk Lagoon.

At first, he tried selling them to American wives and the hotel dining room. He found a ready market in both places. Then he saw that there were enough islanders on Moen working for a wage or salary—with the district administration, TTC, and the Catholic Mission at Tunnuk village—to give him a much broader cash market. He enlarged his garden and his sales.

Gil noticed after a while that the young farmer had acquired a new outboard motor, which he used in delivering his crops by boat. But, Gil told me, the now prosperous farmer wouldn't share his new knowledge or seeds with any other Trukese farmer. He treated it as treasured clan knowledge, and thus kept it secret from all but his own extended family. He wasn't happy when Gil explained that his job was to make those better seeds available to everyone who asked for them. In the end, the youthful farmer reconciled himself to this. His business continued to prosper despite new competitors.

Breadfruit Is Trukese

The Trukese people have, as Frank often pointed out in his lectures to staff members and cultural briefings for visiting officials, a very strong sense of "being Trukese." One of the main manifestations of this is their attitude toward food. To them food means, above all else, breadfruit. It was far and away their favorite food.

A breadfruit is pleasant to the eye and more so to the palate. Shaped like a large ball that has been stretched in the middle, it can be a foot long and eight or nine inches in diameter, has a green, pebbly skin and is cream-colored to light yellow inside. It hangs in clusters of two or three. The breadfruit does more than any other tree, except perhaps the banyan, which we didn't see around Truk, to create shade and a refreshing look and feeling in any tropical village.

Most Americans at Truk really liked breadfruit. We used it as a substitute for fresh potatoes, which were scarce, and as a change from rice. Carolyn sometimes steamed it, like the Trukese did, or she baked it like squash, or cut it into strips and made French fries. Breadfruit has a taste and consistency which is between that of baked squash and a baked potato. Sometimes we followed the Trukese custom of garnishing it with coconut cream. But at our house, different from Trukese families, we always ate it hot, except when we had islander dinner guests.

Because breadfruit was so abundant in the main bearing season, the Trukese preserved some of it for the off-season. They did this by placing peeled, raw chunks into a dug pit lined with stones and leaves. More leaves were placed on top of the breadfruit, then it was covered with stones. There followed a fermenting process which helped preserve it and gave it a sharp, sour smell. The trouble with this system was that if, as frequently happened, it was allowed to stay in the pits too long, those eating it became very sick with gastroenteritis. Clark and his staff often treated such patients during late autumn and winter months. Understandably, all Trukese greatly preferred the taste of fresh breadfruit.

John came in with Russ one day to see me. "We've come up with a good idea for a new project," he said. "Extend the breadfruit season!"

I grinned at his excitement, but I was puzzled.

"You know, Will, how breadfruit's coming out of their ears, at least on the high islands, in the big season—April or May to August. Then in the winter season only a few trees bear."

To call the latter a short season was an exaggeration. Much of the year the people went without fresh breadfruit.

"Our Trukese assistants tell me," he explained, "there are a few varieties that bear later than the main season, and a few that bear earlier. We propose to locate those early and late bearers, propagate them and distribute them around the islands. If we can find enough and the farmers will plant the cuttings, they'll have a longer breadfruit season."

John, Gil and Nori discussed the idea with Trukese farmers. All agreed it would be a most welcome and useful thing—if it could be done. Most Trukese, however, gave the impression that the breadfruit season was God's concern. Just as He had stretched out the heavens and fixed the location of the stars in them, so had he set the breadfruit season, which could no more be changed than the direction the trade winds blow.

Our agriculturists began an intensive search for breadfruit trees to help make the main season last longer. Since there are more than seventy breadfruit varieties in the middle Carolines, this was a slow process.

One day I met John while I was walking around the headquarters area. "We've located a good late-bearing variety!" he said enthusiastically.

"Fine! Are you..."

"Well, it isn't fine—yet," he cut in. "We've only located a couple of this kind of tree so far. Not many Trukese seem to have it or know where we can find more. It's going to take a lot of cuttings to make a real difference."

They searched all the islands. Every time they located a prized tree, they asked for and got roots or limb cuttings. In time they developed little propagation beds, just as they were doing with coconut seedlings, and they gave the sprouting breadfruit cuttings to interested farmers. Because it takes about seven years from the time a new cutting is planted until the tree bears its first crop, John, Gil and I didn't get to see the results.

When Carolyn and I returned to the islands for a visit a couple of decades later, I was dismayed to learn that a year or two after we had left, work to extend the breadfruit season was dropped.

For a couple of years before I left Truk, John Smith, like agriculturists in one or more other districts, had begun to experiment with growing cacao as a possible future cash crop. We kept our work limited and on a trial basis. Not long after I left—and John Smith left about the same time—the Trust Territory headquarters became convinced that cacao indeed was worth developing as a new export crop on some of the high islands. The agriculturists who followed John and Gil shared that conviction. They and their Trukese agricultural agents began to devote the major part of their time to developing cacao, and they dropped work on the much slower moving project to extend the breadfruit season. In the end, cacao didn't work out on Truk—apparently mainly due to sharply changed world market conditions. Breadfruit today still has about the same short bearing season it did when I first came to the islands.

When Gil completed his tour and was transferred to Ponape District, HICOM recruited George Davis as his replacement. George had lived on his parents' farm in Vermont until he went off to the state university to study agriculture. While still in college, he married his childhood sweetheart, Sue, who grew up on a nearby farm. He was twenty-four when he and Sue and their two small boys arrived at Truk. They brought with them strongly ingrained values from their New England farm backgrounds. They liked life on Truk from the start. George developed especially close friendships with two of the Trukese extension agents. Benjamin Frederick, from Dublon Island, was about George's age, and Thomas Sappa, a few years older, was from Fanapenges Island, also in Truk Lagoon. As George and Thomas worked together, they became almost like brothers. George and Sue later named a son for him.

The two young men often went together to islands in the lagoon to work with farmers, staying three or four days at a time. George didn't take along "C" rations or other canned food like the rest of us did. He and Thomas took only a few breadfruit and a little taro or got some on the island. They slept in canoe houses or community buildings. For breakfast they had a drinking coconut and maybe a papaya. They always skipped lunch, Trukese fashion. In the evening they might build a little fire and roast an unpeeled breadfruit for dinner. George learned to speak Trukese better than any of the rest of us, except Frank and Pat Yamasaki, the young American intermediate school teacher trainer Frank married on Truk.

Thomas and George seldom had trouble gathering a circle of farmers around them, or in persuading them to try the coconut seedlings from the Agriculture nurseries. The same was true when they wanted volunteers to help introduce cacao or black pepper plantings as possible new cash crops, or fig plants to add to their own diet.

Of all the fine work George did in the agriculture program, I believe his best and most lasting contribution was to build up the extension agent program into something of a centerpiece of agricultural development in these islands. When he arrived on Moen, we had Nori and one other Trukese extension agent. George saw the importance of a career group of well-trained islanders, so he set about carefully selecting, hiring and training young Trukese to take agricultural information out to the people on all the islands. By the time he left, he had a team of eight Trukese trained to carry on where he and other American agriculturists left off.

Fine Rainy Day

The longer we were at Truk, the more I developed a special feeling for breadfruit—that it was more than just food. It was, as Frank once said to me, part of the essence of being Trukese. It was something material which somehow blended with the spiritual. My feelings about it grew out of simple experiences—like one Chief Justice Furber, Tosiwo Nakayama, and I shared on a field trip together to Fanapanges Island in Truk Lagoon.

We Americans and Trukese alike, I believe, considered the judge to be one of our favorite field trip companions. Because he had to spend so much time riding circuit among the six district headquarters, we always had to limit our trips together to Truk Lagoon, where we'd be out only a day or two at a time. On the second morning of this particular trip, we were awakened by the sound of rain beating down hard on the deck and aft cabin of the boat pool's forty-five foot cabin cruiser. It was the beginning of a most satisfying day.

We had invited Chief Chuemei to have breakfast with us aboard the cabin cruiser. He came down the coral stone and earth-filled pier around eight o'clock. Bare-headed, he was otherwise protected from the rain by a light-weight plastic raincoat he had purchased at TTC. Several children, each well-sheltered, head and back, by a long, wide-banana plant leaf, followed behind him, skipping and chirruping. When they arrived alongside the boat, the chief spoke to them and they frisked away up the pier.

After a leisurely breakfast, during which we continued the previous evening's talk about island matters, Judge Furber peered through a spot he had rubbed clear on the cabin window, streaming with rain on the outside and steamed over inside.

"This appears to be island cook day," he said. "I perceive they are steaming breadfruit."

The chief asked if we'd like to walk over and watch. The judge, Tosiwo and I slipped into our plastic raincoats, and the judge put on his khaki-colored sun helmet—a permanent fixture with him. The chief set the pace by walking slowly along the wide path toward the big community house. Seeming to not notice the rain, he stopped several times along the way to chat with people. By the time we arrived, my head, covered with a blue baseball cap, was nearly as wet as the chief's and Tosiwo's bare heads. We followed the chief into the big, thatched community building with eaves which reached within a few feet of the ground on the sides. It was open at both ends. The place was jumping with activity. A steady din of cheerful voices filled the building as men and women moved about, busy with their tasks. Children raced among them, playing tag and throwing a ball woven from fiber. While rain dripped off the eaves, it was dry and cozy inside. We three visitors were caught up immediately in the good feelings of warmth and friendliness.

We exchanged greetings with the people and walked over with the chief to join several elderly men sitting on mats back from where the others worked. Two of the men we sat with were weaving rope out of coconut fiber. The chief called to two small boys as they ran past us, tossing their ball back and forth. He asked them to bring us seats. They trotted off and returned quickly with some old Navy metal folding chairs.

Several food preparers started the first notes of an island song and other voices joined in, until everyone except our little group was singing. Men and women worked together making *kon* (cooked and pounded breadfruit). In the Truk Lagoon, men did some cooking, especially the heavy, starchy foods. Picking and hauling breadfruit was a man's work because breadfruit is heavy. Men carried them to the village in coconut leaf baskets attached to both ends of shoulder poles, Extended family members often cooked and prepared a

191

week's or more supply at a time.

A cookhouse stood thirty feet from one end of the community building. There we saw, through the rain, a couple of men cooking breadfruit. The cookhouse, open-sided, consisted of four corner poles joined with cross beams and bracings enough to support sheets of rusting corrugated tin, which formed its roof. In the middle of the sand floor was a cooking area ringed with stones. Two men tended a big, soot-blackened iron pot over the fire. Blue smoke struggled upward through the rain.

Tosiwo had left us after a short time and spent part of the day talking with the teachers, health aide, and perhaps others concerned with island government matters in the absence of a full field trip party.

The cooks took turns stirring the steaming contents of the pot with a wooden pole and feeding the fire with dried coconut half-shells and sticks of mangrove. Several ladies sat on the floor near a big pile of breadfruit. Selecting one at a time, they used a cowrie shell to scrape off its green skin. When a lady finished peeling one, a man sliced it with a machete into several chunks and placed them on a woven mat nearby. From time to time one of the cooks carried the slices over to the cookpot. When the breadfruit was cooked, he filled a small metal bucket with the steaming chunks and bore them, half-running, through the pelting rain to the community house. There he deposited them on a rough-woven mat near the three male pounders.

Stripped to their waists and barefooted, each man sat before a long, thick breadfruit wood pounding board. With coral stone pestles, they hammered the chunks into blobs like a baker's bread dough. This was the hardest work. Their bodies glistened with sweat, and their boards made loud, pleasant sounds as the pestles hit wood.

The judge studied all this with as much fascination and pleasure as I did. "The sound of pounding breadfruit on those boards has always been pleasing to my ear," he said in his New England accent.

I was thinking the same. I had read a description by the German ethnologist, Augustin Kramer, of a 1906 Truk scene in which he told of some pounders who were so skilled they could create air pockets in the dough. When the bubbles broke, they made loud, popping sounds and the pounder's companions cheered. I watched and waited, but was disappointed to hear neither pops nor cheers that day. I was pleased, though, when late in the morning one of the pounders stood up, took several pieces of steaming breadfruit from a pan, went over and dipped them into a bowl of coconut cream, coating them generously; then he placed them on pieces of banana leaf used as plates, and gave them to the chief and us visitors.

As each pounder finished a batch of breadfruit, one of the ladies would take it from the board and carry it over to another mat on which several ladies had spread banana leaves. They wrapped the finished product into neat packages and tied them. The breadfruit was ready to be set aside in the extended family's houses and eaten in the days ahead. If someone went on a fishing or other trip, one or more packets went along. Trukese workers on Moen, visiting their home islands on a weekend, might take a package or two back with them to eat.

While rain continued to pour down, the judge and I spent most of the morning observing all that was going on in the big thatched building and cookhouse. We left with some reluctance around noon to walk with Tosiwo and the chief to the village we were going to visit next.

It was a fine rainy day.

Tropical Island Justice

The most important task of a British District Officer—roughly a counterpart to my job—in the Gilbert & Ellice Islands Colony was to supervise the island courts. Part of the Gilbert Islands were not far over the horizon from the southern boundary of the neighboring Marshall Islands. In the Trust Territory, by contrast, the Chief Justice was responsible for the courts system.

Yet, we district administrators had certain work related to the courts. This was particularly true of the community court on each island. I thought of them as the heart of the system. They were the ones which touched the villagers' lives day-by-day. You would find in the Trust Territory's body of laws very little mention of the district administrator's and his staff's duties related to the courts. They were developed in less formal ways.

One morning Chief Justice Furber phoned me and asked if he could come over for a few minutes. There was something he wanted to discuss. "I'll come to your place," I said. He was senior to me in position and grade, and he was about fifteen years older. Offering to come to my office was one more little mark of his graciousness. The quonsets in which the High Court was housed were only a few hundred yards away.

"Well," he responded in his pleasant Boston accent, "I do have a fresh pot

194

of coffee."

The Chief Justice had done both his undergraduate and law studies at Harvard. For years he had practiced law in Watertown, not far from Boston, and sailed for a hobby. From the beginning I found him a very enjoyable working associate, neighbor (their house was next to ours) and friend. His body chemistry and mine seemed to mesh well together.

Our main difference in views about island matters was that I firmly believed in the High Commissioner's policy that all development with which we helped the islanders should be related to the prospects for them to be able to take over and support it some day from their own economy. He thought we should be more generous than that. I did believe, however, that once they became independent, if they still needed technical assistance in developing a productive private economy and continue to improve their programs in education, public health, and to more effectively manage their government, it would be reasonable for our U.S. foreign aid program to help. I took a chair in front of his desk and, after brief small talk, he came right to the point. "I'd like to ask your staff to monitor the work of the community courts."

Chief Justice Furber was a practical man. Islands in our part of the middle Carolines alone are scattered over an ocean area of more than 300 miles from east to west and 600 miles from the equator north. In the Marshalls, the island courts were even more far-flung. There was no way he and Justice Nichols, the only other American High Court judge, could keep in touch with about 100 populated islands in the whole Territory.

Russ, Tosiwo and Sictus, in our Island Affairs office, supervised elections for island judges. The law said judges should be "nominated" by popular vote or some alternate way that was in accord with the people's wishes. If a district administrator wasn't satisfied, he could appoint someone he considered more suitable. I never rejected the people's choice. During my first year or two, the chief and judge were the same man on some islands, particularly in the western part of the district.

Most people on those outer islands were hardly aware that there even existed a Territory-wide body of laws governing them. Following a conference of district administrators in Honolulu near the end of Interior's second year, someone at headquarters summarized our views on this subject:

"Judges in Micronesia should make allowances for ignorance of the law, since it is in large part an alien code derived from Anglo-Saxon and New England sources." Whenever Frank and Trukese members of the Island Affairs staff could take time from their regular work, they were supposed to translate the laws into Trukese. It was a tedious task none of them liked. Judge Furber sometimes pushed me to get more translations made. The resulting collection of loose, single-spaced sheets, mimeographed on legal-size paper, must have seemed overwhelming to island judges—especially those in the western islands.

But there were many good things one could say, too, about that early set of laws: *puken annuk* (judge's book). Many had been drafted by a naval officer who cared deeply-and-wanted to produce something that would make sense in those remote islands. Commander Edward Furber had served in earlier years on the admiral's staff at Guam as a legal officer. This was a year or two before the Navy appointed him Chief Justice for the Trust Territory.

Commander Furber had tried to learn all he could about island customs and traditions. When he could get away from Guam, he spent many hours talking with islanders. He listened to anthropologists, field trip officers, and other Navy staff in the field who worked directly with the people. It isn't surprising, then, that the Interim Regs contained an important provision: *'Due recognition shall be given to local custom in providing a system of law"* (italics mine).

It would have been unthinkable at Truk in the first few decades of U.S. administration for an island judge to bring before his court and punish a member of his own lineage. Never mind. The Interim Regs. anticipated this. They made it possible for an island court judge to invite another judge from a neighboring island to sail over and hear the case.

It would have been equally unthinkable to hold a community court trial by jury. There was no requirement for this, either. Commander Furber and other drafters of those earliest Interim Regs. knew enough about island life to realize it would have been virtually impossible to find three or four—let alone a dozen—impartial jurists on those small islands where everyone knew everyone else well and each extended family stood rock solid together.

Some time after Interior took over from Navy, our new Attorney General for the Territory, Horace "Pony" Marshall, began work to draft a legal code which would tidy up the existing body of law and reflect more fully administration of the islands under the new civilian organization. Pony consulted closely with Judge Furber and others in the field. He told me that besides drawing heavily from the Interim Regs., he found help in the Code of American Samoa.

The new Code of the Trust Territory, as it was officially titled, managed to retain the best of those old Interim Regs. Still, being a compilation of laws, it inevitably contained some mystifying legal terms and references to strange legal papers and records which would make judges on remote tropical islands scratch their heads in puzzlement. Like with the island school teachers' mimeographed lessons, pages of the "Judge's Book" soon became faded and dog-eared, blurred by sun and sand, rained upon, and torn.

Law enforcement in the islands had its informal side. I had been on Moen Island barely two months when word reached me one Sunday morning that a man on neighboring Dublon Island was murdered the night before. A short investigation resulted in the Constabulary's arresting the accused and bringing him over to the district brig, located in one of the two elephant quonsets which were the Constabulary's headquarters.

Manua, who was in his thirties, had, according to the complaint filed by the investigating policeman, got drunk on *achi*, fought with another man and did him in with a machete. He was given a preliminary hearing at the courthouse after the prosecutor, one of the Constabulary men, filed the complaint. The court set his bail at $75.00 and let him return home until the trial began. The judge found him guilty of voluntary manslaughter and sentenced him to prison for five years.

Manua became a regular member of our grass-cutting and road maintenance crew around headquarters, sometimes working with little or no supervision. Like other prisoners, he ate all his meals in the Constabulary's only dining room with the policemen. With a certain amount of prodding from Judge Furber, the parole board I had established reviewed his case after he had served about half his sentence, and recommended release. He was, they noted, a model prisoner. I signed the papers, after which he returned home where he lived quietly and got into no further trouble.

Nearly all court cases revolved around four main themes: land disputes, drinking, fighting, and men getting in trouble over women. One diligent *Truk Tide* reporter wrote a story that gave a fair cross-section of court activity:

Are Tropical Paradises as Peaceful as They Seem

Of approximately 100 criminal cases tried in the Courts during the six-months period July through December, 1952, there was only one case of murder and one involving stealing. Nearly one-fourth of the offenses involved the gentler human foibles, including: absence from the island on island work-day, telling lies, dynamiting fish, getting trochus shells not in season.

There were 30 cases of drinking liquor without permission. Local laws on each island control *achi* drinking; 11 taking liquor between islands; 17 adultery; and 17 assault and battery.

Yosita's Appeal

Hard as Chief Justice Furber and Attorney General Horace "Pony" Marshall tried, how could they fully succeed in making the Code of the Trust Territory—as it was officially titled—simple, clear, and responsive to Micronesian realities? Parts of American law not even directly mentioned in the Code sometimes crept into the islands through the back door. U.S. court decisions became precedents to be cited in future trials to puzzled and amazed villagers standing before the High Court or a district court many thousands of miles out in the Pacific.

One day Yosita, a Truk Trading Company truck driver, ran headlong into this kind of back door law situation. He was charged by the Constabulary after an accident with a company truck he was driving. In due course he found himself facing three Trukese Judges—all respected leaders—who sat as a panel on the district court bench at Moen.

District court judges in those early years handed down some pretty stiff sentences to their own people. As a consequence, a fair number of their decisions were appealed to the High Court. Having felt the sting of this district court, both in its findings and the 30-day prison sentence it handed him, Yosita, after seeking out one of the Trukese legal counsellors—government employees trained by the American public defender, decided to appeal to the High Court.

Yosita looked upon himself, with ample justification, as one of the most skillful and careful drivers on Moen—at that time the only island in the district with vehicles. Didn't he drive a heavy-duty truck four years for TTC, with a fine performance record? Before that, hadn't he been a key worker in the district administration's central garage, emerging with a lot of driving experience and consistently high performance ratings?

He had been charged by the Constabulary with (1) reckless driving, (2) driving without brakes, (3) driving without a license. He vehemently denied the first two allegations but allowed that he had been a bit slow in getting around to renewing his license.

These were the facts of the case as the High Court recorded them: Yosita drove the truck up from the beach road to the commissary and hotel at the district center on a couple of errands for Truk Trading Company. He was accompanied that morning by one male passenger named Iaeko. After leaving the hotel parking strip on Telegraph Hill, Yosita ran into big trouble on his way down to the administration building. That stretch was steep, graveled, rutted, and about 300 feet long. With unmistakable clarity, if not flawless grammar and syntax, Yosita described to the court how sudden peril had descended upon him:

"I start the engine, and while doing it I feel the car moving. I step on the brake. The brake does not work—like I step into the air! At this time I look back and try to cut the car into the open place, but it is too late.... On our way down, I hear someone yelling up and said, 'Iaeko fall off.' I look back and I saw Iaeko lying on the main road. For this reason I come confused and nervous. Suddenly the car stop. I look out. I realize I am in the ditch!"

Truk had no law school graduates then, but a small group of unusually bright, articulate young men worked with either the American roving public prosecutor or the public defender. Some of them developed an impressive knowledge of the Code and court procedure. Andon Amaraich, a quiet, brainy young man from the Mortlocks and a PICS graduate, agreed to represent Yosita before the High Court.

Andon approached the task with his usual thoroughness. He reviewed carefully the district court's trial record. He noted areas in which Yosita's own testimony and that of his witnesses might have been less than clear or failed to underscore salient facts. By talking at length with Yosita, Counsellor Andon developed a thorough understanding of the mechanical problems involved. He went over with his client every part of the driver's trip that landed him in the district court in the first place.

Thus well prepared, Yosita took the stand when the court convened. He stated in his first testimony of the day that on the morning of the accident he had checked the truck's brakes, and found they worked properly. Furthermore, he emphasized, he drove the truck to the commissary, where he stopped to pick up various items. Next, he drove to the hotel on another errand. The foot brakes worked normally when he stopped at both places. His passenger, Iaeko, could vouch for that.

Andon now requested that Rain, a key witness for his client, take the stand. Rain, also a TTC employee, had a considerable audience that day—many of whom were Yosita's friends and relatives. They had come to provide moral support as well as to enjoy a bit of free drama. Rain told the told the High Court justice that he drove the truck in question the very morning of Yosita's accident, and prior to the time Yosita drove it. The brakes at that time were, he pronounced firmly, in good working order.

Next, two pieces of "brake line" (brake oil line) were offered by Counselor Andon for inspection by the Court. Not being objected to by the prosecution, they were received in evidence. The longer piece of tubing had a small hole in it.

Andon requested at this point that his client be recalled to the stand. Yosita now testified, under questioning, that shortly after the accident he had examined the ditched truck to learn what had caused the trouble. He tested the brakes and found they still did not work. The reason became clear. The master brake cylinder was empty, and "the brake line was broke....". In his opinion, he told the Justice, pressure in the line caused the hole from which the brake fluid had drained away.

"The pipe," he concluded, "is too old and rusty and easy to be a hole right there."

Counsellor Amaraich provided other relevant information, then rested his case.

The High Court Justice, after a recess, adjusted his black robes, looked out upon the assembled participants and observers and said he was ready to announce his decision. But first he wanted to cite the section of the Code which requires that every motor vehicle operating on a road must be equipped with brakes adequate to stop the vehicle within a safe distance, and that the brakes must be maintained in good working order.

Next, he introduced a legal concept not directly mentioned anywhere in the Code, but which flowed into it through the back door. It read:

"The common law of England and all Statutes of Parliament in aid thereof in force and effect on July 3, 1776, and as interpreted by American decisions... are declared to be part of the Laws of the Trust Territory, with certain exceptions."

"At common law," the Justice intoned, getting to the meat of his decision, *neither an intent to violate a regulation nor knowledge that it is being violated constitutes an element of the offense. The only question is whether the defendant did the forbidden act.*"(Italics mine). Under the law, then, he announced, Yosita was indeed guilty of driving an unsafe vehicle.

"As to the charge of reckless driving," he went on, "we believe the appellant stands on stronger ground..."

On the first charge, he sentenced Yosita to five days in jail, suspended with certain conditions. He dismissed the reckless driving charge.

Yosita looked first at the Justice, then at Andon in amazement. The faces of his family and well-wishers from his village clouded and registered great puzzlement. Had something gone wrong here? Hadn't Andon and Yosita proved to the full satisfaction of the learned, fair-minded American justice and all others present that Yosita on the morning of the accident didn't want to drive an unsafe vehicle? And did he know it was indeed unsafe? He did not! He had told the High Court Justice that much. Didn't Rain, his fellow TTC worker, testify that he, himself, inspected the truck the morning of the accident and found its brakes worked well?

Why, then, was Yosita guilty? Back in the village, and among Yosita's fellow drivers and other workers at TTC, the puzzle was chewed over for days and weeks later. American law was sometimes a strange and mystifying thing.

Leaving the Islands

From my first months at Truk, I thought how lucky I was—like in my Olympic National Park ranger days—to be getting paid for this kind of work. High Commissioner Delmas Nucker seemed to feel the same way. Once at a conference of district administrators he said, "We have the most unusual and interesting jobs in the entire federal government."

A number of our other staff members went on to spend working careers in international programs such as the Agency for International Development. One became a Peace Corps official.

Still, during my fifth year in the islands I began to think seriously about a new assignment. We were preparing the islanders to handle their own affairs. My staff and I had estimated, late in our first year of civilian administration, that if we did our work well, the Trukese should be able to take over the governing of the district in about ten years. With four years of experience behind us, we had adjusted that estimate to be a total of twelve years from the beginning of civilian administration.

What concerned Carolyn and me most about staying another five or ten years was that when you worked for the Trust Territory government there was no opportunity for periodic rotation to a stateside assignment for two to four years, like there was in the military, U.S. Foreign Service, and most other government agencies with overseas staffs. Marolyn, our oldest daughter, was now nearly seven. Barbara, who was ten weeks old when she arrived in the islands, was now nearly five. Nancy, born on Truk, was three. We thought that in their growing-up years they should have some exposure to life in America—especially American schools.

In terms of working years, I wasn't yet in mid-career. While the Trust Territory offered career service status, it wasn't a typical career-type organization. It offered district administrators no opportunities for further advancement. The only two higher grade positions at headquarters, Deputy High Commissioner and High Commissioner, were political appointments. This meant the incumbents of those jobs had to leave with a change of the administration's political party, unless they were invited to stay on.

For more than a year I had been hearing about a new organization under policy direction of the U.S. Department of State: the International Cooperation Administration. About five years later, with the name changed to Agency for International Development, it became an integral part of State. ICA's main purpose, I learned, was to help people in developing countries—many of them located south of the equator—improve their education, health, agriculture and forestry, industry, public administration, and other aspects of economic and social development. Two of my Maxwell classmates had joined ICA. So had Van Dyke, my former boss in Washington and later in Germany. I wrote to these friends, asking for more information about the agency. When their replies arrived, along with some literature, Carolyn and I read them together with much interest.

I wasn't surprised to learn that ICA's work was, in many ways, like ours here in the Trust Territory. There was one big differences, though. In the islands we were the government at district and headquarters levels. ICA people overseas served in advisory roles to the host governments.

Carolyn and I decided that I should take a short leave and go to Washington, D.C. to look into job opportunities in ICA. My leave request was approved, and I flew to Washington a couple of weeks later. During my visit there, I was interviewed in depth by four mid-level and senior International Cooperation Administration officers. On my fifth day in Washington, a Friday, I received a note at my hotel to phone Mr. Ferris, head of the Office of

South Asian Affairs. One of my most recent interviews had been with him.

"We're nominating you as Deputy Director of our Nepal Mission," he told me when I called. Clearances would take about two months if all went well. I'd be called into Washington about a month after that.

Nepal? At the time I was interviewed by Mr. Ferris, all I knew about the little mountain kingdom in South Asia tucked between north India and Tibet was what I had read in the *National Geographic.* Our U.S. ambassador to India also was accredited to Nepal.

Back at Truk, when I told Carolyn about being offered the assignment to Nepal, she reacted much as she did five years earlier when I first mentioned the South Sea islands to her. Now there was that same timbre in her voice and that same look in her eyes that told me her vote would be "Yes."

"But what about the girls?" she asked, after the first minutes of excited talk about that mountain kingdom. "Wouldn't it be better for them if you get a job in the United States?"

"I thought about that while I was in Washington," I said. "I told the ICA people I'd have to discuss the job offer with you before giving a final answer. They told me that parents in some overseas posts get together and organize an American school, or they help start an international school." And ICA did rotate its staff back to Washington, normally after two to four years out of the country. We agreed that I should accept the assignment.

About two months after my return from Washington, one of our radio operators at Truk walked into my office grinning, and laid a telegram from ICA on my desk. It said the White House had approved my appointment as Deputy Director of the Nepal Mission. I had a month to wind up my affairs and report to Washington for briefings prior to departing for the post.

Now, as I started doing things for the last time, I began to have second thoughts about my decision. On my final field trips to some of the outer islands I found it hard to explain to the chiefs—like to our own Trukese staff—why I was leaving. I kept imagining how my reasons for leaving must sound to them, and I'd wince.

On Puluwat, Chief Romelo walked along the path with me back toward the copra loading area. We talked for the final time about island problems and about his son, in his early twenties. Two years earlier the chief very hesitatingly and sadly had agreed that the young man should be sent to the

American operated leprosarium at Tinian in the Northern Marianas. About a year later the son returned to Puluwat, feeling and looking much better. His disease, seldom seen in the district, was in remission.

As we started to walk back toward the beach area where I'd board our ship's motorboat, Chief Romelo took my hand, a custom in those islands which signifies close male friendship and has no sexual connotations. He had first made this gesture a year earlier and it pleased me. I valued his friendship highly.

Back on Moen when I sat down to talk with Napo, I thought of the untold hours he had spent teaching me Trukese in my first year. I told him I'd come back some day to see him and other Trukese friends. Once I leave Truk, I thought, the language will no longer be useful to me. It was, though. I occasionally used Trukese, written backwards, as a secret code in making notes regarding classified cables when I was preparing to travel to meetings at our embassy in New Delhi or elsewhere.

Keti and Bertelina, our housemaids, moped around and Keti cried a lot the last weeks. They were conditioned by a lifetime of Trukese custom and tradition, in which some children are raised by women who had none of their own, and became as attached to their surrogate children as if they were their own. Nancy had lived with them from a few days after she was born. Barbara was still a babe in arms and Marolyn was less than two when they came to Truk. All three girls thought of Keti and Bertelina as members of our family. For all three girls the parting was a strong emotional experience. They asked us over and over why wouldn't they be leaving with us, too?

The Americans gave a farewell party for us at the hotel, and the Trukese held a dinner at Bokusan's Korean restaurant in Muan village. In the light of Coleman lanterns, we enjoyed one of Bokusan's fine meals and drank tea. Several chiefs and Trukese employees made speeches, and I responded.

"You should stop referring to Americans as '*re uon*,'" (the high ones) I told them a final time. I repeated for the last time that they were, as a group, just as intelligent as any foreigners. It was a matter of continuing to prepare themselves to take over and administer the district.

I went down to say goodbye to Chief Petrus two days before we left. He wasn't at TTC, but someone called out from behind a counter, "Mr. Petrus is working in his garden today." I walked to the field in Muan village, where I found him barefooted—like the first day I had met him in his back yard working on his boat. His shirt was off and his face and body were covered with sweat. He put down his machete and we walked over into the shade of a breadfruit tree, where we sat and talked.

It was no surprise to find him here working on the farm land—this man who was first among all chiefs in the district. He was freely, sometimes awesomely, acknowledged as such by other Trukese leaders. Chief Petrus was very busy as a top board member of Truk Trading Company, Chief of Moen Island, and chairman of the Trukese advisory committee to the district administration, which I had established two years earlier. Yet he still found time to do hard physical work, like repairing his boat or his house, and he worked often in the family garden. I believe he did this because he felt in every cell and tissue of his powerful body that an important part of being Trukese was to keep close to the land.

I had expressed my belief to a number of Americans and Trukese during my island years that Chief Petrus could hold his own very well if he were a member of the U.S. Congress. With all his intelligence, wisdom, and charisma, he was truly a great, yet humble man.

We talked about district projects we had worked on together and matters on which my staff and I often had asked his advice. I spoke half-apologetically about how little we had helped his people accomplish in five years. I said I thought that good progress had been made in health, sanitation, and democratic self-government. More modest but, I believed, solid progress had been made in education and agriculture, but almost none in small industry. And I told him I thought one of my biggest mistakes was not to give stronger encouragement to Trukese leaders to do something about the fast population growth in these islands with limited land. My staff and I had suggested need for such a program to both High Commissioners Midkiff and Nucker. They liked it but the White House didn't.

When I noted that our efforts to help the people earn more dollars through increased copra and breadfruit production and planting trochus shell beds in the Mortlocks would take years to show results, and our work to help get commercial fisheries established here had been fruitless, he looked at me solemnly.

"It is not so bad for us that we have few dollars," he said. "When we have much money our ways will change faster. They change now. The young people begin now to change...."

I recalled again for him what my staff and I had said many times around the district: "We Americans don't encourage you Trukese to be like us. Take only those things that you believe will be good for your people..."

Chief Petrus said it was good that Trukese leaders were being brought more and more into the affairs of district government, and that the Trust Territory headquarters had organized meetings of leaders from all the districts.

"In some things," he said, "change should come slowly, slowly, slowly." He didn't elaborate, but I felt certain he was talking about the culture—perhaps a reference to his earlier observation that a growing cash economy would bring with it faster cultural change. I knew from my years with him that he was uneasy about any changes which might weaken the extended family—heart of the Trukese culture.

When I got up to leave, we shook hands and I said my wife and I would come back to Truk and see him some day.

Nine years later, Chief Petrus and Raymond Setik called on me in my office at the State Department headquarters building in Washington, D.C. They had been invited there under a U.S. Government-sponsored leader grant program. I had known Raymond as the bright young manager of the combined PICS and intermediate school dining room, and later as the assistant finance officer of our Finance and Supply office. During the intervening years he had become one of Truk's leading businessmen, a top political leader in the Congress of Micronesia, and in one of the independent nations which emerged. I went with them to several of their scheduled meetings in Washington, D.C. and they came out to our home in nearby Maryland one evening, along with anthropologist Tom Gladwin, whom we also invited, for dinner and fine talk about the islands. But by the time I got back to visit Truk sixteen years later, Chief Petrus was gone.

Epilogue

When I showed my book manuscript to some friends, including several writers whose opinions I highly respect, most of them asked, "How did it all turn out?"

"That," I told them, "is another whole story—another book or more." Some excellent books have been written covering the years beginning with the early 1960's—start of what has often referred to by Trust Territory observers as *the turnaround period*. I'll try, however, to describe in broad brush strokes some main changes which took place during the rest of the trusteeship period. Those changes have echoed strongly down through the years, altering the lives of islanders in many ways—yet leaving much of the old ways.

Between 1956, when my family and I left the islands, and 1961, policies and programs continued about as they had in the earlier trusteeship years. So did the shoestring appropriations. During 1951-62, they averaged under $6 million a year. Navy's average budget (1945-51) to administer those islands had been even lower. But the Navy was able to draw from other commands staff and stocks of supplies and equipment—some of the latter being war surplus.

When President John Kennedy was elected in 1960, he brought into government a staff of very bright, able, dedicated and, as he liked to say, vigorous people to fill key positions—replacing appointees from the previous administration. Many of the Eisenhower senior staffers being replaced likely had the same qualities, but that's the way the system works for officials appointed on a political basis.

The Department of the Interior got a new top command, including Secretary Stewart Udall, his Assistant Secretary for Land Management, John Carver, Jr., and William Goding, the new High Commissioner for the Trust Territory. Carver was placed in charge of a half-dozen Interior bureaus and offices, one of which was the Office of Territories. Two new developments contributed, beginning in 1961, to help trigger the main changes which rapidly followed in the Trust Territory.

The first was that not long after Carver was appointed in March, 1961, he and his new deputy flew out and visited every district in the Trust Territory for an on-the-ground look. They concluded that conditions generally were unacceptable—not at all befitting a great trustee nation like the United States. They were especially appalled by the education system. Shortly after they returned to Washington, Carver began taking vigorous steps to help the U.S. become a better trustee—especially to change drastically the whole education system in the islands.

When High Commissioner Goding sent to Interior his proposed Trust Territory 1963 fiscal year budget (which began in mid-1962) it was for approximately $10 million—nearly double the previous year's Congressional appropriation. But it contained no new thrust for education. Carver told Goding to redo the budget and build into it provisions to greatly expand and upgrade that whole sector. Goding made frequent trips from the islands to Washington related to the budget and other Trust Territory issues. When he finally finished revising the budget upward, after further consultations with Carver and others, it had reached $18 million.

Goding and Carver, working closely together, were successful in getting the long-standing Congressional appropriations ceiling of $7.5 million—an amount which actual appropriations never had reached in the past—raised to $15 million for 1963 and to $17.5 for the following year. Funds were appropriated in approximately those amounts 1963 and 1964.

As specific segments of plans for the new look in education arrived in the

Trust Territory, Bob Gibson spoke out very strongly against most of them. He told me years later that all those changes coming out of Washington were made by people who knew very little about Micronesia. The Office of Territories staff did, but those plans were being handed down to them from the Assistant Secretary level. Gibson said he believed that the plan to recruit and place American teachers in elementary schools throughout the islands was the wrong thing to do, and it would be most difficult to make it work effectively. He objected equally strongly to Interior's abandoning the existing policy of teaching islander children in their own language for the first three or four years, followed by teaching in English. Interior wanted English to be taught from grade one onward. Bob knew that previous research in the Philippines and other developing countries on the language question supported his position.

If more money was going to be made available for education, he told High Commissioner Goding, one of his top priorities would be to hire more teacher trainers, like Cy Pickerill had been, to travel around the islands, after they had learned something of the language and culture, and help upgrade elementary teachers. Bob's next priority would be to hire several Americans whose full-time jobs would be to develop education materials (books, booklets, other lesson aids) to help provide teaching with island settings.

Interior wanted the Trust Territory government to completely construct modern new school buildings, along with a new wooden house for each American primary teacher to be employed. Gibson told the High Commissioner he believed it was wrong to take away existing responsibility of the people on each island to construct and maintain their own school buildings, with each district administration helping to provide certain materials. He suggested to Goding that if more money became available to spend on school buildings, it should be used first to replace those built entirely of local materials. Secondly, he said, schools which were much better built should be upgraded by adding wood or cement floors and desks made locally of wood. He pointed out that the carpenters trained in Japanese times, plus those who had been trained by the American carpenter shop foreman in each district, could help the people on each island do that work. That way, the islanders would continue to feel that the schools were their own and that they had a continuing responsibility for their upkeep.

Gibson saw virtually complete abandonment in the education sector of the earlier High Commissioners' policy that programs should be developed and carried out in such ways that the islands' own economies could some day support them. Otherwise, he argued, the island people would be dependent upon foreign assistance forever. When his views on all these matters and others were rejected, he resigned and retired in 1964. Some of those changes decreed from Washington in the early 1960's have gone full circle: returning to educational policies and procedures from early post-war years. An example is that today the local language is again being taught in most elementary schools before introducing a foreign language.

The second important happening in spring, 1961 which contributed to bringing about major changes in the Trust Territory was the findings of a United Nations (UN) visiting mission to the islands. Such inspections and evaluations teams were despatched every three years to Micronesia, including two of them during my years at Truk. The 1961 mission wrote a strongly critical report. Their main criticisms were aimed at the education system, although they complimented the existence of universal education at the primary level. The visiting mission also strongly criticized the medical system, poor transportation, and the almost complete lack of economic development. Their report contained one phrase which most strongly jarred people in Washington—administration and Congress—concerned with the trusteeship. The UN mission had found "...*considerable dissatisfaction and discontent*"*among the islanders* (Italics mine).

There continued to exist in Washington in 1961 a belief among high level executive branch officials and many members of Congress that access to those islands for national security purposes was the main U.S. interest in the Trust Territory. Their skimpy appropriations to those islands between 1947-61 seem to suggest that there existed during those years a casual attitude, a lack of understanding, or both by the Congress, related to U.S. trusteeship responsibilities and what should be done in relation to our security interests there. Those years came to be referred to by observers and writers about Micronesia as the era of "benign neglect."

The U.N. visiting mission report had the effect of making Washington movers and shakers concerned decide they should take a whole new look at the situation. Some day the U.S. government would need to sit down with

Micronesian leaders to negotiate their future political status. The 1947 Trusteeship agreement with the U.N. provided for future "...independence or self-government." Our government had both a moral and legal obligation to honor this.

The White House then turned to the National Security Council (NSC), which includes the President, Vice-President, Secretary of State, and Secretary of Defense. The Chairman of the Joint Chiefs of Staff and the Director of the CIA also attend as advisers to the Council.

The NSC concluded their review of Micronesia by issuing a secret paper in mid-1962, designated National Security Council Action Memorandum 145. While it remained secret, information became available through the years about parts of it. The paper seemed to reflect the Council's belated realization that since the Trusteeship began in 1947, Congress and the administration had indeed done far too little to help the islanders prepare for independence. The U.N. criticism reminded them of what they already surely knew: if the U.S. hoped to maintain adequate security arrangements in that part of the Pacific in the future, they must build a better relationship with the leaders and people of Micronesia, whose agreement they'd need to obtain regarding those security matters.

That same NSC document sharply decreased the Navy's strong security control over the islands, which meant that, with some exceptions, outsiders could travel more freely to and from them, and more shipping would have access to them—still excluding such places as our Navy missile testing range at Kwajalein. That helped create a better atmosphere to begin bringing in foreign commercial fisheries firms to work with the islanders, and to develop tourism and other economic activities in cooperation with potential foreign investors.

Wisely, the memorandum didn't state specific programs and projects to carry out. It did indicate that much more attention should be paid to education, health, transportation and that a Trust Territory-wide Micronesian Council should be created. It also cancelled Navy's responsibility to administer the Northern Mariana Islands District. That duty had been reassigned to the Navy about a year after the 1951 beginning of civilian administration. Now it again became the High Commissioner's civil administration responsibility to manage under Interior.

That document strongly supported, in broad terms, initiatives Carver and his staff already had taken. Carver worked with Secretary Udall to create in November, 1962 an appointed islander Council of Micronesia. That twelve-member advisory council held two sessions in calendar year 1963, both of which devoted "major time" preparing recommendations to Interior concerning the formation of a territory-wide legislature. In September, 1964 Secretary Udall approved the creation of the Congress of Micronesia, with veto powers resting in the High Commissioner. Its first members were chosen by territory-wide elections in 1965.

By 1965, every district also had its own legislative body. During the same year the High Commissioner appointed Dwight Heine, a Marshallese and one of the most talented Micronesian education leaders, as the first islander District Administrator. By 1973, the High Commissioner had appointed islander district administrators in all districts except Yap. Thus, by the early 1970's government at the district level—legislative and administrative—was largely in the hands of the islanders, subject to the High Commissioner's veto power. Since early Navy years, each district had its own islander judges and a district court.

The Congress of Micronesia now became the focal point in pressing the U.S. government to begin negotiations on the Trust Territory people's political future. In 1967, it requested the U.S. government to begin such talks. The first negotiations between the Micronesian delegation and the U.S. government took place in 1969 in Washington.

The great Chief Petrus Mailo became the first Vice-Speaker of the Congress of Micronesia's House of Representatives and served there until he resigned in 1968. Two young Trukese former district officials, Tosiwo Nakayama and Raymond Setik, emerged over the years among the strongest leaders in the Congress. Chief Petrus had nominated Tosiwo Nakayama to become the first President of the new Congresss, and he was elected. Raymond Setik, formerly in our district Finance and Supply office, years later became an outstanding businessman in Truk and a leader in the new nation of which the Truk District became a part. Both Tosiwo Nakayama and Raymond Setik spoke up for independence from the beginning of negotiations.

In 1972 there took place the first breakaway from a Micronesian united front approach in negotiations for their political future. Until then there appeared to be an expectation on the part of islander leaders that eventually there would emerge from the six districts one new nation. But in that year leaders in the Northern Mariana Islands (NMI) openly changed course. First, they tried to become annexed to Guam, only to find rejection of that proposal by the Guamanian people. They next approached the U.S., asking for separate negotiations regarding their political future. The U.S. government responded favorably. In March, 1976, after extensive status negotiations, the Covenant to establish the U.S. Commonwealth of the Northern Mariana Islands was signed by the President and approved by the U.S. Congress. The first constitutional government of the CNMI took office in January, 1978. Upon completion of other legal steps, the Covenant entered fully in force in November, 1986. The people of the Northern Mariana Islands are now U.S. citizens. The Commonwealth is self-governing for internal matters. The U.S. government retains responsibility for foreign relations and defense.

Father Francis X. Hezel, S.J., is a man of many talents. He played a major part in developing the Catholic territory-wide Xavier High School for boys on Moen (now Weno) Island in Truk Lagoon into one of the best in Micronesia. He also founded the impressive and flourishing Micronesian Seminar, a research center and think tank based in Pohnpei. He is author of two definitive history books on Micronesia titled *The First Taint of Civilization* (history of the pre-colonial period) and *Strangers In Their Own Land* (Micronesia's colonial period under Spain, Germany and Japan).

He is one of the keenest observers and commentators on developments in the former Trust Territory during the *turnaround period* and the years that followed. His writings on those changes and their consequences have been published in books, magazines and newspapers. Eighteen of his papers were issued in 1982 with the title, *Reflections on Micronesia*. His writings, based on more than thirty-five years of on-the-ground observation and experience, continue to represent some of the most common sense analysis available.

U.S. yearly funding increased from $7 million in 1962 to $70 million in 1975. Those sharp increases in U.S. dollars flowing into the islands were utilized mainly for education and health programs, along with new public buildings, roads, airfields, water, electric utilities, and sewage facilities—the latter mainly for people on islands close to headquarters towns. Francis Hezel began expressing strong concern about the high costs to future budgets when all the repair and maintenance costs for the new physical plant construction related to those programs were factored in. He worried that such a small part of all that new spending was accompanied by productive economic development. There was a strong need to create in the private sector permanent jobs, contrasted with small services type businesses that did appear: restaurants, more stores, movie theatres, bars, car sales, and taxis—made possible very largely by the pay checks flowing from sharply increased government employment.

He also was greatly concerned about the startling increases in the numbers of high school and college graduates being turned out each year with no wage or salaried jobs available to them, and their let-down feelings which followed. He wrote that in 1965 there was a single moderate-sized high school serving the entire Truk District; by 1978 there were no fewer than six. In 1965 there was a total of 200 Trukese with high school diplomas; by 1978 there were more than 2,300. A single senior class at Truk High School by 1978 produced more graduates than were turned out during the entire first twenty years of American administration (1945-64). In 1965 there were 35 Trukese away at colleges; by 1978 there were over 600 studying abroad.

"Truk is almost literally awash with the young graduates that its schools have been mass-producing for some years now," he wrote back in 1978. From the Truk High School graduating class of 1966, for example, 25 out of 37 found jobs in education, almost all of them on their home islands. "More recently, however, teaching jobs in village schools have become much more difficult to obtain; they have long since been filled by the earlier waves of high school graduates. And there is virtually no other salaried employment available in the villages."

If there are no jobs for them on Moen, he observed, most young people eventually leave for their own island where they can at least live off the land and count on the support of their families. Some may dally in the bright lights of the district center for a year or two to "catch a piece of the action" while they half-heartedly hunt for a job, but they soon tire of this footloose life and return to their home islands. There they would keep listening for news of a job opening anywhere. When they did hear of something, they would quickly apply.

"Some will keep a close lookout for an opportunity to get to college, perhaps to temporarily escape the tedium of life on a small island or possibly to improve their chances of finding a job in the future. Most, however, simply marry, have children, and settle into the quiet village life that they had known before their high school days.... The facts show that over 60 percent of all high school graduates not currently in college are now living on their home islands.... Of the 400 (30 percent of all high school graduates) who have taken up residence on Moen, all but 70 have found full salary employment." He speculated back then that in the years ahead there would be a big out-migration by those who could find no jobs which came even close to fitting their educational qualifications. His predictions proved right.

Father Hezel also noted another effect of the greatly increased flow of dollars into the islands: the multiplication of government jobs. Total wages paid to government-employed Micronesians swelled from $2.5 million in 1961 to about $25 million by 1975. The value of the Trust Territory's total exports in 1975 was $2.5 million—about the same as it had been in 1961—while the value of imports jumped from $4.5 million to $30 million in the same time period. "In less than fifteen years, Micronesia moved from a subsistence economy to a parasitic one that draws on large U.S. annual subsidies to sustain it." (By the turn of the century the FSM is still running large trade deficits, with trade goods imports running around five times exports.)

He pointed out that back in the early 1970s the Congress of Micronesia enacted a Single-Pay Plan, which established the same base salary for Micronesians and expatriates (Americans and other foreigners) who worked for the Trust Territory government. That sounds egalitarian. But could the Micronesian economy then—even now, nearly three decades later, support islander salaries close to or at U.S. salary levels? The facts at hand suggest no.

He expressed his own strong, clear view on the matter at the time. "The Single Pay Plan would appear to be nothing short of economic folly, given the nature of the economic problems that Micronesian faces now." He reported that foreign business people coming to look at investment possibilities have been discouraged by the high islander wage scales. "As the wage gap widens, he added, "employment in productive industries such as farming and fishing will become even more undesirable by contrast with government employment."

After the people of the Northern Mariana Islands broke away from the rest of the districts, future political status negotiations for the other five dragged along in the 1970s and early 1980s. Spokesmen for the Marshallese and the Palauan people announced that they, too, wanted separate negotiations. Some American observers familiar with those negotiations believe that, among other considerations, the Marshallese didn't want to share with less wealthy districts the substantial income their district government was receiving related to U.S. missile testing range headquarters at Kwajalein Island. The Palauans believed they had a good chance for U.S. Marine Corps training facilities to be established in their islands, and by then they already had agreed to have Van Camp Seafoods, on the U.S. West Coast, establish in their islands a major tuna fishing operation. Thus, they, too, foresaw a relatively much stronger economic position for themselves than most other districts would have. Like the Marshallese, they didn't want to share it with the other districts.

The former Truk District (now Chuuk State) joined together with three other former districts in 1979 to create a new island nation, the Federated States of Micronesia (FSM). Its capitol is on Pohnpei Island—about 400 miles east of Chuuk Lagoon. It includes Pohnpei State (formerly Ponape District), Kosrae State (formerly a big island of the Ponape District, which became a separate state in 1978, just before the FSM voted in its new Constitution in 1979), Chuuk State (formerly Truk District), and Yap State (formerly Yap District). Shortly before those four States united, the Trukese people had decided to return to their historic name: Chuuk.

When protracted negotiations for a Compact of Free Association, as agreements between each new Micronesian nation and the U.S. are officially called, finally were completed and signed, two of them came fully into force in 1986. At that time the FSM and the Republic of the Marshall Islands each became a fully self-governing nation. An Interior, OIA 1999 report stated that in the case of the FSM, the inherent sovereignty of the people and their constitutional government had never been owned by a metropolitan power. Tosiwo Nakayama, from Chuuk, was elected the first President of the FSM.

Compact negotiations with the former Palau District were finally completed in 1994, containing quite similar terms, with one important exception: the Palau Compact agreement runs for a period of fifty years. The Republic of Palau then became the third sovereign nation to emerge from the former

Trust Territory. Shortly afterward, the Trust Territory ceased to exist.

Under terms of the Compacts, each of those three new Pacific islands nations agreed to grant to the U.S. authority and responsibility for their security and defense. The U.S. agreed, for its part, to provide economic assistance over a fifteen-year period: 1986-2001. Included in the FSM and Marshalls Islands agreements was a provision for a two-year grace period after the Compact agreements expired in October 2001. It gives time to negotiate a new agreement. The Compacts further provided that any islanders who wish to do so may enter, reside, and work in the United States, though they do not become U.S. citizens. Now diplomatic relations between each of those three new nations and the U.S. government are carried out through their own diplomatic channels and ours.

Interior, Office of Insular Affairs' 1999 annual report states that grants to the FSM under the Compact agreement started at $60 million a year beginning in 1986, then dropped to $51 million a year in 1991, and to $40 million a year from 1996—2001. It also noted that, overall U.S. assistance, however, includes a number of Federal programs and technical assistance which, currently, adds a value of approximately $50 million annually to the package. These payments were intended to help the FSM move from a consumption to a productive economy.

The same report further states that other foreign country donors such as Japan, China and Australia, initiated their own assistance programs. Japan has been the second largest donor, providing about $10 million a year. Most of that aid is focused on physical plant development, mainly on port construction, fisheries and transport. Its assistance is provided to each of the four states on an annual rotation basis. Other donors are the People's Republic of China (PRC) and Australia. The PRC's aid, beginning in 1992, is in the form of two scholarships a year to the FSM for higher education and or technical training in China. Australia's aid to the FSM is about $1 million a year.

By 2001, the U.S. government's involvement with those islands had spanned about forty years during the Trust Territory period and another fifteen years under the Compact of Free Association. A number of highly respected observers and chroniclers of America's efforts to help the FSM people have a better life, keep pointing to the lack of a *productive growing economy*. It is necessary, they usually emphasize, to do so to help support health, education, public safety, and other social services programs, including related basic infrastructure. Some economists have bluntly referred to it as an *upside-down economy,* where government spending fuels the private economy instead of vice-versa (Italics mine.)

A 1995 Bank of Hawaii report on the economic situation in those islands stated, "Essentially, the FSM economy has remained unchanged since Bank of Hawaii's first report on the economy of the islands in 1989. It is as dependent on outside payments as it was then."

From the *turnaround period* until the middle 1990s, some conditions continued much as Father Hezel had described them in his writings decades earlier: high schools turning out large numbers of graduates, college graduates returning from abroad, with very few opportunities for salaried positions, bloated government staffs, unreasonably high government salaries, imports greatly exceeding exports.

How Trukese (Chuukese) Culture Has Changed Over the Years

When we asked Trukese people back in the 1950s about their felt needs which they believed we weren't addressing, one of their first responses would be, "Can you help us find ways for our people to earn more cash?" But in those years, as related in earlier chapters, our Truk District staff, with Bob Gibson's help, had to fight hard and long to finally get one of several much needed roving teacher trainers—positions like the one Cy Pickerill eventually filled. Other District Administrators and I had to create a joint voice from the field to persuade our Honolulu headquarters to cancel plans to close down PICS— the only high school in the Trust Territory. We couldn't get a development loan of a few thousand dollars to help Chief Ennis and his Fefan Island people purchase a simple, small engine-powered boat to begin commercial fishing.

More than once when we discussed in staff meetings the problem of the Truk District's having almost no cash economy, Frank Mahony told us such future changes would come at a price to the culture. We even saw an inkling of this with our own Trukese staff and those at Truk Trading earning regular salaries.

As readers already know, the extended family—*eterenges*—has been the centerpiece of Chuukese culture. Matrilineally based, it usually involves thirty to fifty or more members spanning three generations, most of them living nearby each other in the same village. It has been economically based on its communally held lands. The most senior women in the *eterenges* normally had the final voice in decisions regarding land use assignments and to dispose of any such land. The oldest brother would supervise men in working the land, while the senior woman supervised women's work. One of its golden rules has been for family members to share with one another worldly goods, work time to meet their food, shelter and other needs, and some non-material things of value.

The Bank of Hawaii's FSM Economic Report, issued in 1995, neatly summarized the impact of the culture on economic development programs. "Institutionally FSM is a communal economy based on the concept of extended family, where the individual's economic productivity, regardless of amount and value, belongs to the family. This aspect of the culture and economy, not unique to FSM or the Pacific, weakens the entreprenurial drive inherent in market economies. Most entrepreneurs in FSM, not surprisingly, are expatriates. As foreign as the communal culture may appear to those accustomed to a market economy, it is the essence of FSM's cultural and economic stability. To the extent that economic change requires stability it is a major advantage, but economic change in a communal culture takes place at a very slow pace."

Tosiwo Nakayama and a number of other Chuukese have told me that now, at the turn of the century, the extended family is still moderately intact, and in more remote areas little touched by change. The degree of change from one island to another varies considerably depending upon how close each is to the government center Moen (Weno) with its cash-paying jobs and accompanying bright lights of modernity. The farther islanders live from the built-up center, the more likely they are to be living today mainly in a subsistence farming and fishing economy. Even in Chuuk Lagoon, though, islands more distant from Weno still have a mix of subsistence economies alongside at least a few wage earners. Some of the latter work on Weno and commute home by passenger boat.

Responses from a number of Chuukese men and women either living or visiting here in the Pacific Northwest or Hawaii, regarding my questions about life in the islands today, are in general agreement with what Tosiwo and others have told me. They say that people with cash paying jobs and higher education are the ones most likely to build their own homes, usually on their extended family lands, and they now begin increasingly to exist as nuclear families. Despite such changes, more often than not one or two older needy relatives from either the wife's or husband's extended family may be living with them.

Today, in those situations where *eterengeses* are still largely intact, more often a new bride is likely to go and live with or near her husband's family, and they will do quite a bit of visiting back and forth with her mother's family. They agree, too, that at Weno on payday some—though fewer—relatives keep coming, as they did with Sergeant Kumio back when we were in the islands. And salaried employees keep handing over at least a small part of their pay— probably much smaller amounts than in the past—to extended family members in need. They further agree that the bride's older brother in an *eterenges* sometimes still will approach the husband of one of his sisters who is living with his wife and children in a *nuclear* family and ask him for some material thing, like one long ago asked Sergeant Kumio for his new aloha shirt.

A family enjoying a good cash income is likely to live in a modern house with a kitchen, living room, and several bedrooms. Carolyn and I saw during our return visits to Chuuk early stages of such housing and other changes. The nuclear family is likely to be cooking, on a small kerosene stove, food purchased at Truk Trading Company or one of the other big stores. If they have some extra food or other necessities, they may share a part with one or more extended family member and even with a related nuclear family in which the breadwinner has lost his job. Other modern touches in today's nuclear family home may include electric lights and a refrigerator. Most of Weno Island is electrified today and has been for a couple of decades.

Father Hezel recently has had published a book, *The New Shape of Old Island Cultures: A Half Century of Social Change in Micronesia.* It describes in a section titled The Absent Father, the changing role of a father toward his son in a nuclear family, compared with earlier times in an extended family. The oldest brother in many *eterengeses* no longer can involve in food production any of his sisters' husbands who, with their wives and children have become members of nuclear families living economically on their own. In the past, a son might go with his father to help on *eterenges* tasks. The big brother, not the father, was the son's boss, too. In today's nuclear families the father represents much more strongly than in the past the authority figure.

Father Hezel wrote that today in Chuuk and other groups in Micronesia, conscientious sons in many households studiously avoid the presence of their fathers. This is practicing "...what anthropologists might call classic respect avoidance, a strategy employed everywhere in the Pacific. Respect is shown today, as it always has been, by acknowledging the social distance separating the authority figure and the subject. This is often done by avoiding familiarity with the person in authority."

Wife beating appears to be increasing in some areas and families and diminishing in at least some others. Father Hezel wrote that where it is increasing, some look to the rise of alcohol abuse among men for the explanation, while some others attribute it to a growing permissiveness in today's island societies. Still others blame it on some men's explosive rage stemming from frustrations. Few seem to look for the explanation in the weakening of social controls that once effectively checked the tendency of males to take out their rage on their wives. A brother is often in no position to see to his married sister's welfare, because she and her husband may have moved to town or to some distant place like Guam or Saipan. This offers an abusive husband freedom from earlier social controls. He also points out that to help address the problem today some churches are offering marriage courses which cover the subject of wife beating.

Several lady informants who lived until recently in different villages on Weno, told me they believe that, along with certain other Western ways, some Chuukese returning from abroad seem to have brought with them a changed attitude about how men should treat their wives. Today many husbands realize, too, that their wives are better-educated than in the past and will not tolerate wife beating like their mothers and grandmothers did. Despite the diminished role of the wife's oldest brother, he still steps in sometimes, they say, to stop abuse of one of his sisters. He might get her to leave her husband or to divorce him. Or he may get the husband to agree to treat his wife better.

The roles of the man and woman have shifted, too, in nuclear families. The salaried husband does little or no gardening. The family may eat breadfruit in season, but will likely eat rice or other store-bought substitutes the rest of the year. (Back in early trusteeship years, Dr. Richardson and his staff saw many patients with very painful intestinal upsets due to eating spoiled preserved breadfruit which Trukese ate after the breadfruit season ended.) If both husband and wife work, the husband may share the housework.

I asked Sabino Asor, a very bright and thoughtful young man from Uman Island in Chuuk Lagoon, who studied law at an American university, for his views on how much the great increase in the number of high school and college graduates and relatively many more people with cash paying jobs have affected the extended family. What does he see as the future outlook for the institution of the *eterenges*? This is what he told me.

"I do believe in the *eterenges* as one of the valuable aspects of Trukese culture. I would hate to see it erode by the influence of time. The *eterenges* does serve many functions for the Trukese people, such as a social security system, a check and balance on individual anarchy, as an economic network, and generally as a stabilizing force in Trukese society.

"Through the *eterenges,* Trukese people learn their duties for the care and welfare of one another... One could not go around enjoying life by him or herself knowing a grand aunty or uncle in the *eterenges* is being neglected, unable to care for him or herself. It is always the responsibility of the *eterenges* members to take such an uncle or auntie and care for him or her as a member of the family....

"The mutuality of needs and responsibilities among *eterenges* members also provide good emotional security and stability. No one feels neglected or unwanted because the rest of the members will include you in their lives, care for and support each other when visited with poor health or other unfortunate circumstances. The company of relatives always provides the emotional support needed under such circumstances...

"Most young men usually weigh their individual actions by their effects on the *eterenges* and the possible reaction of *eterenges* elders... It is true that people are beginning to perceive resulting tensions between the roles of the *eterenges* and the new individualism associated with modern education and travel. Some islanders now begin to wonder if the new emphasis on individual liberties are inherently inimical to the values espoused in the *eterenges*... For example, most young Trukese who finish college go back, establish a business or find employment, build a home and family. That of course is a capsulized version of the 'American Dream': to make it on your own for yourself. But if one looks at it closely, in most respects there is no need for tension unless one does not appreciate the necessity to reconcile the two. Like the new Trukese families making it on their own through modern education, they still rely on the *eterenges* for their emotional support, and for the distribution and entitlement to *eterenges* land on which to establish their new families. In short, the reconciliation of the old Trukese *eterenges* with the changing times does pose an interesting challenge for the generations of Trukese and friends of Trukese people."

Tosiwo Nakayama told me that one of the biggest cultural changes—again mainly at or near developed centers—is that nearly all young women will go to the government hospital to have a baby, and many islanders go there instead of to the *sounsafei* for most other serious medical problems. One main exception, my informants agree, is when a man or boy falls out of a coconut tree and is injured; then they first consult the local medicine man.

When I asked several of my Pacific Northwest Chuukese lady informants to what extent love magic still exists, they all giggled. Each of them has either lived on Weno until recently or has been back for a visit. They agree that such magic still exists, but to a much more limited extent. A young man wishing to win the affection of his heart's desire may still write her flowery love letters, delivered by a trusted secret messenger. When the young suitor is first trying to attract her attention, he may put love magic lotions on his body, as of yore, and be certain to place himself, as he passes her on a path or road, so that she is downwind from him and smells the fragrance. If she is interested, she may agree to meet him in some secluded place on the island.

One lady informant told me, in the presence of several other lady relatives, that in situations where a married woman has left her husband and he wants her back, he may ask a love magic man to intervene on his behalf. One way the magic man may proceed is to pluck a coconut leaf spine, dip it into sea water and perform special love magic chants while doing so. Another way is to have a love magic man prepare a special potion with a strong fragrance. This is very similar to actions described in the Love Magic chapter; but here it is the abandoned husband, instead of the young swain, who wears it. His wife can smell its fragrance. "It makes magic with her," my lady informant explained.

Chuukese with whom Carolyn and I have talked in recent years, including some who were in Hawaii at the same times as our visits there, agree that the custom remains almost universally intact for a young man who wants to marry his sweetheart to ask permission from the girl's family, including parents and other older family members.

Earlier ways of courting are being replaced by new ones introduced by Chuukese students or others returning home after studying or working abroad, and also by movies and TV films. Among the most popular are young men openly dating their girl friends, calling on them at their homes, and taking them to a movie, a bar or disco, or they just to go together for a walk. As with some other customs and traditions, these new ways take place most often, in the case of Chuuk, on Weno, with its dollar paying jobs and the related bright lights which follow them. Discos, electricity and other marks of modernity have so far invaded very few places beyond the headquarters island. All my informants agree that when young people date today they are still expected, as in the past, to be circumspect in their pre-marital relations and not promiscuous. Faithfulness is still valued: that is, not having an affair with more than one person at a time.

I asked a young Chuukese college student here in the U.S. for his views on the serious problem of beer and other drinking in Chuuk State—especially on Chuuk Lagoon islands today. This was his reply. "Alcohol in the islands is a social question. Complicating the matter is the fact that Truk State believes it needs the revenue from the alcohol business but is ineffective in administering existing laws regulating the sale and consumption of alcohol... I personally often find it hard to understand how some of my acquaintances in the islands could find money for a bottle of rum when there was no money for cough syrup for their children or laundry detergent for the household."

Past belief in ghosts, reef, island, and other spirits which were always lurking and ready to bring down terrible consequences on some hapless islander who displeased that spirit, are giving way fairly extensively to strong religious faith. Again, this seems to be particularly true for the more educated islanders. Yet several informants agreed in a recent discussion that some villagers still keep a light burning at night to help ward off such trouble. I have wondered if Chuukese coming to the U.S. and noticing the numerous security lights glowing at night, might look at each other and nod their heads knowingly.

Some aspects of island cultures in most former FSM districts—now states—have not fitted well so far in response to limited efforts to build private productive economies. A 1998 booklet written by Jay Dobbs and Francis Hezel, titled *Sustainable Human Development,* and issued by the Micronesian Seminar in its The Micronesian Counselor series, illustrates this point as it relates to the need to sharply reduce government staffs.

"Government funds," they wrote, "can be considered as income to families in the form of salaries, rather than as a resource to be used for the overall public good. Similarly, when there are cutbacks, the perception is that the impact should be felt and shared by all employees. The result is that, rather than cut back to a lower number of people getting a good wage, governments will keep on more employees at reduced wages for all. Thus, salaries and employment are the very last thing to be reduced even if, by keeping more employees hired there is no remaining money with which to do anything...*The priority of jobs above services is a critical cultural dimension of the local economy*" (italics mine).

During our five years living and working with the Trukese people, my staff and I and other headquarters staff, like Bob Gibson, stationed at Truk greatly benefited by having available the guidance and counsel of anthropologist Frank Mahony. He, and we in turn, were enriched by the cultural knowledge of early Navy anthropologists. The Navy, during its post-war occupation period in the Pacific, had the good judgment and foresight to hire cultural anthropologists to help them understand the very different cultures with which they were not familiar. Those people's basic beliefs and values, customs and traditions guided and directed their daily lives and shaped their judgments and decisions.

After leaving the Trust Territory in 1956, I spent the rest of my working career with assignments in Washington and in developing countries in Africa and Asia. In one African country, the forerunner to the Agency for International Development permitted me to add a cultural anthropologist to my staff. Predictably, he proved invaluable. In other countries I missed greatly the lack of a Frank Mahony type to help our host country officials and my staff to much better understand each other's ways. A specific example would be to understand why certain types of development projects under consideration would or wouldn't work. Similarly, certain international policies under consideration which their government would like us to support or our government would like them to support—like some issue before the UN—might

227

be accepted more readily when we have a better understanding of each other's culture.

The former U.S. Information Agency (known abroad as the U.S. Information Service) did fine work informing foreign countries about the U.S. culture. But after nearly a decade of budget cuts in the 1990s, its staff levels and support funds were greatly diminished. In late 1999 it was integrated into the State Department's Office of Public Diplomacy and Public Affairs. Now Public Affairs officers are assigned to embassies but they have much smaller operations than in the past due to those budget cuts.

State's Foreign Service Institute has done excellent work through the years in conducting foreign language studies for foreign service officers and support personnel of the foreign affairs community. It also has conducted in the Washington area cultural orientation programs, while individual embassies have arranged in-country orientation for new arrivals and their families. However, it is desirable to have an anthropologist at the post to provide in-depth cultural orientation and be continuously available to help build bridges between the two cultures. He or she should be there to explain certain specific situations which may from time to time arise out of lack of cultural understanding. The anthropologist is never a pleader for either the host country or the Americans. The anthropologist is, I repeat, a neutral cultural bridge builder.

I recommend that wherever the U.S. government has staff posted abroad, particularly in developing countries, arrangements be made to provide cultural anthropologist support. At different times in the past the Departments of Defense and Interior have used cultural anthropologists abroad with mutual benefit to both the host government and its people and to ours. To a more limited extent the State Department, U.S. Agency for International Development and, in more recent years, the latter's contractors, referred to as Private Voluntary Organizations (PVOs) have used such help with positive results.

The Population Problem

Population growth rates are among the most important problems to which the FSM's four states—especially the Chuukese—and future donors need to give more emphasis. Chuuk State, with more than 53,300 people in 1994, had about half of FSM's total population of 105,500, and the least land. It had that year a population density of 1,088 per square mile. By comparison, Pohnpei State then had a density of 255, closely followed by Yap, with a density of 243. Kosrae, the smallest FSM state had a density of 170.

FSM's 1994 census, from which most data in this section were taken, was carried out with advice and assistance from the U.S. Bureau of Census, Interior's Office of Territorial and International Affairs (now the Office of Insular Affairs), United Nations Fund for Population Activities, and the South Pacific Commission.

The report stated that the FSM had a total fertility rate of 4.6 and Chuuk State had a TFR of 5.6—highest in the FSM. TFR is defined as the total live births by a woman in her lifetime. The report concluded that, "This is high by world standards and creates a rapidly growing population. However, fertility rates in the FSM are continuing to decrease, as they have been for the past two decades. *If the growth rate stays at the 1994 level the population of the FSM will double in about 30 years*" (italics mine). It added that, "Also, given the high current age specific fertility rates, it appears that the uses of family planning, which usually initially lowers fertility in the older age groups, is still rather limited."

The census report further stated that mortality and migration also play large roles in the population situation of the FSM. Crude death rate was calculated to be about four per thousand. Regarding this, it commented that, "The analysis on mortality data suggested that, given results of the 1994 census alone, the high level of infant mortality rate should be a real worry for FSM policy makers, particularly in the health sector." Dr. Michael Levin, one of the main U.S. Bureau of the Census consultants, believes the reported death rate of four per thousand is much lower than is actually the case. For example, many Micronesians go to Hawaii when they are seriously ill and quite a number die there and are not always reported back to their sending countries. Thus it is not picked up later in the FSM's population data.

A section on international out-migration concluded that in the previous forty years the population of Chuuk grew at a rate of around four percent a year. (That would represent one of the world's highest population growth rates.) It more than doubled, from 25,000 in 1967 to 53,300 by 1994.

After the census data were gathered and analyzed, Dr. Levin and Father

Hezel wrote an article, published in 1996, about the results of a special analysis they undertook related to out-migration. In it they noted that data collected on family members residing outside the FSM at the time of the census were not complete. Reviewing that problem and other information related to out-migration, they expressed their belief that the data on FSM-persons abroad in 1994 were understated. They concluded that the total number abroad actually was, "...in the region of 15,000," and, taking this into account, that the FSM's annual population growth rate was under 1.5%.

A report titled, The FSM Planning Framework 1999-200l (FSM:PF '99—'01) prepared with the help of a private U.S. economic consulting firm, represents the collective efforts of public and private citizens in each of the four States and their national government. Particularly, it is based on policies and strategies which emerged from the first and second FSM Economic Summits held in 1995 and 1999, and those later convened in each of the four States. Resulting policies and strategies were endorsed by political leaders of the central government and the four State governments In a section on Economic Growth Performance, it states that real GDP grew by an annual average of 2.5 percent during the FY 87-FY99 period.... "Clearly, the high rates of population growth experienced in the FSM, especially in the early period, erode the gains made in real GDP growth and indicate the need for the FSM to implement effective population policies and programs to improve the likelihood of real welfare gains for the people of the FSM."

That report's section on Environment cited a half-dozen main categories described as key threats to the FSM's biodiversity. First on the list was "Rapid population growth."

The Bank of Hawaii's Federated States of Micronesia Economic Report, issued July, 2000, noted: that "FSM's population was an estimated 116,268 in 1999, up 19.1 percent from 1990. The annual growth rate of 2.0 percent in 1990—99 was lower than in the previous decades, but still considered rapid." The report also showed Chuuk State's estimated 1999 population was nearly 59,400.

Back in 1952, economist Donald J. O'Connor visited all districts of the Trust Territory at the High Commissioner's request to study and make recommendations regarding economic prospects. While at Truk, he spoke to me with strong conviction about the importance of trying to get some kind of family planning program started in the islands. After discussing this with the staff, I strongly urged its support to High Commissioner Midkiff and to his successor, Delmas Nucker. Both responded pretty much in the same words: President Eisenhower believed it was not an appropriate area for expenditure of U.S. government funds. Years later, Dr. Ravenholt confirmed that President Eisenhower had indeed strongly held that view. At Truk, prior to my first approaches to headquarters, I talked about the problem with some of our American Jesuit priest friends. They told me they would offer no objection to the rhythm method of contraception. That is considered among family planning experts to be the least effective.

Dr. Reimert Ravenholt, a world authority on population problems, and former Director of the U.S. Agency for International Development's Office of Population, reviewed what is known concerning FSM's birth, death, migration, and, broadly, its economic situation, including its natural resources. He suggested one may conclude that although the out-migration of young adults tends to mute the impoverishment caused by high fertility rates, the living standards of its population would be considerably improved if the total fertility rate were cut in half—to 2.3 births per woman. Thus the FSM's—and especially Chuuk State's—limited resources wouldn't need to be stretched even more thinly to feed more people, provide more schools, hospitals, jobs and other human daily needs.

Dr. Ravenholt believes the best measure of a nation's population problems is not just population density but, as he expresses in a formula: A nation's resources divided by its population equals the people's well-being.

The United Nations Family Planning Agency (UNFPA) sub-regional office was set up in Suva, Fiji in 1976 and provides assistance to fourteen Pacific islands countries, including the FSM, Marshall Islands and Palau. Their budget totals $10 million for the four-year period, 1998-2001. But almost none of that money, Dr. Levin told me, goes to the FSM, Republic of the Marshall Islands or Palau. Approximately 86% of those funds have been allocated towards ensuring quality health/family planning/sexual health information and services to some Pacific Island countries. The current assistance program has moved from traditional maternal and child health and family planning programs towards focusing on the broader aspects of reproductive health. Dr. Ravenholt believes it would be highly desirable for any family planning program in a developing country to provide ample contraceptives at the village and household levels, along with clear family planning information. At the beginning of the new century the FSM is falling far short of meeting that need.

Trying for an Economic Turnaround

Some positive steps were taken in the late 1970s and beyond to start building up sustainable productive economies. Modest progress was made in getting commercial fishing started, including some fish processing, and small but encouraging steps were taken to build up tourism. In addition, by 1999 there were twenty-two private, FSM-owned construction companies employing mostly local labor. Fifty percent of all housing in the FSM has been newly constructed in the last dozen years, largely by those companies. The houses are built mostly of typhoon-proof materials. Some infrastructure projects involved building up water, sewage and electrical services to many communities—mostly those in or fairly near population centers.

Now at the end of the century and the start of the new millennium, what needs to be done to help the people become as self-supporting as possible? Are there any new promising ideas, plans, programs? If so, what is being done about them?

Interior, Office of Insular Affairs' (OIA) annual report to Congress, *A Report on the State of the Islands, 1996,* provided some encouraging change-of-course information on the subject. Noting that many obstacles were hindering the pace of economic development and that dependence on U.S. aid was not diminishing at the rate desired, it stated that the U.S. in 1993 initiated a process through the Asian Development Bank (ADB) to analyze the FSM's situation and assist its leaders in designing and carrying out effective strategies to improve the economy.

As things then stood, the OIA report observed, a sudden cutoff of Compact assistance after 2001 would produce an overnight drop in per capita gross domestic product from about $1,445 to around $300. "Obviously," it added, "something had to be done." A decline that steep in per capita income would have put them in a class with some of the very poorest countries in the world.

Beginning in early 1995, the ADB, with financial help from the U.S. government and Japan, sent to the FSM a team of advisors to make on-the-ground studies of the situation in each of the four states and the central government. Special emphasis was placed on government policies and programs strongly affecting the economy. In late 1995, after extensive discussions with and support from the ADB team, the FSM government convened an "Economic Summit" at Pohnpei. Those attending included national and state leaders and businessmen from throughout the country. A major summit agreement was that *the national and state governments should downsize on a priority basis.*

A follow-on ADB report titled, *The FSM Economy: 1996 Economic Report,* issued in March, 1997, highlighted three other key findings, partly based on the FSM 1994 census data:

"The public service accounts for approximately half of total employment. The same ratio was found constant across the four States.

"Median income from employment in the national public service was more than three times greater than income from private sector employment. It was five times greater than income from being self-employed. While wage levels in each of the four State governments were much lower than at national level, they were 70% greater than from private sector employment.

"Between 1987 and 1995, *total government expenditures averaged 88% of GDP.*

"The problems lie in the slow pace of economically productive growth in the private sector and the large government payrolls (italics mine). This has resulted in a situation where most economic activity is in infrastructure development, services and sales of consumer goods—all largely dependent on continued outside financial assistance."

What happened to those 1995 ADB and FSM Economic Summit findings that government should down-size on a priority basis? In 1995, total Chuuk government employment, based on Social Security data, was 2,577 persons. By the end of 1999 it totaled 2,303—a decrease of about 10.5%. During the same period, its payroll dropped from $21.9 million to $14.0 million—a decrease of about 36%. The *FSM's total government staff* dropped from 6,842 to 6,204—a cut of about 9%. During the same period, its payroll dropped from $62.9 million to $52.2 million—a decrease of about 17%. One main reason staffs and payrolls dropped that much is that the government ran its voluntary Early Retirement Program. The second main reason is some of the FSM's four states dropped wages partly by shifting to a 32-hour week instead of forty.

The FSM '99—'01 report noted an unfortunate side to the staff down-sizing program. By making cuts across the board, some essential parts of government may have suffered unduly, while other less essential aspects have remained intact. It pointed particularly to the medical staffs, which were cut 10—30%. "Unfortunately, little thought as to health system requirements appears to have taken place prior to approval for early retirement and many essential personnel were retired prematurely and/or inappropriately." It concluded that "Further structural adjustment is best achieved through more rapid economic growth in the private sector rather than by further large-scale reductions in government. Clearly relying on the latter can achieve the result of reducing dominance of Government in the economy, but is tantamount to winning the battle and losing the war."

The ADB has been and continues to be helpful by working with Interior's OIA in bringing together representatives from foreign aid donor countries—referred to collectively as a Consultative Group. Its 1996 Economic Report concluded, and FSM's PF '99—'01 report reaffirmed—as did most previous economic consultants' studies in Micronesia—that sectors which seem to offer the most potential for near-term income generation are Fisheries and Tourism. Agriculture has some potential, particularly for intra-FSM trade, but the small land area sharply limits large-scale farming for export. It suggests that the central and state governments should change their roles in economic development. Instead of direct involvement in production it should create a favorable environment that is attractive to investors and which will support private development.

Agriculture

Arable land is Micronesia's scarcest natural resource. The ADB's 1996 Economic Report noted that, "In all States there is an increasing realization concerning the importance of ensuring a greater degree of self-sufficiency before the end of the Compact. States are placing priority on self-sufficiency and import substitution in view of rising food imports. A clearer understanding is required as to how producers, especially at the subsistence and semi-commercial levels, can be mobilized to meet domestic food requirements."

Dr. Levin told me that the FSM never has had a successful agricultural census. Thus it doesn't know whether it can feed itself or not. It goes into the new Compact negotiations without this knowledge. Palau, he added, had a good agricultural census in 1994.

After noting that outer islands have limited opportunities for cash generation, and that copra provides an important year-round potential source of cash income, the 1995 Economic Summit identified, and the 1999 Summit agreed on, the critical role of coconuts in outer islands' economies and the urgent need for a replanting program to replace old, poorly producing trees. But the facts show that in the years since those Summits, very little replanting of such coconut trees has taken place. The main reason given: world copra prices are sharply down, and this dampens incentive.

FSM's PF'99—'01 report states that recent attempts to stimulate commercial production for import substitution of introduced commodities including broiler chickens and pork, have failed, despite direct and indirect government subsidies. Failures, the report states, suggest inadequate understanding of competitiveness and inadequate business practices by government services and farmers. Still, it expresses the belief that there are prospects to market agricultural products in the region, including FSM states, Guam, Saipan, the Marshalls and Palau. This may be true for the few larger islands within the FSM and Palau—especially those in developed areas like State capitols—but my own observations during five years of visiting Chuuk State's small outer islands suggest that the latter will have little more than copra to sell for cash, and only the proceeds from such sales to purchase food and other needs from distant islands when their own food supplies run low.

During a recent get-together in California with former FSM President Tosiwo Nakayama, I asked him about any candidate crops to replace coconuts, and thus copra, as a cash earner on outer islands. He replied that there were none in sight.

Agriculturists in the early post-war years sought to identify new crops which might help promote export earnings. Experiments were carried out, especially at the central agricultural research station on Ponape, to produce for export pepper, citrus fruits, and cacao. Results have been relatively small. For some years pepper was bringing in annual earnings of around $100,000.

But the Pohnpei State Government put the private pepper company out of business, and the government did not arrange for continued pepper production. When my wife and I revisited Chuuk State in 1981, with its sharply increased population, some fruits were not adequately available even for people in Chuuk State. Cacao became unprofitable when world prices plummeted.

Leo Migvar, an American, spent most of his long career as an agriculturist for the Trust Territory. He served in positions ranging from agricultural teacher in Palau and District Agriculturist in Ponape, to serving for seventeen years as Assistant Director of Agriculture for the entire Trust Territory. After retirement he served in those islands as a representative for the U.S. Federal Emergency Management Agency (FEMA) and in other consulting assignments until near the turn of the century. He is very knowledgeable regarding the current agricultural situation and prospects in the FSM and some other parts of the former Trust Territory.

During recent discussions with him about agriculture and its prospects in the FSM, he emphasized that there is indeed heavy pressure on the relatively very limited land suitable for agriculture. He estimated that Pohnpei Island, largest in the FSM, has around 10% available for food crops and perhaps another 20% or slightly more for tree crops. In the Mortlocks, 50 to 150 miles southeast of Chuuk Lagoon, the food situation is so difficult that even a breadfruit tree often is divided to give one or two branches to one person and one or two to another person. He believes that virtually all the food the people can produce is going to be needed within the FSM. These are his main suggestions:

First, some islands can still benefit by adding giant swamp taro. It takes two years to grow. Then the farmer can get a crop any time he wants it for the next seventeen to twenty years. It is one of the best food bank accounts. Secondly, row crop farming can produce on one acre ten times as much food as some tree crops. He suggested growing Chinese cabbage, green peas, radishes, string beans, okra, and eggplant. He noted that sweet potatoes and many kinds of melons already are grown. He then acknowledged wryly that, "The slowest change in a culture is the people's food habits."

Fisheries

Fish, along with productive land, are the FSM's greatest natural resources. There is an abundance of factual information showing that ocean areas reserved by international agreements for fishing by the people of those island nations are rich with tuna—the primary resource—and other fish prized for commercial fisheries. Each of those new island nations now is very fortunate to have a 200-mile exclusive ocean fishing right, known as an Exclusive Economic Zone (EEZ). Those were agreed upon by the International Law of the Sea Conference, under UN sponsorship. The FSM's EEZ became effective by 1980. It covers approximately 2.6 million square kilometers (nearly 1.6 million square miles) of the Western Pacific Ocean. It is one of the largest such zones in the Pacific Region.

Tuna catches from FSM-controlled waters during years 1991-98 have averaged nearly 150,000 metric tons a year. Current estimates indicate that those landings are within sustainable limits. Yearly target tuna catches during that period ranged from a high of about 249,000 metric tons in 1995 to a low of approximately 46,000 tons in 1998. The target annual tuna catch declined markedly and consistently since 1995. Raymond Clarke, a fishery biologist with the Honolulu office of the National Marine Fisheries Service, told me that one of the main reasons fish catch volume in the EEZ varies greatly from year to year is due to the migration of tuna stocks, which are importantly affected by *el nino* and *la nina*. The catch Information above is from the *FSM Fisheries Review, Working Paper NFR-5*, prepared by Tim Park and issued by the Micronesian Maritime Authority, FSM.

Interior, OIA's annual report for 1999 stated, "FSM has for some years earned $18 to $24 million annually in licensing fees paid by foreign vessels for tuna fishing in FSM's EEZ."

Readers interested in more detailed information on fisheries in Micronesia may wish to read the Asia Development Bank's study issued in early 1997, *The Pacific's Tuna: The Challenge of Investing in Growth*. Geographic areas covered by the report include, along with the FSM, Marshall Islands, and Palau, six other Pacific islands nations—together referred to as the ADB's Pacific Developing Member Countries (PDMCs). Interested readers also may want to study the ADB's *The FSM Economy: 1996 Economic Report*, issued in early 1997. The latter, while its section on fisheries draws from the ADB's *Pacific Tuna* report, focusses mainly on FSM fisheries. The following are a few highlights of those studies:

Offshore resources—mainly tuna—are being exploited by foreign capital using modern technology and highly capital-intensive methods. By contrast, inshore fishing utilizes traditional low capital and labor intensive methods.

Fishing fleets participating, at least periodically, have included Japan, Taiwan, South Korea, USA, Philippines, People's Republic of China and Australia. The FSM and other former Trust Territory areas receive payment in the form of license fees, from around 3 to 5 percent of the total gross annual value of the tuna harvested in their EEZs.

In sharp contrast to much of the rest of the world's oceans, which are seriously over-fished, according to the U.N.'s Food & Agriculture Organization, the Pacific ocean's tuna stocks constitute the last of the world's great fisheries areas largely under-fished.

There is significant participation by the FSM's central government and its four state governments in commercial fisheries. They have made investments in direct fishing and in some places have provided docking, unloading and trans-shipment, ice storage, refuel, supplies, repair and maintenance and other related services. Various estimates place investments by the FSM's central and four state governments at more than $100 million by 1998. Some such operations were making a profit and some were failing.

Development is plagued by surveillance limitations against illegal fishing by foreign fleets, lack of skills, high domestic costs, and past inappropriate investment decisions. The ADB's 1997 fisheries report examined a whole range of problems and opportunities and concluded by considering possible options for participating in the fishery industry in the three Micronesian nations and other nations covered in the study.

FSM's '99—'01 report's section on the nation's fisheries situation includes a review of both the inshore and oceanic fisheries, followed by reporting on policies determined by the Fisheries Summit held on Pohnpei Island in 1997 and strategies for carrying them out. Those policy determinations range from making the private sector responsible for all commercial fisheries investment and operations to reforming laws and regulations inhibiting private fisheries development.

Tourism

Tourism has become a huge segment of the economy in the Commonwealth of the Northern Mariana Islands, and to a much lesser extent but still impressive in the Republic of Palau. Interior, OIA's annual report, 1999, stated that

238

tourism has increased significantly in recent years, but, "...the challenge in terms of large-scale tourism investment is to overcome limitations of air transportation, land use issues and competition with other island destinations closer to tourist markets." The latter reference is to places like Guam and the Northern Mariana Islands, which have, by comparison with the four FSM states and the Marshall Islands, excellent air service from Japan, the Philippines and some other countries in Southeast Asia, as well as from the U.S. Japanese have made large investments in hotels on Guam and the Northern Marianas. Many thousands of Japanese tourists and somewhat smaller numbers of those from other countries in Southeast Asian nations and the U.S. vacation there. Of the three new island nations which emerged from the former Trust Territory, Palau has made the most progress in tourism development.

The OIA report also noted that a number of new, small hotels have opened in Pohnpei, Yap and Kosrae with support facilities for diving and other tourist activities. An earlier report mentioned that in Chuuk State about two decades previously, Continental Airlines built a hotel consisting of several two-story buildings on Moen (Weno) Island's south shore. It was drawing a good business, partly from scuba diving enthusiasts, who find the Chuuk Lagoon one of the world's finest for such sport. They later sold to private investors that hotel and several others they had built in Micronesia.

The FSM's PF '99—'01 report states that tourism has the possibilities of becoming a major driving force for economic development and growth in the FSM. It notes that, unlike agriculture and fisheries, the governments have correctly avoided direct public involvement in hotels and other industry businesses. The FSM is a tropical island destination in close proximity to Asia Pacific countries. The more than one million visitors a year to Guam should be seen as an opportunity for onward travel to exotic FSM destinations. And it points to the need for much more and better tourism promotion.

Some writers on Micronesia over the years, beginning with Willard Price, who visited Truk in 1925, during Japanese occupation years, have characterized the islands in Truk (Chuuk) Lagoon as the most beautiful of all island groups in Micronesia. In the late 1990s, Raymond Setik, introduced to readers earlier, started construction of a modern five-story, 150-room hotel not far from the water on Weno (Moen) Island. Unhappily, Raymond died before the hotel was completed. His family, with help from some hotel professionals, took over its management. A major international hotel firm—the Castle Group—began financing the renovation of Chuuk's Blue Lagoon Resort, (formerly the Continental Hotel) and have assumed direct control and management of the operation. There are also several smaller, comfortable hotels on Moen and one very small one in the Mortlocks.

A Micronesian Seminar 1998 booklet titled *Sustainable Human Development in Micronesia*, by Dobbs and Hezel, also commented on the status of FSM tourism. It reported that in 1995 there was a total of about 23,000 visitors in all four states. The natural beauty is there, it observed, but the tourist infrastructure of fine roads, luxury hotels, exquisite cuisine, meaningful tours are not there—with a few notable exceptions. The infrastructure and the tourist industry will not support the general package tours that are the backbone of the Saipan prosperity. Cottage type tourist accommodations, blending a combination of spectacular scenery in simple thatched settings, have been successful on Pohnpei and Yap. A restored "traditional" village was popular on Yap. Pohnpei's ancient ruins of Nan Madol are accessible by motor launch tour.

Summary

The biggest single problem facing the FSM is to turn around their "upside down" economy. Now it is necessary, the FSM government with ADB advice has concluded, to build upon a small start in the Tourism and Fisheries industries, and to improve subsistence agriculture with, hopefully, at least a small amount to export. To accomplish this, the ADB's 1995 report to potential donors stated—and the second Economic Summit in 1999 largely reaffirmed—the FSM needs to carry out those main policies and actions identified and agreed upon.

The Bank of Hawaii's annual reports on the FSM are based on knowledge derived from thorough on-the-ground study of the region. It offered in its FSM Economic Report, issued July, 2000, as it has in earlier annual issues, perceptive comments on the FSM's economic future. "FSM is in a critical stage of economic and political evolution, especially in relation to the United States. Both sides know the limitations and potentials of what may and may not work to put the FSM economy on a track to greater self-sufficiency."

"Institutionally, FSM is a rather closed economy, especially to foreign capital in areas other than basic activities such as banking and finance, transportation and communications. Few joint ventures have been attempted...." It added that FSM leaders are keenly aware of the pressure on them by the U.S. government to become efficient and less costly to American taxpayers. It further states that for the FSM to try to get the best possible future Compact and other U.S. assistance, it needs to adopt an economic change strategy based on institutional reform and explicit and irrevocable commitment to market principles and openness, including in the public sector.

In the best of circumstances it is going to be difficult for the FSM, like most other small Pacific islands nations, to bring about such changes. Some of those nations have been independent longer than the FSM, Republics of the Marshall Islands and Palau. Examples are Western Samoa, Kiribati, and Tonga. Most of them, too, still have subsistence farming and fishing along with cash economies struggling to grow, and relatively large government payrolls. A few have commercial fishing programs and thriving tourist incomes. Several produce clothing, but by the time they bring in the raw materials to produce garments, and unless wages for imported foreign labor are at or near sweat shop levels, those operations have not, with few notable exceptions such as in Yap, been very profitable. Most of those island nations have some families receiving remittances from relatives who are sailors on ships or live and otherwise work abroad.

While considering the FSM's economic future, the Bank of Hawaii came close to paraphrasing statements by former U.S. Congressman (later Senator) Mike Mansfield (D) Montana, in 1947, and one of the U.S. Navy, Pacific Command's final reports on the Trust Territory. The Bank wrote, *'The notion of FSM becoming a self-sufficient economy is not based on a realistic assessment of its current resources.''* (Italics mine). The Bank also stated in the report quoted above, "As former colonial sponsors have found elsewhere in the Pacific, self-sufficiency in the Pacific island economies can be elusive..."

Those other island nations' examples mentioned above, and still others like them, struggle with many of the same built-in handicaps as former Trust Territory areas: isolation from markets, small, scattered populations which do not permit production and marketing with economy of scale, and sharing extended family cultures. They have insufficient productive agricultural land to permit substantial exports.

The U.S. General Accounting Office, after a field audit of the FSM and Marshalls Compact funds in the year 2000, was very critical of the ways much of them were handled. One of its major recommendations to the U.S. Congress was that the "full faith and credit" provisions of Compact funding, which have guaranteed U.S. payment each year since 1986, be removed from any future agreements in order to help the U.S. better insure accountability.

At least a small number of Micronesian high level officials, past and present, strongly believe that the new Compacts should include language which provides for much greater control over how the grant funds will be spent. Past experience, they say, shows it is necessary to help insure the most effective use of that money in the best interests of all the people. At least a few other high level Micronesian leaders have voiced equally strong belief that the grant money is payment by the U.S. government of yearly rent under their Compact agreements that the U.S. will provide security and defense in that region. Thus, they reason, how the money is to be spent should rest entirely with the islanders.

Some Micronesian leaders, past and present, and other observers have pointed to the need to separate rental type payments from grants, since the latter are foreign aid. Thus it is possible and reasonable to place the latter under much more effective controls. Considering the FSM's—including its four member states'—past record of U.S. funds management, it would seem both reasonable and necessary at this point in time to build in tighter controls on the use of U.S. government funds and those of other foreign donors. An arrangement worth considering is to separate the "rental" aspect of U.S. funds paid them. Then urge them to put on those rental funds controls to insure that such money will be used in the best interest of all the people. Make annual audit results widely available to the general public. Make the point clearly to FSM leaders, including those at the states level, that how much foreign aid type money the U.S. government will make available will be determined by the quality of their stewardship of the rent money.

Further negotiations to reach a jointly acceptable solution to that problem is a must if future funds from foreign sources are to be used for the long-term benefit of all the people. Hopefully, the Micronesian people will show the wisdom to accept the best and most reasonable of modern public finance and other management ways. Like Frank Mahony used to say, the people are going to need to change their culture some as they acquire more modern services and other ways of living.

Micronesians' history has proved that they are sturdy and enduring. Their ancestors coped through centuries and millennia with nature's strongest elements and survived—in many ways with a good life. They continue to demonstrate clearly to Americans and others in contact with them since WWII that they are as intelligent as we are. Many have shown, too, that they are willing to work hard when they see good reasons for doing so. They continue to need friendly foreign countries to help them make the best use of their natural resources and to further develop needed skills. Proceeding in those ways, they can and will make a better life for themselves.

As the late James Michener wrote back in 1991 about those former Trust Territory islands, "We will continue to hear much about them."

Index